Sole trader partnership accounts

Tutorial

David Cox

osborne
BOOKS

Published by Osborne Books Limited
Unit 1B Everoak Estate
Bromyard Road
Worcester WR2 5HP
Tel 01905 748071
Email books@osbornebooks.co.uk
Website www.osbornebooks.co.uk

Design by Laura Ingham
Cover and page design image © Istockphoto.com/Petrovich9

Printed by CPI Antony Rowe Limited, Chippenham

British Library Cataloguing in Publication Data
A catalogue record for this book is available from the British Library

ISBN 978 1905777 297

Contents

Acknowledgements

The publisher wishes to thank the following for their help with the reading and production of the book: Jean Cox, Maz Loton, Mike Gilbert and Cathy Turner. Thanks are also due to Roger Petheram for his technical editorial work and to Laura Ingham for her designs for this series.

The publisher is indebted to the Association of Accounting Technicians for its help and advice to our authors and editors during the preparation of this text.

Author

David Cox has more than twenty years' experience teaching accountancy students over a wide range of levels. Formerly with the Management and Professional Studies Department at Worcester College of Technology, he now lectures on a freelance basis and carries out educational consultancy work in accountancy studies. He is author and joint author of a number of textbooks in the areas of accounting, finance and banking.

Introduction

what this book covers

This book has been written specifically to cover the two Learning Areas 'Accounts Preparation I' and 'Accounts Preparation II' which combine five QCF Units in the AAT Level 3 Diploma in Accounting:

- Principles of accounts preparation

- Extending the trial balance using accounting adjustments

- Prepare accounts for partnerships

- Prepare final accounts for sole traders

- Accounting for fixed assets

The book contains a clear text with worked examples and case studies, chapter summaries and key terms to help with revision. Each chapter has a wide range of activities, many in the style of the computer-based assessments used by AAT.

The book is divided into two sections, each dealing with a separate Learning area.

Accounts Preparation 1 begins with a review of double-entry book-keeping skills and knowledge. It then develops the trial balance in extended form to show the year end financial statements (final accounts), and taking note of accounting adjustments.

Other important areas covered are the rules of accounting, recording and accounting for non-current (fixed) assets, the use of control accounts, and the correction of errors.

Accounts Preparation 2 focuses on the preparation of conventional layout financial statements (final accounts) for sole traders and partnerships. The financial statements of partnerships include the appropriation of profits, capital and current accounts, and the accounting treatments for admission of a partner, change in profit sharing ratios, and the retirement of a partner.

Incomplete records are where full double-entry accounts are not available. Techniques such as control accounts, bank statements, and margins and mark-ups are used to calculate the figures needed for the financial statements.

Downloadable blank documents for use with this text are available in the Resources section of www.osbornebooks.co.uk

Osborne Workbooks

Osborne Workbooks contain practice material which helps students achieve success in their assessments. 'Sole Trader and Partnership Accounts Workbook' contains a number of paper-based 'fill in' practice exams in the style of the computer-based assessment. Please telephone the Osborne Books Sales Office on 01905 748071 for details of mail ordering, or visit the 24-hour online shop at www.osbornebooks.co.uk

International Accounting Standards (IAS) terminology

In this book the terms set out below are quoted as follows when they first appear in a chapter (and elsewhere where it seems appropriate): IAS terminology (UK terminology), ie:

> trade receivables or receivables (debtors)
>
> trade payables or payables (creditors)
>
> inventory (stock)
>
> non-current assets (fixed assets)
>
> carrying amount (net book value)
>
> revenue or sales revenue (sales)
>
> financial statements (final accounts)
>
> income statement (profit and loss account)
>
> profit for the year (net profit)
>
> statement of financial position (balance sheet)

Section 1

Accounts Preparation 1

This section begins with a review of basic double-entry skills and knowledge. It then develops the trial balance in extended form to show the year end financial statements (final accounts), including making adjustments for inventories (stock), accruals and prepayments, depreciation of non-current (fixed) assets, irrecoverable debts and allowance for doubtful debts.

Other important areas covered are the rules of accounting, the accounting and recording of non-current (fixed) assets, the use of control accounts, and the correction of errors.

The accounting system

Before studying sole trader and partnership accounts in detail, it is important to take an overview of the accounting system. Every organisation is unique and therefore no one accounting system will be exactly the same as another. This chapter provides:

- *an introduction to business transactions*

- *an explanation of how the transactions are recorded in an accounting system*

- *an introduction to some of the terms used in accounting*

SOLE TRADERS AND PARTNERSHIPS

In this book we cover the accounting systems and year end financial statements of sole traders and partnerships:

- *sole traders* are people who run their own businesses – they run shops, factories, farms, garages, local franchises, etc, and are often small businesses

- *partnerships* normally consist of between two and twenty partners, and are often larger businesses than those run by sole traders

The other type of business in the private sector is the limited company – which can be either a private limited company (ltd) or a public limited company (plc). Limited company financial statements are not covered in this book, but some of the business transactions we will see may refer to limited companies.

ACCOUNTING AND THE ACCOUNTING SYSTEM

what is accounting?

Accounting involves keeping financial records up-to-date and the preparation of financial statements. It includes:

- recording business transactions in financial terms
- reporting financial information to the owner or managers of the business and other interested parties
- advising the owner how to use the financial reports to assess the past performance of the business, and to make decisions for the future

why keep accounts?

Accounting is essential to the recording and presentation of financial records and financial statements. It is important for:

- *internal control*, to ensure that all financial transactions are correctly recorded so as to show the true financial position of the business, and to help prevent fraud
- *measuring business performance*, by means of financial reports and the year end financial statements
- *obtaining credit/financing*, by providing lenders with the current financial position of the business
- *statutory requirements*, to provide the information for VAT returns and income tax returns to HM Revenue and Customs, and for other financial reports

the role of the accountant

The accountant's job is to check, summarise, present, analyse and interpret the accounts for the benefit of the owner and other interested parties. There are two types of specialist accountant:

- *financial accountant*, mainly concerned with external reporting
- *management accountant*, mainly concerned with internal reporting

The function of the *financial accountant* is concerned with financial transactions, and with taking further the information produced by the person who 'keeps the books'. The financial accountant extracts information from the accounting records in order to provide a method of control, for instance over receivables (debtors), payables (creditors), cash and bank balances. The role also requires the preparation of year end financial statements (final accounts).

The *management accountant* obtains information about costs – eg the cost of materials, labour and overheads (expenses) – and interprets it and prepares reports for the owner or managers of the business.

manual and computer accounts

This book is concerned with the preparation of financial records and their use in the year end financial statements. Financial records are kept either in handwritten form or on a computer. Computer accounting systems are sensibly backed up by handwritten records, in case of computer disasters such as total loss of data. The main record in a handwritten system is *the ledger* which, at one time, would be a weighty leather-bound volume, neatly ruled, into which the book-keeper would handwrite each business transaction into individual accounts.

The major advantage of computer accounting is that it is a very accurate method of recording business transactions. The word 'ledger' has survived into the computer age but, instead of being a bound volume, it is used to describe data files held on a computer disk.

Whether business transactions are recorded by hand, or by using a computer, the basic principles remain the same. In the first few chapters of this book we will concentrate on these basic principles.

keeping accounts – practical points

When maintaining financial accounts you should bear in mind that they should be kept:

- accurately
- up-to-date
- confidentially:
  - not revealed to people outside the business (unless authorisation is given)
  - revealed only to those within the business who are entitled to the information

Maintaining financial accounts is a discipline, and you should develop disciplined accounting skills as you study with this book.

the stages of the accounting system

The diagram on the next page shows the stages of the accounting system – these will have been covered in your earlier studies. Topics such as financial documents, books of prime entry, and some aspects of double-entry book-keeping will have been explained in Osborne Books' introductory texts. In this book we will focus on the double-entry accounts system, the trial balance in its extended form, and the preparation of year end financial statements (final accounts) for sole traders and partnerships. If you should at any time lose sight of where your studies are taking you, refer back to this chapter, and the diagram, and it should help to place your work in context.

the accounting system

FINANCIAL DOCUMENTS

invoices – issued and received

credit notes – issued and received

bank paying-in slips

cheques issued

BACS documents

sources of accounting information

BOOKS OF PRIME ENTRY

day books

journal

cash book (also used in double-entry)

gathering and summarising accounting information

DOUBLE-ENTRY BOOK-KEEPING

sales ledger – accounts of customers

purchases ledger – accounts of suppliers

general ledger

– 'nominal' accounts for sales, purchases, expenses, capital, loans etc

– 'real' accounts for items, eg non-current (fixed) assets, inventory (stock)

cash book

– cash book for bank and cash transactions

recording the dual aspect of business transactions in the accounting system

TRIAL BALANCE

a summary of the balances of all the accounts

– extended to produce data for financial statements

arithmetical checking of double-entry book-keeping

FINANCIAL STATEMENTS (FINAL ACCOUNTS)

• income statement (profit and loss account)

and

• statement of financial position (balance sheet)

statement measuring profit or loss for an accounting period

statement of assets, liabilities and capital at the end of an accounting period

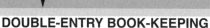

We will now look at each of the stages of the accounting system in turn.

FINANCIAL DOCUMENTS

Business transactions generate documents. In this section we link the main documents to the type of transaction involved.

sales and purchases – the invoice

When a business buys or sells goods or services the seller prepares an invoice stating:

- the amount owing
- when it should be paid
- details of the goods sold or service provided

cash and credit sales, cash and credit purchases

A sale by one business is a purchase by another business. The difference between cash and credit transactions is:

- *cash sales and cash purchases* – where payment is immediate, whether by cash or by bank payment.
- *credit sales and credit purchases* – where payment is to be made at a later date (often 30 days later)

A *receivable (debtor)* is a person who owes you money when you sell on credit.

A *payable (creditor)* is a person to whom you owe money when you buy on credit.

Note that the total of sales, both cash and credit, for a particular time period is referred to as *revenue* or *sales revenue*.

return of goods – the credit note

If the buyer returns goods which are bought on credit (they may be faulty or incorrect) the seller will prepare a credit note which is sent to the buyer, reducing the amount of money owed. The credit note, like the invoice, states the money amount and the goods and services to which it relates.

bank transactions – cheques, giro credits, BACS

Businesses need to pay in money, draw out cash and make payments. Paying-in slips and cheques are used as financial documents for bank account transactions as are documents generated by the BACS inter-bank computer payments system (eg customers paying direct into the bank).

BOOKS OF PRIME ENTRY

Many businesses issue and receive large quantities of invoices, credit notes and banking documents, and it is useful for them to list these in summary form, during the course of the working day. These summaries are known as *books of prime entry*. The books of prime entry include:

- *sales day book* – a list of credit sales made, compiled from invoices issued
- *purchases day book* – a list of credit purchases made, compiled from invoices received
- *sales returns day book* – a list of returns in, ie goods returned by credit customers, compiled from credit notes issued
- *purchases returns day book* – a list of returns out, ie goods returned by the business to credit suppliers, compiled from credit notes received
- *cash book* – the business' record of cash and bank transactions, compiled from receipts, paying-in slips, BACS documents and cheques
- *journal* – a record of non-regular transactions, which are not recorded in any other book of prime entry (the journal is covered in Chapter 11)

DOUBLE-ENTRY ACCOUNTS: THE LEDGER

The basis of many accounting systems is the *double-entry book-keeping system* which is embodied in a series of records known as the *ledger*. This is divided into a number of separate *accounts*.

double-entry book-keeping

Double-entry book-keeping involves making two entries in the accounts for each transaction: for instance, if you are paying wages by BACS you will make an entry in bank account and an entry in wages account. If you are operating a manual accounting system you will make the two entries by hand, if you are operating a computer accounting system you will make *one* entry on the keyboard, but indicate to the machine where the other entry is to be made by means of a numerical code.

accounts

The books of prime entry are the sources for the entries you make in the accounts. The ledger into which you make the entries is divided into separate accounts, eg a separate account for sales, purchases, each type of business expense, each receivable (debtor), each payable (creditor), and so on. Each account is given a specific name, and a number for reference purposes.

computer accounts

As noted earlier, many small businesses and all large businesses use computers to handle their business transactions. Using an accounting program, transactions are input into the computer and stored on disk. The separate accounts are represented by data files held on disk. The principles of double-entry book-keeping remain the same; an input code is used to identify the two accounts involved in each transaction.

division of the ledger

Because of the large number of accounts involved, the ledger has traditionally been divided into a number of sections. These same sections are used in computer accounting systems.

- *sales ledger* – personal accounts of receivables (debtors), ie customers to whom the business has sold on credit

- *purchases ledger* – personal accounts of payables (creditors), ie suppliers to whom the business owes money

- *cash book* – comprising cash account and bank account); note that cash book is also a book of prime entry for cash transactions

- *general ledger* – the remainder of the accounts: *nominal accounts*, eg sales, purchases, expenses, and *real accounts* for items owned by the business, eg non-current (fixed) assets, inventory (stock)

Note that, when control accounts (see Chapter 10) are in use, the sales ledger and purchases ledger are *subsidiary ledgers* to the general ledger. When this happens, *sales ledger control account* and *purchases ledger control account* are used in general ledger as totals accounts to represent the accounts contained in sales ledger and purchases ledger. The diagrams in Chapter 10 – on pages 177 and 178 – show the relationship between general ledger and the subsidiary ledgers.

TRIAL BALANCE

Double-entry book-keeping, because it involves making two entries for each transaction, is open to error. What if the person keeping the books writes £45 in one account and £54 in another? The trial balance – explained fully in Chapter 3 – effectively checks the entries made over a given period and will pick up most errors. It sets out the *balances* of all the double-entry accounts from the general ledger, ie the totals of the accounts to date. As well as being an arithmetical check, it is the source of valuable information which is used – in the *extended trial balance* – to help in the preparation of the *financial statements* of the business.

FINANCIAL STATEMENTS

The financial statements (final accounts) of a business comprise the income statement (profit and loss account) and the statement of financial position (balance sheet).

income statement

income	minus	expenses	equals	profit
eg sales revenue		eg running costs		which adds to capital

The income statement of a business calculates the profit due to the owner/owners of the business after the cost of purchases and other expenses have been deducted from the sales revenue.

The figures for these calculations – sales, purchases, expenses of various kinds – are taken from the double-entry system. Income statements are discussed in more detail in Chapter 4, and later in the book.

statement of financial position

The statement of financial position is so called because it shows the assets, liabilities and capital of a business in numerical (money) terms:

assets	minus	liabilities	equals	capital
what a business owns		what a business owes		how the business has been financed

The double-entry system contains figures for:

assets   items the business owns, which can be:

- non-current (fixed) assets – items with a life span of more than one year which are bought for use in the business, eg premises, vehicles, computers
- current assets – items needed for the everyday running of the business, eg inventory (stock), receivables (debtors) ie money owed by customers, and money in the bank

liabilities   items that the business owes, which can be :

- current liabilities – short-term liabilities repayable within twelve months, eg payables (creditors) ie money owed to suppliers, bank overdrafts

- non-current liabilities – longer-term liabilities repayable in more than twelve months, eg bank loans, mortgages

capital   money or assets introduced by the owner(s) of the business; capital is in effect owed by the business to the owner(s)

Statements of financial position are discussed in more detail in Chapter 4 and later in the book.

the accounting equation

The statement of financial position illustrates a concept important to accounting theory, known as the *accounting equation*. This equation has been explained above, namely:

   assets   minus   **liabilities**   equals   **capital**

Every business transaction will change the statement of financial position and the equation, as each transaction has a *dual effect* on the accounts. However, the equation will always balance. Study the following financial transactions made through the business bank account and see how the accounting equation is affected by each of the transactions.

TRANSACTION	EFFECT ON EQUATION
Business pays a supplier	• decrease in asset (bank) • decrease in liability (money owed to supplier)
Comment: assets and liabilities both decrease by the amount of the payment; capital remains unchanged.	
Business buys a computer	• increase in asset (computer) • decrease in asset (bank)
Comment: assets remain the same because the two transactions cancel each other out in the assets section: value is transferred from the asset of bank to the asset of computer.	
The owner introduces new capital by paying a cheque into the bank	• increase in asset (bank) • increase in capital (the owner's investment in the business)
Comment: both sides of the equation increase by the amount of the capital introduced.	

In conclusion, every business transaction has a *dual aspect*, as two entries are involved: this is the basis of the theory of double-entry book-keeping.

Note that the accounting equation is often set out as:

assets　　equals　　　**capital**　　　plus　　　**liabilities**

It is in this form that we will see it used in the extended trial balance (Chapter 4, and later chapters).

Chapter Summary

- ■ Accounting is used to record business transactions in financial terms
- ■ Financial accounts are used by the owner and managers of the business and also by other interested parties.
- ■ The accounting system comprises a number of specific stages of recording and presenting business transactions
  - – financial documents
  - – books of prime entry
  - – the double-entry system of ledgers
  - – the trial balance and extended trial balance
  - – financial statements (final accounts)
- ■ The statement of financial position uses the accounting equation:

  assets　*minus*　liabilities　*equals*　capital

- ■ The extended trial balance uses the accounting equation:

  assets　*equals*　capital　*plus*　liabilities

Key Terms

In the course of this chapter a number of specific accounting terms have been introduced. You should now study this section closely to ensure that you are clear about these terms:

accounts	financial records, where business transactions are entered
ledger	the set of accounts of a business
assets	items owned by a business
liabilities	items owed by a business
capital	the amount of the owner's (or owners') stake in the business
receivables (debtors)	individuals or businesses who owe money in respect of goods or services supplied by the business
payables (creditors)	individuals or businesses to whom money is owed by the business
purchases	goods bought, either on credit or for cash, which are intended to be resold later

credit purchases	goods bought, with payment to be made at a later date
cash purchases	goods bought and paid for immediately
sales	the sale of goods, whether on credit or for cash, in which the business trades
credit sales	goods sold, with payment to be received at an agreed date in the future
cash sales	goods sold, with immediate payment received in cash, by cheque, by credit card, or by debit card
revenue	the total of sales, both cash and credit, for a particular time period
profit	the gain made by a business from selling goods or services during a particular time period
expenses	the costs of running the business, eg wages, rent, rates, telephone, etc
trial balance	list of the balances of all the double-entry accounts from the general ledger

Activities

1.1   Write out and complete the following sentences.

(a)   The set of double-entry accounts of a business is called the ....

(b)   A .... is a person who owes you money when you sell on credit.

(c)   A .... is a person to whom you owe money when you buy on credit.

(d)   The .... is a list of sales made, compiled from invoices issued.

(e)   The business' record of bank account and amount of cash held is kept in the ....

(f)   Accounts such as sales, purchases, expenses are kept in the ....

(g)   The accounting equation is: .... minus .... equals ....

1.2 Distinguish between:
- (a) assets and liabilities
- (b) receivables and payables
- (c) purchases and sales
- (d) credit purchases and cash purchases

1.3 Show the dual aspect, as it affects the accounting equation (assets – liabilities = capital), of the following transactions (which follow one another) for a particular business (ignore VAT):
- (a) owner starts in business with capital of £8,000 in the bank
- (b) buys a computer for £4,000, paying by cheque
- (c) obtains a loan of £3,000 by cheque from a friend
- (d) buys a van for £6,000, paying by cheque

1.4 Fill in the missing figures:

	Assets £	Liabilities £	Capital £
(a)	20,000	0	....
(b)	15,000	5,000	....
(c)	16,400	....	8,850
(d)	....	3,850	10,250
(e)	25,380	....	6,950
(f)	....	7,910	13,250

1.5 The table below sets out account balances from the books of a business. The columns (a) to (f) show the account balances resulting from a series of transactions that have taken place over time. You are to compare each set of adjacent columns, ie (a) with (b), (b) with (c), and so on and state, with figures, what accounting transactions have taken place in each case. (Ignore VAT).

	(a) £	(b) £	(c) £	(d) £	(e) £	(f) £
Assets						
Office equipment	–	2,000	2,000	2,000	2,000	2,000
Van	–	–	–	10,000	10,000	10,000
Bank	10,000	8,000	14,000	4,000	6,000	3,000
Liabilities						
Loan	–	–	6,000	6,000	6,000	3,000
Capital	10,000	10,000	10,000	10,000	12,000	12,000

2 Double-entry book-keeping

We saw in Chapter 1 that book-keeping is the basic recording of business transactions in financial terms. Before studying financial accounting in detail it is important to study the principles of double-entry book-keeping, as these form the basis of all that we shall be doing in the rest of the book.

In Chapter 1 we looked briefly at the dual aspect of accounting – each time there is a financial transaction there are two effects on the accounting equation. This chapter shows how the dual aspect is used in the principles of book-keeping. In particular, we shall be looking at accounts used when:

- starting a business

- dealing with cash and bank transactions

- paying expenses and receiving income

- buying and selling goods

- dealing with returned goods, carriage costs and discounts

- dealing with Value Added Tax

DOUBLE-ENTRY ACCOUNTS

In this book we will use a simple account layout shown as follows:

Dr		Bank account		Cr
20-4	£	20-4		£
22 April Sales	1,450	23 April Wages		790

This layout is often known in accounting jargon as a 'T' account; it separates in a simple way the two sides of the account – debit (Dr) and credit (Cr). Note that each side records three items – the date, the nature of the transaction and the money amount.

debits and credits

The principle of double-entry book-keeping is that for every business transaction:

• one account is *debited* with the money amount of the transaction, and

• one account is *credited* with the money amount of the transaction

Debit entries are on the left-hand side of the appropriate account, while credit entries are on the right. The rules for debits and credits are:

• *debit entry* – the account which gains value, or records an asset, or an expense

• *credit entry* – the account which gives value, or records a liability, or an income item

This is illustrated as follows:

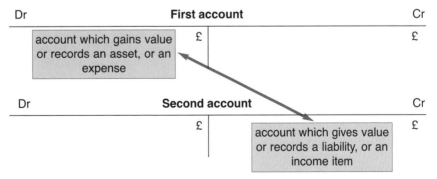

When one entry has been identified as a debit or credit, the other entry will be on the *opposite* side of the other account.

DOUBLE-ENTRY INVOLVING BANK ACCOUNT

In order to see how accounts are used, we will look at the business transactions undertaken by a new business which was set up by Jayne Hampson on 1 September 20-4 (and is not registered for VAT):

1 Sep	Started in business with capital of £5,000: a cheque from Jayne Hampson paid into the business bank account
4 Sep	Bought office equipment £2,500, paying by cheque
7 Sep	Paid rent of office £500, by cheque
10 Sep	Received commission of £100, by cheque
14 Sep	Withdrew £250 from the bank for own use (drawings)
16 Sep	Received a loan of £1,000 from James Henderson by cheque

All of these transactions involve the bank, and the business will enter them in its *bank account*. The bank account records money in the form of bank receipts and payments, ie cheques, standing orders, direct debits, BACS transfers and debit card transactions. Note that most businesses also use a *cash account* to record transactions which involve money in the form of cash. These two accounts – bank account and cash account – are usually combined in a *cash book*.

In a cash book, the rules for debit and credit are:

- *money in* is recorded on the debit side
- *money out* is recorded on the credit side

Using these rules, the bank account of Jayne Hampson's business, after entering the transactions listed above, appears as:

Dr			Bank account	Cr	
20-4		£	20-4		£
1 Sep	Capital	5,000	4 Sep Office equipment		2,500
10 Sep	Commission	100	7 Sep Rent paid		500
16 Sep	J Henderson: loan	1,000	14 Sep Drawings		250

Money in   Money out

Note: the bank account shows the firm's record of how much has been paid into, and drawn out of, the bank – it may not be exactly the same as the record of receipts and payments kept by the bank.

To complete the double-entry book-keeping transactions we need to:

*   identify on which side of the bank account the transaction is recorded – debit (money in), or credit (money out)
*   record the other double-entry transaction on the *opposite side* of the appropriate account
*   note that business transactions involving cash will be entered in the cash account

The other accounts involved can now be recorded, and we shall look at the principles involved for each transaction.

CAPITAL ACCOUNT

Capital is the amount of money invested in the business by the owner (or owners). The amount is *owed* by the business back to the owner, although it is unlikely to be repaid immediately as the business would cease to exist. A *capital account* is used to record the amount(s) paid into the business; the book-keeping entries are:

*   **capital introduced**
    *   *debit* bank account, as in the case of Jayne Hampson, or cash account, or a non-current (fixed) asset account – see below – where these form part of the capital)
    *   *credit* capital account

> ### example transaction
>
> 1 Sep 20-4   Started in business with capital of £5,000, a cheque paid into the bank.

Dr			Capital account			Cr
20-4		£	20-4			£
			1 Sep	Bank		5,000

Note: The dual aspect is that bank account has gained value and has been debited already (see page 16); capital account records a liability (to the owner) and is credited. Note that the business is a *separate entity* from the owner, and this book-keeping entry looks at the transaction from the point of view of the business. The introduction of capital into a business is often the very first business transaction entered into the books of account.

NON-CURRENT ASSETS

Non-current (fixed) assets are items purchased by a business for use on a semi-permanent basis. Examples are premises, vehicles, machinery and office equipment. All of these are bought by a business with the intention that they will be used for some time. Without non-current assets, it would be difficult to continue in business, eg without machinery it would prove difficult to run a factory; without delivery vans and lorries it would be difficult to transport the firm's products to its customers.

When a business buys non-current assets, the expenditure is referred to as *capital expenditure*. This means that items have been bought for use in the business for some years to come. By contrast, *revenue expenditure* is where the items bought will be used by the business quite quickly. For example, the purchase of a car is capital expenditure, while the cost of repair of the car is revenue expenditure.

The importance of the difference between capital expenditure and revenue expenditure is covered in Chapter 9.

non-current assets and double-entry book-keeping

When non-current assets are bought, a separate account for each type of non-current asset is used, eg premises account, vehicles account, machinery account, etc. The book-keeping entries are:

• **purchase of a non-current asset**

   – *debit* non-current asset account (using the appropriate account)

   – *credit* bank account (or cash account)

---

example transaction

4 Sep 20-4   Bought office equipment £2,500, paying by cheque.

Dr		Office equipment account		Cr
20-4		£	20-4	£
4 Sep	Bank	2,500		

The other part of the dual aspect of this transaction is a credit to bank account: this has been entered already (see account on page 16). Notice how the name of the other account involved in the double-entry transaction is always used in the details column as a description – this helps to cross-reference transactions.

EXPENSES

Businesses pay various running expenses, such as rent, wages, electricity, telephone, vehicle running expenses, etc. These day-to-day expenses of running the business are termed revenue expenditure. A separate account is used in the accounting system for each main class of revenue expenditure, eg rent paid account, wages account, etc.

The book-keeping entries are:

• **payment of an expense**

    –   *debit* expense account (using the appropriate account)

    –   *credit* bank account (or cash account)

---

example transaction

7 Sep 20-4   Paid rent of office £500, by cheque.

Dr			Rent paid account		Cr
20-4		£	20-4		£
7 Sep	Bank	500			

Note: The accounting rules followed are that we have debited the account which has gained value (rent – the business has had the use of the office for a certain time). The account which has given value (bank) has already been credited (see page 16).

INCOME

From time-to-time a business may receive amounts of income, such as rent received, commission received, or fees received. These are recorded in separate accounts for each category of income, eg rent received account, commission received account. The book-keeping entries are:

- **receipt of income**
  - *debit* bank account (or cash account)
  - *credit* income account (using the appropriate account)

---

example transaction

10 Sep 20-4   Received commission of £100, by cheque.

Dr	Commission received account		Cr
20-4	£	20-4	£
		10 Sep Bank	100

Note: We have already debited the account which has gained value (bank – see page 16) and credited the account which has given value (commission received).

OWNER'S DRAWINGS

Drawings is the term used when the owner takes money, in cash or by cheque (or sometimes goods), from the business for personal use. A drawings account is used to record such amounts; the book-keeping entries for withdrawal of money are:

- **owner's drawings**
  - *debit* drawings account
  - *credit* bank account (or cash account)

---

example transaction

14 Sep 20-4   Withdrew £250 from the bank for own use.

Dr	Drawings account		Cr
20-4	£	20-4	£
14 Sep Bank	250		

The other part of the dual aspect of this transaction is a credit to bank account: this entry has been made already (see page 16).

LOANS

When a business or organisation receives a loan, eg from a relative or from the bank, it is the cash account or bank account which gains value, while a loan account (in the name of the lender) records the liability.

- **loan received**
    - *debit* bank account (or cash account)
    - *credit* loan account (in name of the lender)

---

example transaction

16 Sep 20-4   Received a loan of £1,000 from James Henderson by cheque

---

Dr		James Henderson: loan account		Cr
20-4	£	20-4		£
		16 Sep Bank		1,000

The debit entry has already been made in bank account (see page 16).

FURTHER TRANSACTIONS

Using the accounts which we have seen already, here are some further transactions:

- **loan repayment**
    - *debit* loan account
    - *credit* bank account (or cash account)
- **sale of a non-current asset, or return of an unsuitable non-current asset**
    - debit bank account (or cash account)
    - credit non-current asset account
- **withdrawal of cash from the bank for use in the business**
    - *debit* cash account
    - *credit* bank account
- **payment of cash held by the business into the bank**
    - *debit* bank account
    - *credit* cash account

PURCHASES AND SALES

purchases account and sales account

Buying and selling goods or services are common business transactions. They are recorded in *purchases account* and *sales account* respectively. These two accounts are used to record the purchase and sale of the goods or services in which the business trades. For example, a shoe shop will buy shoes from the manufacturer and will record this in purchases account; as shoes are sold, the transactions will be recorded in sales account.

The normal entry on a purchases account is on the debit side – the account has gained value, ie the business has bought goods for resale. The normal entry on a sales account is on the credit side – the account has given value, ie the business has sold goods.

When a business buys an item for use in the business, eg a computer, this is debited to a separate account, because a non-current asset (see page 18) has been purchased. Likewise, when a non-current asset is sold, it is not entered in the sales account.

Case Study

TEMESIDE TRADERS: PURCHASES AND SALES

situation

To show the double-entry book-keeping for purchases and sales, we will look at some financial transactions undertaken by Temeside Traders, a business which started trading on 1 October 20-6:

1 Oct	Started in business with capital of £7,000 paid into the bank
2 Oct	Bought goods for £5,000, paying by cheque
5 Oct	Sold some of the goods for £3,000, a cheque being received
6 Oct	Bought equipment for use in the business, £700, paying by cheque
12 Oct	Bought goods for £2,800, paying by cheque
13 Oct	Sold some of the goods for £5,000, a cheque being received
15 Oct	Paid rent £150, by cheque

Note: Temeside Traders is not yet registered for Value Added Tax

solution

The entries into the book-keeping system are shown on the next page.

Dr		Bank account			Cr
20-6		£	20-6		£
1 Oct	Capital	7,000	2 Oct	Purchases	5,000
5 Oct	Sales	3,000	6 Oct	Equipment	700
13 Oct	Sales	5,000	12 Oct	Purchases	2,800
			15 Oct	Rent paid	150

Dr		Capital account			Cr
20-6		£	20-6		£
			1 Oct	Bank	7,000

Dr		Purchases account			Cr
20-6		£	20-6		£
2 Oct	Bank	5,000			
12 Oct	Bank	2,800			

Dr		Sales account			Cr
20-6		£	20-6		£
			5 Oct	Bank	3,000
			13 Oct	Bank	5,000

Dr		Equipment account			Cr
20-6		£	20-6		£
6 Oct	Bank	700			

Dr		Rent paid account			Cr
20-6		£	20-6		£
15 Oct	Bank	150			

Notes:

- A purchases account and a sales account are used to record the two different movements of the goods or services in which a business trades.
- The equipment is a non-current asset, so its purchase is entered to a separate equipment account.
- The purchases and sales made in the transactions above are called cash purchases and cash sales, because payment is immediate.

CREDIT PURCHASES AND SALES

credit transactions

We have just looked at the book-keeping for cash purchases and cash sales, ie where payment is made immediately. However, in business, many transactions for purchases and sales are made on credit, ie the goods or services are bought or sold now, with payment to be made at a later date. It is an important aspect of double-entry book-keeping to record the credit transaction as a purchase or a sale, and then record the second entry in an account in the name of the payable (creditor) or receivable (debtor), ie to record the amount owing by the firm to a supplier, or to the firm by a customer.

Businesses usually record credit transactions in appropriate books of prime entry:

- credit purchases are entered in the purchases day book
- credit sales are entered in the sales day book

At regular intervals – daily, weekly or monthly – the totals and amounts from the day books are transferred into the double-entry accounts.

credit purchases

Credit purchases are goods obtained from a supplier, with payment to take place at a later date. From the buyer's viewpoint, the supplier is a *trade payable (creditor)*.

The book-keeping entries are:

- **credit purchase**
    - *debit* purchases account
    - *credit* payable's (supplier's) account

When payment is made to the supplier the book-keeping entries are:

- **payment made to trade payable**
    - *debit* payable's account
    - *credit* bank account or cash account

Many businesses keep their payables' accounts as subsidiary accounts in the purchases ledger and use a *purchases ledger control account* as part of the double-entry system. The use of control accounts is covered in Chapter 10.

credit sales

With credit sales, goods or services are sold to a customer who is allowed to settle the account at a later date. From the seller's viewpoint, the customer is a *trade receivable (debtor)*.

The book-keeping entries are:

- **credit sale**
  - – *debit* receivable's (customer's) account
  - – *credit* sales account

When payment is received from the customer the book-keeping entries are:

- **payment received from trade receivable**
  - – *debit* bank account or cash account
  - – *credit* receivable's account

Many businesses keep their receivables' accounts as subsidiary accounts in the sales ledger and use a *sales ledger control account* as part of the double-entry system. The use of control accounts is covered in Chapter 10.

Case Study

1.850

1.600

WYVERN WHOLESALERS: CREDIT TRANSACTIONS

situation

A local business, Wyvern Wholesalers, has the following transactions:

20-7

18 Sep	Bought goods, £250, on credit from Malvern Manufacturing, with payment to be made in 30 days' time
21 Sep	Sold goods, £175, on credit to Strensham Stores, payment to be made in 30 days' time
16 Oct	Paid £250 by cheque to Malvern Manufacturing
20 Oct	Received a cheque for £175 from Strensham Stores

Notes:

- *Wyvern Wholesalers is not registered for Value Added Tax*
- *day books are not used*

solution

These transactions will be recorded in the book-keeping system as follows (previous transactions on accounts, if there are any, are not shown here) :

Dr			Purchases account		Cr
20-7		£	20-7		£
18 Sep	Malvern Manufacturing	250			

Dr			Sales account		Cr
20-7		£	20-7		£
			21 Sep	Strensham Stores	175

Dr			**Malvern Manufacturing**		Cr
20-7		£	20-7		£
16 Oct	Bank	250	18 Sep	Purchases	250

Dr			**Strensham Stores**		Cr
20-7		£	20-7		£
21 Sep	Sales	175	20 Oct	Bank	175

Dr			**Bank account**		Cr
20-7		£	20-7		£
20 Oct	Strensham Stores	175	16 Oct	Malvern Manufacturing	250

Note: the name of the other account involved has been used in the details column as a description.

balancing off accounts

In the Case Study above, after the transactions have been recorded in the books of Wyvern Wholesalers, the accounts of Malvern Manufacturing and Strensham Stores have the same amount entered on both debit and credit side. This means that nothing is owing to Wyvern Wholesalers, or is owed by it, ie the accounts have a 'nil' balance. In the course of trading, accounts will often *not* have a nil balance. We will explain in Chapter 3 how to 'balance' an account to show the 'total' of that account.

non-current assets bought on credit

Non-current (fixed) assets are often purchased on credit terms. As with the purchase of goods for resale, an account is opened in the name of the supplier, as follows:

- **purchase of a non-current asset on credit**
    - *debit* non-current asset account
    - *credit* payable's (supplier's) account

When payment is made to the supplier the book-keeping entries are:

- **payment made to trade payable**
    - *debit* payable's account
    - *credit* bank account or cash account

The book of prime entry for the purchase of non-current assets on credit is the journal – see Chapter 11.

PURCHASES RETURNS AND SALES RETURNS

From time-to-time goods bought or sold are returned, perhaps because the wrong items have been supplied (eg wrong type, size or colour), or because the goods are unsatisfactory. The book-keeping entries for returned goods are explained below.

purchases returns

Purchases returns (or *returns out*) is where a business returns goods to a supplier.

The book-keeping entries are:

– *debit* payable's (supplier's) account

– *credit* purchases returns (or returns outwards) account

Purchases returns are normally kept separate from purchases, ie they are entered in a separate purchases returns account rather than being credited to purchases account.

sales returns

Sales returns (or *returns in*) is where a customer returns goods to the business.

The book-keeping entries are:

– *debit* sales returns (or returns in) account

– *credit* receivable's (customer's) account

Sales returns are normally kept separate from sales, ie they are entered in a separate sales returns account rather than being debited to sales account.

Businesses usually record returns transactions (of goods or services originally bought/sold on credit) in appropriate books of prime entry:

• purchases returns are entered in the purchases returns day book

• sales returns are entered in the sales returns day book

The totals and amounts from these day books are transferred into the double-entry accounts at regular intervals.

Now read the Case Study which follows on the next page. It shows how the double-entry book-keeping for purchases and sales returns is carried out.

SUDBURY SUPPLIERS: PURCHASES RETURNS AND SALES RETURNS

situation

Sudbury Suppliers has the following transactions:

20-8

  7 Oct   Bought goods, £280, on credit from B Lewis Limited

  9 Oct   Returned unsatisfactory goods, £30, to B Lewis Limited

12 Oct   Sold goods, £125, on credit to A Holmes

19 Oct   A Holmes returned goods, £25

26 Oct   Paid the amount owing to B Lewis Limited by cheque

29 Oct   A Holmes paid the amount owing in cash

Notes:
* *Sudbury Suppliers is not registered for Value Added Tax*
* *day books are not used*

solution

The transactions will be recorded in the book-keeping system (previous transactions on accounts, if any, not shown) as follows:

Dr		Purchases account		Cr
20-8		£	20-8	£
7 Oct	B Lewis Limited	280		

Dr		B Lewis Limited		Cr
20-8		£	20-8	£
9 Oct	Purchases returns	30	7 Oct Purchases	280
26 Oct	Bank	250		

Dr		Purchases returns account		Cr
20-8		£	20-8	£
			9 Oct B Lewis Limited	30

Dr		Sales account		Cr
20-8		£	20-8	£
			12 Oct A Holmes	125

Dr		A Holmes		Cr
20-8	£	20-8		£
12 Oct	Sales	125	19 Oct	Sales returns	25
			29 Oct	Cash	100

Dr		Sales returns account		Cr
20-8	£	20-8		£
19 Oct	A Holmes	25			

Dr		Bank account		Cr
20-8	£	20-8		£
			26 Oct	B Lewis Limited	250

Dr		Cash account		Cr
20-8	£	20-8		£
29 Oct	A Holmes	100			

CARRIAGE IN AND CARRIAGE OUT

Carriage in (inwards) is where the buyer pays the carriage (transport) cost of purchases, eg an item is purchased by an internet order, and the buyer has to pay the additional cost of delivery (and possibly packing also).

Carriage out (outwards) is where the seller pays the carriage charge, eg an item is sold to the customer and described as 'post free'.

Both carriage in and carriage out are expenses and their cost should be debited to two separate expenses accounts, *carriage in account* and *carriage out account* respectively:

- **carriage in**
  - *debit* carriage in account (alternatively, purchases account could be debited)
  - *credit* payable's account, or bank account/cash account

- **carriage out**
  - *debit* carriage out account
  - *credit* bank account/cash account

Tutorial note: the reason for using two separate expenses accounts is because they are dealt with differently in the conventional format income statement (Chapter 12).

SETTLEMENT DISCOUNT IN THE BOOK-KEEPING SYSTEM

Settlement discount (or cash discount) is an allowance off the invoice amount for quick settlement, eg 2% settlement discount for settlement within seven days. (Do not confuse settlement discount with *trade discount* – an amount sometimes allowed as a reduction in price when goods are supplied to other businesses – or with *bulk discount* – a reduction in price when large quantities of goods are supplied.) A business can be involved with settlement discount in two ways:

- discount allowed to customers
- discount received from suppliers

Case Study

R PATEL: DISCOUNTS ALLOWED AND RECEIVED

situation – discount allowed

R Patel sells TV and computer equipment. When settlement discount allowed is taken by one of his customers it is entered into the accounts as shown by the following transactions:

20-9

12 Oct   Sold goods, £100, on credit to P Henry, allowing her a settlement discount of 2% for payment within 7 days (note: the seller of the goods is not VAT-registered)

16 Oct   P Henry pays £98 by bank transfer

solution

Dr		Sales account		Cr
20-9		£	20-9	£
			12 Oct P Henry	100

Dr		P Henry		Cr
20-9		£	20-9	£
12 Oct	Sales	100	16 Oct Bank	98
			16 Oct Discount allowed	2
		100		100

Dr		Bank account		Cr
20-9		£	20-9	£
16 Oct	P Henry	98		

Dr		Discount allowed account		Cr
20-9		£	20-9	£
16 Oct	P Henry	2		

Notes:

- *The amount of the payment received from P Henry is debited to the bank account and credited to the receivable's account.*
- *The amount of discount allowed – an expense to the business – is debited to discount allowed account and credited to the receivable's account.*

situation – discount received

R Patel is allowed settlement discount by his suppliers. The following transactions show how discount received is entered into the accounts.

20-9

20 Oct   Bought goods, £200, on credit from H Singh Limited; 2.5% settlement discount is offered for payment by the end of October (note: the seller of the goods is not registered for VAT)

30 Oct   Paid H Singh Limited £195 by bank transfer

solution

Dr		Purchases account			Cr
20-9		£	20-9		£
20 Oct	H Singh Limited	200			

Dr		H Singh Limited			Cr
20-9		£	20-9		£
30 Oct	Bank	195	20 Oct	Purchases	200
30 Oct	Discount received	5			
		200			200

Dr		Bank account			Cr
20-9		£	20-9		£
			30 Oct	H Singh Limited	195

Dr		Discount received account			Cr
20-9		£	20-9		£
			30 Oct	H Singh Limited	5

Notes:

- *The business is receiving settlement discount from H Singh Limited, and the amount is entered as: debit payable's account, credit discount received account.*
- *Discount received account is an income account, because it represents a benefit given to the business by suppliers.*

VAT AND DOUBLE-ENTRY ACCOUNTS

When a business is registered with HM Revenue and Customs for Value Added Tax, it is normally able to claim back VAT paid on purchases of goods, non-current assets and expenses – this is known as *input tax*. A VAT-registered business must also charge VAT – *output tax* – whenever it supplies goods and services (except for zero-rated and exempt goods and services). A separate account is opened for VAT.

When a VAT-registered business buys, for example, non-current assets it will enter the amount of input VAT direct to the debit side of VAT account.

example transaction

On 16 April 20-1, Osborne Paints Limited, a company which is registered for Value Added Tax, buys a new computer at a cost of £1,000 + VAT of £200 (at 20%), paying £1,200 by bank transfer.

This is recorded in the double-entry accounts as:

Dr			Computer account			Cr
20-1		£	20-1			£
16 Apr	Bank	1,000				

Dr			Value Added Tax account			Cr
20-1		£	20-1			£
16 Apr	Bank	200				

Dr			Bank account			Cr
20-1		£	20-1			£
			16 Apr	Computer		1,200

Similarly when Osborne Paints Limited sells its paints to a customer it will charge *output VAT* on the goods. For example, the entries for a sale of £720 (£600 + VAT at 20%) will be:

- *debit* customer's account £720 – this is the amount owed
- *credit* VAT account £120 – this is the VAT charged on the sale
- *credit* sales account £600 – this is the value of the goods sold

Chapter Summary

- Business transactions are recorded in ledger accounts using double-entry book-keeping principles.

- Each double-entry book-keeping transaction involves a debit entry and a credit entry.

- Entries in the bank account and cash account are:
  - *debit* money in
  - *credit* money out

- Non-current (fixed) assets are items purchased by a business for use on a semi-permanent basis, eg premises, vehicles, machinery and office equipment. The purchase of such items is called *capital expenditure*.

- Running expenses of a business, such as rent paid, wages, electricity, etc are called *revenue expenditure*.

- Other accounts are opened in the book-keeping system for: capital, non-current assets, expenses, income, drawings and loans.

- Purchases account is used to record the purchase of goods in which the business trades: the normal entry is on the debit side.

- Sales account is used to record the sale of goods or services in which the business trades: the normal entry is on the credit side.

- The purchase of goods is recorded as:
  - *debit* purchases account
  - *credit* bank/cash account or, if bought on credit, payable's account

- The sale of goods or services is recorded as:
  - *debit* bank/cash account or, if sold on credit, receivable's account
  - *credit* sales account

- Purchases returns (or returns out) are recorded as:
  - *debit* payable's account
  - *credit* purchases returns account

- Sales returns (or returns in) are recorded as:
  - *debit* sales returns account
  - *credit* receivable's account

- 'Carriage' is the expense of transporting goods:
  - *carriage in (inwards)* is the cost of carriage paid on purchases
  - *carriage out (outwards)* is the cost of carriage paid on sales

- Settlement discount allowed (cash discount) is entered in the accounts as:
  - *debit* discount allowed account
  - *credit* receivable's account

- Settlement discount received is entered as:
  - *debit* payable's account
  - *credit* discount received account

- VAT account will record the amounts of input VAT (VAT on purchases and expenses) and output VAT (VAT on sales of goods and services).

<table>
<tr><td rowspan="20">**Key Terms**</td></tr>
<tr><td>**ledger accounts**</td><td>where double-entry book-keeping transactions are recorded</td></tr>
<tr><td>**debit entry**</td><td>the account which gains value, or records an asset or an expense</td></tr>
<tr><td>**credit entry**</td><td>the account which gives value, or records a liability, or an income item</td></tr>
<tr><td>**capital**</td><td>the amount of money invested in the business by the owner (or owners)</td></tr>
<tr><td>**non-current (fixed) asset**</td><td>item purchased by a business for use on a semi-permanent basis</td></tr>
<tr><td>**capital expenditure**</td><td>the purchase of non-current assets for use by the business</td></tr>
<tr><td>**revenue expenditure**</td><td>the expenses incurred in the day-to-day running of the business</td></tr>
<tr><td>**drawings**</td><td>money taken from the business by the owner, in the form of cash or cheque (or sometimes goods) for personal use</td></tr>
<tr><td>**purchases account**</td><td>used to record the purchase – whether on credit or for cash – of the goods in which the business trades</td></tr>
<tr><td>**sales account**</td><td>used to record the sale – whether on credit or for cash – of the goods in which the business trades</td></tr>
<tr><td>**credit purchases**</td><td>goods bought, with payment to be made at a later date</td></tr>
<tr><td>**credit sales**</td><td>goods sold, with payment to be received at an agreed date in the future</td></tr>
<tr><td>**purchases returns**</td><td>where a business returns goods to a supplier</td></tr>
<tr><td>**sales returns**</td><td>where a customer returns goods to the business</td></tr>
<tr><td>**carriage in**</td><td>the cost of carriage paid on purchases</td></tr>
<tr><td>**carriage out**</td><td>the cost of carriage paid on sales</td></tr>
<tr><td>**settlement discount**</td><td>an allowance off the invoice amount for quick payment</td></tr>
<tr><td>**discount allowed**</td><td>settlement discount allowed to customers</td></tr>
<tr><td>**discount received**</td><td>settlement discount received from suppliers</td></tr>
</table>

Activities

2.1 The payment of wages in cash is recorded in the accounts as:

	Debit	Credit
(a)	wages account	drawings account
(b)	cash account	wages account
(c)	capital account	wages account
(d)	wages account	cash account

Answer (a) or (b) or (c) or (d)

2.2 A loan is received by cheque from John Box. This is recorded in the accounts as:

	Debit	Credit
(a)	bank account	capital account
(b)	bank account	John Box: loan account
(c)	drawings account	John Box: loan account
(d)	John Box: loan account	bank account

Answer (a) or (b) or (c) or (d)

2.3 The owner of a business withdraws cash for her own use. This is recorded in the accounts as:

	Debit	Credit
(a)	drawings account	bank account
(b)	bank account	cash account
(c)	wages account	cash account
(d)	drawings account	cash account

Answer (a) or (b) or (c) or (d)

2.4 James Anderson has kept his bank account up-to-date, but has not got around to the other double-entry book-keeping entries. Rule up the other accounts for him, and make the appropriate entries.

Dr			**Bank account**			Cr
20-4		£		20-4		£
2 Feb	Capital	7,500		6 Feb	Computer	2,000
13 Feb	Bank loan	2,500		9 Feb	Rent paid	750
20 Feb	Commission received	145		12 Feb	Wages	425
				23 Feb	Drawings	200
				25 Feb	Wages	380
				27 Feb	Van	6,000

Note: James Anderson is not registered for Value Added Tax

3 Balancing accounts and the trial balance

this chapter covers...

With the 'traditional' form of account (the 'T' account) that we have used so far, it is necessary to calculate the balance of each account from time-to-time, according to the needs of the business, and at the end of each financial year.

The balance of an account is the total of that account to date, eg the amount of wages paid, the amount of sales made. In this chapter we shall see how this balancing of accounts is carried out.

We shall then use the balances from each account in order to check the double-entry book-keeping by extracting a trial balance, which is a list of the balances of all the general ledger accounts, including cash book (which contains bank account and cash account).

BALANCING THE ACCOUNTS

At regular intervals, often at the end of each month, 'T' accounts are balanced in order to show total amounts to date, for example:

- owing to each trade payable
- owing by each trade receivable
- cash and credit sales (referred to in total as 'revenue' or 'sales revenue')
- purchases
- sales returns (returns in)
- purchases returns (returns out)
- expenses incurred by the business
- non-current assets, eg premises, machinery, etc owned by the business
- bank and cash
- capital and drawings of the owner of the business
- liabilities, eg loans

The reason for balancing accounts is to enable the balances to be used in the trial balance (see page 41), which is a check on the accuracy of the double-entry book-keeping and also the starting point for the preparation of year end financial statements.

METHOD OF BALANCING ACCOUNTS

Set out below is an example of a traditional format double-entry account which has been balanced at the month-end:

Dr			**Bank account**			Cr
20-1		£	20-1			£
1 Sep	Capital	5,000	2 Sep	Computer		1,800
4 Sep	J Jackson: loan	2,500	7 Sep	Purchases		500
10 Sep	Sales	750	11 Sep	Drawings		100
			15 Sep	Wages		200
			30 Sep	Balance c/d		5,650
		8,250				8,250
1 Oct	Balance b/d	5,650				

The steps involved in balancing accounts are shown on the next page.

Step 1

The entries in the debit and credit money columns are totalled; these totals are not recorded in ink on the account at this stage, but can be written either as sub-totals in pencil on the account, or noted on a separate piece of paper. In the example on the previous page the debit side totals £8,250, while the credit side is £2,600.

Step 2

The difference between the two totals is the balance of the account and this is entered on the account:

- on the side of the smaller total
- on the next available line
- with the date of balancing (often the last day of the month)
- with the description 'balance c/d', or 'balance carried down'

In the example shown, the balance carried down is £8,250 – £2,600 = £5,650, entered in the credit column.

Step 3

Both sides of the account are now totalled, including the balance which has just been entered, and the totals (the same on both sides) are entered *on the same line* in the appropriate column, and double underlined. The double underline indicates that the account has been balanced at this point using the figures above the total: the figures above the underline should not be added in to anything below the underline.

In the example shown, the totals on each side of the account are £8,250.

Step 4

As we are using double-entry book-keeping, there must be an opposite entry to the 'balance c/d' calculated in Step 2. The same money amount is entered *on the other side of the account* below the double underlined totals entered in Step 3. We have now completed both the debit and credit entry. The date is usually recorded as the next day after 'balance c/d', ie often the first day of the following month, and the description can be 'balance b/d' or 'balance brought down'.

In the example shown, the balance brought down on the bank account on 1 October 20-1 is £5,650 debit; this means that, according to the firm's accounting records, there is £5,650 in the bank.

a practical point

When balancing accounts, use a pen and not a pencil (except for Step 1). If any errors are made, cross them through neatly with a single line, and write the corrected version on the line below. Avoid using correcting fluid – it may hide errors, but it can also conceal fraudulent transactions.

further examples of balancing accounts

Dr		Wages account				Cr
20-1		£	20-1			£
9 Apr	Bank	750	30 Apr	Balance c/d		2,250
16 Apr	Bank	800				
23 Apr	Bank	700				
		2,250				2,250
1 May	Balance b/d	2,250				

This wages account has transactions on one side only, but is still balanced in the same way. The account shows that the total amount paid for wages is £2,250.

Dr		B Lewis Limited			Cr
20-1		£	20-1		£
10 Apr	Purchases returns	30	7 Apr	Purchases	280
27 Apr	Bank	250			
		280			280

This payable's (creditor's) account has a 'nil' balance after the transactions for April have taken place. The two sides of the account are totalled and, as both debit and credit side are the same amount, there is nothing further to do, apart from entering the double underlined total.

Dr		A Holmes			Cr
20-1		£	20-1		£
1 Apr	Balance b/d	105	10 Apr	Bank	105
10 Apr	Sales	125	13 Apr	Sales returns	25
			30 Apr	Balance c/d	100
		230			230
1 May	Balance b/d	100			

This receivable's (debtor's) account has a debit balance at the start of the month of £105 brought down from March. After the various transactions for April, there remains a debit balance of £100 owing at 1 May.

Dr		Office equipment account			Cr
20-1		£	20-1		£
13 Apr	Bank	2,000			

This account has just the one transaction and, in practice, there is no need to balance it. The account clearly has a debit balance of £2,000, which represents office equipment (a non-current asset).

Dr		Malvern Manufacturing Company			Cr
20-1		£	20-1		£
29 Apr	Bank	250	17 Apr	Purchases	250

This payable's account has a 'nil' balance, with just one transaction on each side. All that is needed here is to double underline the amount on both sides.

CONTROL ACCOUNTS

There is one further type of account to mention before looking at the accounts listed in the trial balance – a control account.

A control account is a summary account or master account, which records the totals of entries to a particular set of accounts.

Sales ledger control account shows the total of all the receivables' accounts in the sales ledger and tells the owner of the business how much in total is owing from trade receivables.

Purchases ledger control account shows the total of all the payables' accounts in the purchases ledger and tells the owner of the business how much in total is owing to trade payables.

Value Added Tax control account brings together totals of VAT from books of prime entry, such as the day books and cash books, and tells the owner of the business how much in total is owing to (the usual situation for most businesses), or owing from, HM Revenue and Customs.

The use of control accounts is covered in more detail in Chapter 10.

control accounts and the trial balance

The trial balance (see next page) is the listing of all the account balances in two columns: debit balances on the left, credit balances on the right.

It is the balances of the control accounts which are taken to the trial balance rather than the individual receivables and payables account balances, which would clutter it up and make it very long. The description in the trial balance is 'sales ledger control account' (debit balance on the left) and 'purchases ledger control account' (credit balance on the right). This is illustrated in the following diagram.

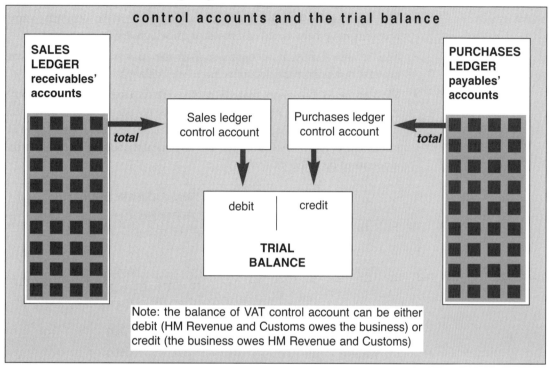

EXTRACTING A TRIAL BALANCE

The purpose of a trial balance, which is taken from the accounting records – either manually or by generation of a computer report – is to:

- check the accuracy of the double-entry book-keeping, ie that the total of debit entries equals the total of the credit entries

- form the basis for the preparation of the year end financial statements of the business

A trial balance is a list of the balances of every account from the general ledger, (including cash book) setting out debit balances and credit balances in separate columns.

A trial balance is extracted at regular intervals – often at the end of each month. An example is shown on the next page.

Note the following points:

- The debit and credit columns have been totalled and are the same amount. Thus the trial balance proves that the accounting records are *arithmetically* correct – the total of the debits equals the total of the credits. (For types of errors, see page 45.)

- The heading for a trial balance gives the name of the business whose accounts have been listed and the date on which it was extracted.

- The balance for each account listed in the trial balance is the figure brought down after the accounts have been balanced.

- Most of the trial balances that you will see in Assessments are listed with the accounts in alphabetical order. There is no need for you to do this when preparing trial balances – unless, of course, you are instructed to do so, or are given an accounts list already in alphabetical order with the amounts to be filled in.

TARA SMITH, TRADING AS "THE FASHION SHOP"
Trial balance as at 31 December 20-4

	Dr £	Cr £
Opening inventory (stock)	12,500	
Purchases	105,000	
Sales revenue		155,000
Administration expenses	6,200	
Wages	23,500	
Rent paid	750	
Telephone	500	
Interest paid	4,500	
Travel expenses	550	
Premises	100,000	
Shop fittings	20,000	
Sales ledger control (receivables)	10,500	
Bank	5,450	
Cash	50	
Capital		75,000
Drawings	7,000	
Loan from bank		50,000
Purchases ledger control (payables)		14,500
Value Added Tax		2,000
	296,500	296,500

DEBIT AND CREDIT BALANCES – GUIDELINES

Certain accounts always have a debit balance, while others always have a credit balance. You should already know these, but the lists set out below will act as a revision guide, and will also help in your understanding of trial balances.

debit balances

- cash account
- purchases account
- sales returns account (returns in)
- non-current asset accounts, eg computers, vehicles, machinery, etc
- expenses accounts, eg wages, telephone, rent paid, carriage in, carriage out, etc
- drawings account
- sales ledger control account (the total of the receivables' accounts)

credit balances

- sales or sales revenue account
- purchases returns account (returns out)
- income accounts, eg rent received, discount received, fees received, etc
- capital account
- loan account, eg loan from bank
- purchases ledger control account (the total of the payables' accounts)

Note that:
- *Bank account* can be either debit or credit – it will be debit when the business has money in the bank, and credit when it is overdrawn.
- *Value Added Tax account* can be either debit or credit – it will be debit when VAT is due to the business and credit when the business owes VAT to HM Revenue and Customs.

IF THE TRIAL BALANCE DOESN'T BALANCE . . .

If the trial balance fails to balance, ie the two totals are different, there is an error (or errors):
- *either* in the addition of the trial balance
- *and/or* in the double-entry book-keeping

The procedure for finding the error(s) is as follows:

- check the addition of the trial balance

- check that the balance of each account has been correctly entered in the trial balance, and under the correct heading, ie debit or credit

- check that the balance of every account from the general ledger (including cash book) has been included in the trial balance

- check the calculation of the balance on each account

- calculate the amount that the trial balance is wrong, and then look in the accounts for a transaction for this amount: if one is found, check that the double-entry book-keeping has been carried out correctly

- halve the amount by which the trial balance is wrong, and look for a transaction for this amount: if it is found, check the double-entry book-keeping

- if the amount by which the trial balance is wrong is divisible by nine, then the error may be a reversal of figures, eg £65 entered as £56, or £45 entered as £54

- if the trial balance is wrong by a round amount, eg £10, £100, £1,000, the error is likely to be in the calculation of the account balances

- if the error(s) is still not found, it is necessary to check the book-keeping transactions since the date of the last trial balance, by going back to the prime documents (invoices, cheques, etc) and the books of prime entry (day books and cash book)

- we will look at how to correct errors shown by the trial balance in Chapter 11, for example

  - one-sided entry (ie only one of the two parts of a double-entry transaction has been recorded)

  - entry duplicated on one side, nothing on the other (ie two debits or two credits have been recorded for a transaction)

  - unequal entries (ie different amounts have been recorded for the debit and credit entries)

  - account balance incorrectly transferred to the trial balance

ERRORS NOT REVEALED BY A TRIAL BALANCE

As mentioned earlier, a trial balance does not prove the complete accuracy of the accounting records. There are six main types of errors that are not revealed by a trial balance.

error of principle

This is when a transaction has been entered in the wrong type of account. For example, the cost of fuel for vehicles has been entered as a debit to vehicles account, and as a credit to bank account. The error is that vehicles account is a non-current asset and the transaction should have been debited to the vehicle expenses account. If not corrected, such an error of principle will show a false financial position for the business.

mispost/error of commission

Here, a transaction is entered to the wrong person's account. For example, a sale of goods on credit to A T Hughes entered as a debit to A J Hughes' account. The double-entry book-keeping has been completed, but the error will be discovered when A J Hughes complains about the incorrect charge.

error of original entry

Here, the correct accounts have been used, and the correct sides: what is wrong is that the amount has been entered incorrectly in *both* accounts. This could be caused by a 'bad figure' written on a financial document, eg an invoice, or it could be caused by a 'reversal of figures', eg an amount of £45 being entered in both accounts as £54. Note that where both debit and credit entries have been made incorrectly the trial balance will still balance; if one entry has been made incorrectly and the other is correct, then the error will be revealed.

error of omission

Here a transaction has been completely omitted from the accounting records, ie both the debit and credit entries have not been made.

reversal of entries

With this error, the debit and credit entries have been made in the accounts but on the wrong side of the two accounts concerned. For example, a cash sale has been entered wrongly as a debit to sales account, and as a credit to cash account. (This should have been entered as a debit to cash account, and a credit to sales account.)

compensating error

This is where two separate errors cancel each other out. For example, if the balance of purchases account is calculated wrongly at £10 too much, and a similar £10 error has occurred in calculating the balance of sales account, the the two errors will compensate each other, and the trial balance will not show the errors

Correction of errors is covered fully in Chapter 11.

IMPORTANCE OF THE TRIAL BALANCE

A business will extract a trial balance on a regular basis to check the arithmetical accuracy of the book-keeping. More importantly, the trial balance is used as a basis for the preparation of the *financial statements* of a business. These financial statements, which are prepared once a year (often more frequently) comprise:

- income statement (profit and loss account)
- statement of financial position (balance sheet)

The financial statements show the owner(s) how profitable the business has been, what the business owns, and how the business is financed. The preparation of financial statements is an important aspect of accounting and one which we shall be developing in the remainder of this book.

In the next chapter we will see how the two-column trial balance is extended and the figures entered into further columns as a method of preparing the financial statements.

Chapter Summary

- The traditional 'T' account needs to be balanced at regular intervals – often at the month-end.

- When balancing accounts, the book-keeper must adhere strictly to the rules of double-entry book-keeping.

- When each account in the ledger has been balanced, a trial balance can be extracted.

- A trial balance does not prove the complete accuracy of the accounting records; errors not revealed by a trial balance are:
  - error of principle
  - mispost/error of commission
  - error of original entry
  - error of omission
  - reversal of entries
  - compensating error

- The trial balance is used as the starting point for the preparation of a business' financial statements.

Key Terms	balance of account	the total amount of the account to date
	control account	summary or master account which records the totals of entries to a particular set of accounts; examples are: – sales ledger control account – purchases ledger control account – Value Added Tax control account
	trial balance	list of the balances of every account forming the general ledger (including cash book), distinguishing between those accounts which have debit balances and those which have credit balances
	error of principle	transaction entered in the wrong type of account
	error of original entry	wrong amount entered incorrectly in accounts
	error of omission	business transaction completely omitted from the accounting records
	reversal of entries	debit and credit entries made on the wrong side of the accounts

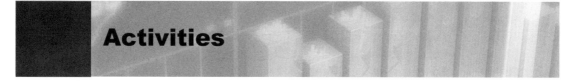

Activities

3.1   A firm's bank account is as follows:

Dr			Bank account			Cr
20-7		£	20-7			£
1 Jan	Capital	1,000	9 Jan	Computer		500
19 Jan	Sales	650	12 Jan	Purchases		400
			27 Jan	Purchases		350
			29 Jan	Electricity		75

At 31 January 20-7, the balance of the account is:

(a)   credit £325

(b)   debit £1,650

(c)   debit £325

(d)   credit £1,325

Answer (a) or (b) or (c) or (d)

3.2   Which one of the following accounts normally has a debit balance?

(a)   capital account

(b)   purchases account

(c)   sales account

(d)   purchases returns account

Answer (a) or (b) or (c) or (d)

3.3   Which one of the following accounts normally has a credit balance?

(a)   purchases account

(b)   premises account

(c)   capital account

(d)   wages account

Answer (a) or (b) or (c) or (d)

3.4   The following are the business transactions of Andrew Johnstone, a retailer of computer software, for the months of January and February 20-4:

Transactions for January

1 Jan	Started in business with £10,000 in the bank
4 Jan	Paid rent on premises £500, by cheque
5 Jan	Bought shop fittings £1,500, by cheque
7 Jan	Bought stock of computer software £5,000, on credit from Comp Supplies Limited
11 Jan	Software sales £1,000 paid into bank
12 Jan	Software sales £1,250 paid into bank
16 Jan	Software sales £850 on credit to Rowcester College
20 Jan	Paid Comp Supplies Limited £5,000 by cheque
22 Jan	Software sales £1,450 paid into bank
25 Jan	Bought software £6,500 on credit from Comp Supplies Limited
27 Jan	Rowcester College returns software £100

Transactions for February

2 Feb	Paid rent on premises £500 by cheque
4 Feb	Software sales £1,550 paid into bank
5 Feb	Returned faulty software, £150 to Comp Supplies Limited
10 Feb	Software sales £1,300 paid into bank
12 Feb	Rowcester College pays the amount owing by cheque
15 Feb	Bought shop fittings £850 by cheque
19 Feb	Software sales £1,600 paid into bank
22 Feb	Paid Comp Supplies Limited the amount owing by cheque
24 Feb	Bought software £5,500 on credit from Comp Supplies Limited
25 Feb	Software sales £1,100 paid into bank
26 Feb	Software sales £1,050 on credit to Rowcester College

You are to:

(a)   record the January transactions in the double-entry accounts, and balance each account at 31 January 20-4

(b)   draw up a trial balance at 31 January 20-4

(c)   record the February transactions in the double-entry accounts, and balance each account at 28 February 20-4

(d)   draw up a trial balance at 28 February 20-4

Notes

*   *Andrew Johnstone is not registered for Value Added Tax*

*   *day books are not required*

*   *Andrew Johnstone's accounting system does not use control accounts*

*   *make sure that you leave plenty of space for each account – particularly sales, purchases and bank*

3.5   Prepare the trial balance of Samantha Wilkes as at 31 March 20-4. You are to fill in the missing figure for her capital in order to balance the trial balance.

	£
Bank overdraft	2,750
Purchases	14,890
Sales	35,680
Purchases returns	440
Purchases ledger control	2,360
Office equipment	8,000
Vehicle	14,000
Opening inventory (stock)	2,810
Sales returns	550
Sales ledger control	3,840
Administration expenses	12,060
Value Added Tax owing	1,420
Carriage out	740
Discount received	210
Capital	?

4 Financial statements – the extended trial balance

this chapter covers...

So far we have looked at the techniques of recording different types of financial transactions in the books of account. The financial accountant will use the information from the accounting system, summarised in the two-column trial balance, to produce the year end financial statements of the business: income statement (profit and loss account) and statement of financial position (balance sheet).

In this chapter we see how these financial statements can be produced using an extended trial balance (ETB). This sets out debit and credit columns for:

- *the ledger balances*

- *adjustments to the figures*

- *the financial statements where the figures are used: income statement and statement of financial position*

Later in the chapter we study the link between double-entry book-keeping and the financial statements.

FINANCIAL STATEMENTS

At regular intervals the owner/owners of a business and other interested parties need to know how the business is progressing. To meet this need, financial statements are prepared which comprise:

- *income statement (profit and loss account)* – showing the profitability and performance of the business during the accounting period
- *statement of financial position (balance sheet)* – showing what the business is worth (in terms of assets, liabilities, and capital) at the end of the accounting period

In this chapter we will see how the figures for the financial statements are prepared by means of the *extended trial balance* which takes the figures from the two-column trial balance explained in the last chapter and sets them out in columns ready for the preparation of the income statement and statement of financial position. To illustrate this process we will look at the accounts of a sole trader shop owner, Tara Smith.

In the three chapters which follow we will be developing the extended trial balance of Tara Smith to deal with accounting adjustments for accruals and prepayments, depreciation of non-current assets, irrecoverable debts and allowance for doubtful debts. Such adjustments are used to present a more realistic view of the business' financial statements.

ACCOUNTING PERIODS

There is a link between the financial statements: an income statement covers a specific time period, and a statement of financial position shows the state of the business on the last day of that time period. For example:

- income statement **for the year ended** 31 March 20-6
- statement of financial position **as at** 31 March 20-6

The time period covered by the income statement is known as an *accounting period*. Generally, for each business, an accounting period covers the same length of time, for example the year ended 31 March 20-6, year ended 31 March 20-7, and so on. The last day of one accounting period is immediately followed by the first day of the next accounting period. While accounting periods can cover any length of time, the most common are:

- *monthly or quarterly* – used within a business to monitor activity and profitability in the accounting period, and the state of the business, in terms of assets and liabilities, at the end of the period

- *half-yearly* – often produced by public limited companies as information for their shareholders
- *annually* – the most common accounting period (but not always to fit the calendar year) used by virtually every business from sole traders and partnerships, through to the largest public limited companies

FINANCIAL STATEMENTS AND THE TRIAL BALANCE

As we have seen in earlier chapters, the book-keeping system records day-to-day business transactions. At regular intervals a trial balance is extracted to prove the arithmetical accuracy of the book-keeping. It is the trial balance that provides the starting point in the preparation of financial statements. There are two trial balance formats:

- the two-column trial balance (shown opposite)
- the trial balance *extended* into a number of columns (see page 55)

Note that the income statement is an 'account' in terms of double-entry book-keeping. This means that an amount recorded in this account must be recorded elsewhere in the book-keeping system, eg a debit to the income statement is recorded as a credit to another account, in order to complete double-entry. By contrast, the statement of financial position is not an account, but is a list of account balances remaining after the income statement has been prepared.

To understand the preparation of the extended trial balance you should now read the Tara Smith Case Study which follows.

Case Study

TARA SMITH: THE EXTENDED TRIAL BALANCE

situation

Tara Smith runs a designer clothes shop called 'The Fashion Shop'. Her book-keeper has just extracted the year end trial balance shown opposite. You will see that the trial balance includes the inventory value at the *start* of the year, while the end-of-year inventory valuation is noted *after* the trial balance. For the purposes of financial accounting, the inventory of goods for resale is valued by the business at the end of each financial year, and the valuation is subsequently entered into the book-keeping system (see page 58).

We will go through the process of preparing the financial statements using an extended trial balance (ETB) – this is the next stage on from the two-column trial balance and is often presented in a spreadsheet format. We will go through this process before explaining adjustments for items such as accruals, prepayments, depreciation of non-current assets, irrecoverable debts, and allowance for doubtful debts (each of which will be dealt with in Chapters 5 to 7).

TARA SMITH, TRADING AS "THE FASHION SHOP"

	Dr	Cr
	£	£
Opening inventory (stock)	12,500	
Purchases	105,000	
Sales revenue		155,000
Administration expenses	6,200	
Wages	23,500	
Rent paid	750	
Telephone	500	
Interest paid	4,500	
Travel expenses	550	
Premises at cost	100,000	
Shop fittings at cost	20,000	
Sales ledger control (receivables)	10,500	
Bank	5,450	
Cash	50	
Capital		75,000
Drawings	7,000	
Loan from bank		50,000
Purchases ledger control (payables)		14,500
Value Added Tax		2,000
	296,500	296,500

Note: closing inventory was valued at £10,500

The layout on page 55 shows how an extended trial balance uses columns and rows to prepare the financial statements of Tara Smith. The steps to complete the extended trial balance are as follows:

step 1 Enter the trial balance details into the account name and ledger balances columns. Total the debit and credit columns of ledger balances to show that the trial balance proves the arithmetical accuracy of the book-keeping. Note that the blank lines after premises at cost and shop fittings at cost will be used for accumulated depreciation amounts – dealt with in Chapter 6.

step 2 Deal with adjustments – in this example, the only adjustment is for the valuation of closing inventory (at 31 December 20-4). In the adjustments columns the amount of closing inventory is credited to the income statement and debited to the statement of financial position (see page 58 for the book-keeping entries for closing inventory). Transfer the adjustment for closing inventory to:

- income statement – credit column
- statement of financial position – debit column

Now total the debit and credit adjustment columns; note that the totals are the same, ie they balance. We shall be using the other adjustment items (eg accruals and prepayments) in the next few chapters.

step 3

Transfer to the income statement columns the rows for

- opening inventory at the start of the year
- purchases made by the business
- sales made by the business (together with small amounts of income, if any)
- expenses (revenue expenditure) of the business, such as administration expenses, wages, rent paid, interest paid, travel expenses

Ensure that debit balances from the trial balance rows are entered in the debit column of the income statement; credit balances are entered in the credit column.

step 4

Transfer to the statement of financial position columns the remaining rows from the trial balance (keeping debit and credit figures in the correct columns). These figures represent:

- assets (amounts owned by the business) such as premises, shop fittings, sales ledger control, bank, cash
- liabilities (amounts owed by the business) such as bank overdraft, purchases ledger control, loans, Value Added Tax due to HM Revenue and Customs
- capital (the amount of the owner's finance in the business)
- drawings (the amount withdrawn from the business by the owner during the year)

step 5

In the income statement columns, total the money amounts and then, just like balancing an account, enter the amount required to make both debit and credit sides equal: here it is £12,000. If the amount is entered on the debit side, it represents the profit of the business for the accounting period; if on the credit side, it is a loss. For Tara Smith, it is a profit of £12,000 for the financial year.

step 6

Enter the profit or loss for the year in the statement of financial position columns, but on the opposite side to that in the income statement. For example, with Tara Smith's business, the amount of the profit row is £12,000, which is *debited* in the income statement column and *credited* in the statement of financial position column.

Now total the debit and credit statement of financial position columns. They balance with the same total – here £153,500 – which proves that the statement of financial position balances.

points to note about the extended trial balance

Each account balance from the trial balance is entered into the financial statements once only – either to the income statement (income and expenses), or to the statement of financial position (assets, liabilities, capital and drawings). The additional items of closing inventory and profit or loss for the year are entered into both financial statements – this ensures that the double-entry book-keeping rules of one debit and one credit entry for each transaction are maintained.

There are blank rows below the items of premises and shop fittings. These are intentionally left blank and will eventually show accumulated depreciation amounts (see Chapter 6).

EXTENDED TRIAL BALANCE TARA SMITH TRADING AS "THE FASHION SHOP" **31 DECEMBER 20-4**

Account name	Ledger balances Dr £	Ledger balances Cr £	Adjustments Dr £	Adjustments Cr £	Income statement Dr £	Income statement Cr £	Statement of financial position Dr £	Statement of financial position Cr £
Opening inventory	12,500				12,500			
Purchases	105,000				105,000			
Sales revenue		155,000				155,000		
Administration expenses	6,200				6,200			
Wages	23,500				23,500			
Rent paid	750				750			
Telephone	500				500			
Interest paid	4,500				4,500			
Travel expenses	550				550			
Premises at cost	100,000						100,000	
Shop fittings at cost	20,000						20,000	
Sales ledger control	10,500						10,500	
Bank	5,450						5,450	
Cash	50						50	
Capital		75,000						75,000
Drawings	7,000						7,000	
Loan from bank		50,000						50,000
Purchases ledger control		14,500						14,500
Value Added Tax		2,000						2,000
Closing inventory: income statement				10,500		10,500		
Closing inventory: statement of financial position			10,500				10,500	
Accruals								
Prepayments								
Depreciation charge								
Irrecoverable debts								
Allowance for doubtful debts								
Allowance for doubtful debts:adjustment								
Profit/loss for the year					12,000			12,000
	296,500	296,500	10,500	10,500	165,500	165,500	153,500	153,500

Revenue expenditure (the payment of expenses) is shown in the income statement, while *capital expenditure* (the cost of non-current assets, such as premises, vehicles and equipment) is shown in the statement of financial position. Note that if, for example, the cost of buying a new vehicle was wrongly recorded as an expense in the income statement, then

- profit would be understated (or even a loss sustained)
- the statement of financial position would not show the value of a non-current asset owned by the business

This means that both financial statements would fail to show the correct state of the business' finances. Thus it is important to show revenue expenditure in the income statement, and capital expenditure in the statement of financial position – we will look in more detail at these two types of expenditure in Chapter 8.

EXTENDED TRIAL BALANCE – LAYOUT

The extended trial balance gives an understanding of the principles of financial statements by showing

- the profit (or loss) made by the business during the accounting period
- the assets, liabilities and capital of the business at the end of the accounting period

The extended trial balance format is often used by accountancy firms as a step towards preparing year-end financial statements for their clients. When the adjustments have been completed, it provides a posting sheet for making transfers in the general ledger (see the book-keeping entries in the section which follows).

To help with your practice of extended trial balances, a layout or pro-forma is included in the Appendix. This may be photocopied (it is advisable to enlarge it up to A4 size); alternatively, the layout can be downloaded from the website www.osbornebooks.co.uk

Note that the layout used for the extended trial balance includes space for a number of other adjustments (eg accruals and prepayments) – these will be covered in the later chapters.

DOUBLE-ENTRY BOOK-KEEPING AND THE FINANCIAL STATEMENTS

We have already noted that the income statement forms part of the double-entry book-keeping system. Therefore, each amount recorded in this must have an opposite entry in the general ledger. In preparing the income statement we are, in effect, emptying each account that has been storing up a record of transactions during the course of the financial year and transferring it to the income statement.

Tutorial note: Each of the transfers shown below requires a journal entry – see Chapter 11. This records the amount of the transfer in a book of prime entry and gives the book-keeper the authority to record the transactions in the double-entry accounts.

purchases, sales and inventory

In the accounts of Tara Smith the balance of purchases account will be transferred to the income statement as follows *(debit* income statement; *credit* purchases account):

Dr		**Purchases account**		Cr
20-4	£	20-4		£
31 Dec Balance b/d (ie total for year)	105,000	31 Dec Income statement	105,000	

The account now has a nil balance and is ready to receive the transactions for next year.

The balances of sales account (and also, where used, sales returns and purchases returns accounts) will be cleared to nil in a similar way and the amounts transferred to the income statement, as debits or credits as appropriate.

Inventory account, however, is dealt with differently. Inventory is valued for financial accounting purposes at the end of each year (it is also likely to be valued more regularly in order to provide management information). Only the annual inventory valuation is recorded on inventory account, and the account is not used at any other time. After the book-keeper has extracted the trial balance, but *before* preparation of the income statement, the inventory account appears as follows:

Dr		**Inventory account**		Cr
20-4	£	20-4		£
31 Dec Balance b/d	12,500			

This balance, which is the opening inventory valuation for the year, is transferred to the income statement to leave a nil balance, as follows *(debit* income statement; *credit* inventory account):

Dr		Inventory account			Cr
20-4		£	20-4		£
31 Dec Balance b/d		12,500	31 Dec Income statement		12,500

The *closing* inventory valuation for the year – for Tara Smith it is £10,500 – is now recorded on the account as an asset *(debit* inventory account; *credit* income statement):

Dr		Inventory account			Cr
20-4		£	20-4		£
31 Dec Balance b/d		12,500	31 Dec Income statement		12,500
31 Dec Income statement		10,500	31 Dec Balance c/d		10,500
20-5			20-5		
1 Jan Balance b/d		10,500			

The closing inventory figure is shown on the statement of financial position, and will be the opening inventory in next year's income statement. In the extended trial balance the closing inventory figure is normally put through the adjustments columns; however, some trial balances in Activities and Assessments may already incorporate the closing inventory adjustments – see Activity 4.6 on page 63 for an example of this.

expenses

The expenses or overheads of running the business are transferred from the double-entry accounts to the income statement. For example, the wages account of Tara Smith has been storing up information during the year and, at the end of the year, the total is transferred to the income statement *(debit* income statement; *credit* wages account):

Dr		Wages account			Cr
20-4		£	20-4		£
31 Dec Balance b/d (ie total for year)		23,500	31 Dec Income statement		23,500

The wages account now has a nil balance and is ready to receive transactions for 20-5, the next financial year.

profit/loss for the year

After the income statement has been completed, the amount of profit (or loss) for the year is transferred to the owner's capital account. The book-keeping entries are:

- profit for the year
  - *debit* income statement
  - *credit* capital account
- loss for the year
  - *debit* capital account
  - *credit* income statement

Profit increases the owner's stake in the business by adding to capital account, while a loss decreases the owner's stake.

Note that profit for the year and loss for the year are often referred to as net profit and net loss.

At the same time the account for drawings, which has been storing up the amount of drawings during the year is also transferred to capital account:

- *debit* capital account
- *credit* drawings account

Thus the total of drawings for the year is debited to capital account.

When these transactions are completed, the capital account for Tara Smith appears as:

Dr			Capital account			Cr
20-4		£	20-4			£
31 Dec	Drawings for year	7,000	31 Dec	Balance b/d		75,000
31 Dec	Balance c/d	80,000	31 Dec	Income statement (profit for year)		12,000
		87,000				87,000
20-5			20-5			
			1 Jan	Balance b/d		80,000

Note: Although the balance of capital account at the end of the year, £80,000, does not appear on the extended trial balance, the constituent figures are shown, ie capital £75,000, profit £12,000, drawings £7,000.

statement of financial position

Unlike the income statement, the statement of financial position is not part of the double-entry accounts. The statement of financial position is made up of those accounts which remain with balances at the end of the financial year, after the income statement transfers have been made. Thus it consists of asset and liability accounts, not forgetting the asset of closing inventory, together with the owner's capital and drawings.

Chapter Summary

- The financial statements of a business comprise:
  - income statement
  - statement of financial position

- The extended trial balance method of preparing financial statements starts with the trial balance and then transfers each account balance to one of the financial statements.

- Each account balance from the trial balance is entered into the financial statements once only; the additional items of closing inventory and profit or loss for the year are entered into both financial statements – this ensures that the double-entry rules of one debit and one credit entry for each transaction are maintained.

- The income statement forms part of the double-entry system; amounts entered must have the opposite entry recorded in the appropriate general ledger account.

- The statement of financial position is not part of the double-entry system; it lists the balances of accounts for assets, liabilities and capital at a particular date.

- The extended trial balance gives an understanding of the principles of financial statements. It is often used by accountancy firms as a step towards preparing year-end financial statements for their clients.

Key Terms

financial statements — accounting statements, comprising income statement and statement of financial position, produced at least once a year, which give information to the owner(s) and other interested parties on how the business is progressing

income statement — shows the profit (or loss) of the business for the accounting period

statement of financial position — shows the assets, liabilities and capital of the business at the end of the accounting period

extended trial balance — a spreadsheet format used as a method of preparing the financial statements

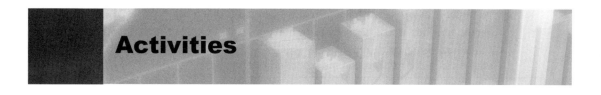

Activities

> **Extended trial balance format:** a blank photocopiable extended trial balance is included in the Appendix – it is advisable to enlarge it up to full A4 size. Alternatively you can set up a computer spreadsheet – but remember to allow for all the rows shown on the layout – they will be needed in later chapters.

4.1 Which one of the following does not appear in the income statement?

(a) salaries

(b) vehicles

(c) fuel for vehicles

(d) profit for the year

Answer (a) or (b) or (c) or (d)

4.2 Profit for the year is:

(a) assets minus liabilities

(b) sales revenue minus purchases

(c) closing bank balance minus opening bank balance

(d) income minus expenses

Answer (a) or (b) or (c) or (d)

4.3 You are to fill in the missing figures for the following businesses:

	Income	Expenses	Profit or loss*	Assets	Liabilities	Capital
	£	£	£	£	£	£
Business A	100,000	60,000	....	250,000	150,000	....
Business B	80,000	....	10,000	200,000	....	100,000
Business C	....	50,000	20,000	....	40,000	50,000
Business D	60,000	....	(15,000)	130,000	....	70,000
Business E	90,000	100,000	....	....	60,000	40,000

* Note: loss is indicated by brackets

4.4 Complete the table below for each item (a) to (g) indicating with a tick:
- whether the item would normally appear in the debit or credit column of the trial balance
- in which financial statement the item would appear at the end of the accounting period and whether as a debit or credit in the extended trial balance

| | | TRIAL BALANCE | | FINANCIAL STATEMENTS | | | |
| | | | | INCOME STATEMENT | | STATEMENT OF FIN POS | |
		Debit	Credit	Debit	Credit	Debit	Credit
(a)	Salaries						
(b)	Purchases						
(c)	Sales ledger control						
(d)	Sales returns						
(e)	Discount received						
(f)	Vehicle						
(g)	Capital						

4.5 The following trial balance has been extracted by Nick Johnson on 31 December 20-3:

	Dr £	Cr £
Opening inventory	25,000	
Purchases	210,000	
Sales revenue		310,000
Administration expenses	12,400	
Wages	41,000	
Rent paid	7,500	
Telephone	1,000	
Interest paid	9,000	
Travel expenses	1,100	
Premises at cost	200,000	
Machinery at cost	40,000	
Sales ledger control (receivables)	31,000	
Bank	900	
Cash	100	
Capital		150,000
Drawings	14,000	
Loan from bank		100,000
Purchases ledger control (payables)		29,000
Value Added Tax		4,000
	593,000	593,000

Note: closing inventory was valued at £21,000

You are to prepare the extended trial balance of Nick Johnson for the year ended 31 December 20-3.

4.6   The following trial balance has been extracted by the book-keeper of Alan Harris at 30 June 20-4:

	Dr	Cr
	£	£
Opening inventory	13,250	
Capital		70,000
Premises at cost	65,000	
Vehicle at cost	5,250	
Purchases	55,000	
Sales revenue		85,500
Administration expenses	850	
Wages	9,220	
Rent paid	1,200	
Telephone	680	
Interest paid	120	
Travel expenses	330	
Sales ledger control (receivables)	1,350	
Purchases ledger control (payables)		6,400
Value Added Tax		1,150
Bank	2,100	
Cash	600	
Drawings	8,100	
Closing inventory – income statement		18,100
Closing inventory – statement of financial position	18,100	
	181,150	181,150

Tutorial note: this trial balance already incorporates the closing inventory adjustments

You are to prepare the extended trial balance of Alan Harris for the year ended 30 June 20-4.

5 Accruals and prepayments

this chapter covers...

In the last chapter we have looked at the preparation of financial statements – or final accounts – using the extended trial balance, or spreadsheet, approach.

There are a number of adjustments which are made to the financial statements at the year end in order to show a more realistic view of the state of the business. This chapter is concerned with the adjustments to be made for accruals and prepayments of expenses and income.

To illustrate the effect of adjustments for accruals and prepayments on financial statements we shall be referring to the extended trial balance of Tara Smith seen in the previous chapter.

ACCRUAL OF EXPENSES

An accrual is an amount due, or the calculation of an amount due, in an accounting period which is unpaid at the end of that period, eg an insurance premium or an electricity bill not yet paid.

In the financial statements, accrued expenses are:

- added to the expense account (eg insurance account, electricity account) shown in the trial balance, before it is listed in the income statement
- shown as a liability in the year end statement of financial position

The reason for dealing with accruals in this way is to ensure that the income statement records the expense that has been incurred for the year, instead of simply the amount that has been paid. In other words, the expense is adjusted to relate to the time period covered by the income statement. The year end statement of financial position shows a liability for the amount that is due, but unpaid.

journal entry

A journal entry – see Chapter 11 – is made at the end of the financial year for accruals of expenses. The journal entry records the amounts of accruals in a book of prime entry and gives the book-keeper the authority to record the transactions in the double-entry accounts.

Case Study

TARA SMITH: ACCRUAL OF AN EXPENSE

The trial balance of Tara Smith at 31 December 20-4 (see page 53) shows a debit balance for telephone expenses of £500. Before preparing the final accounts, a telephone bill for £100 is received on 4 January 20-5, ie early in the new financial year. An examination of the bill shows that it is for costs incurred in 20-4, therefore an adjustment needs to be made in the final accounts for 20-4 to record this accrued expense.

accruals – the extended trial balance

The accrual is shown in the extended trial balance as follows:

- in the adjustments columns
  - record £100 on the debit side of the telephone row
  - record £100 on the credit side of the accruals row
- on the debit side of the income statement column the total cost of the telephone row is now £600 (ie £500 from the trial balance, plus £100 accrual)
- on the credit side of the statement of financial position column £100 from the accruals row is shown as a liability of the business

This adjustment is shown on Tara Smith's extended trial balance (page 70): the figures affected by the accrual (and also the prepayment – see below) are shaded for ease of reference.

accruals – the double-entry book-keeping

In the double-entry accounts, the amount of the accrual and the transfer of the year's expense to income statement are shown. The telephone account in the records of Tara Smith will appear as follows:

Dr		**Telephone account**		Cr
20-4	£	20-4		£
31 Dec Balance b/d	500	31 Dec Income statement		600
31 Dec Balance c/d	100			
	600			600
20-5	£	20-5		£
		1 Jan Balance b/d		100

Notes:

- The book-keeper's trial balance showed the debit side balance brought down of £500 on telephone account

- As £100 is owing for telephone expenses at the end of the year, the transfer to income statement is the expense that has been incurred for the year of £600

- The amount of the accrual is carried down to the credit side of telephone account; it is listed on the statement of financial position at 31 December 20-4 as a liability

Later on, for example on 15 January 20-5, the telephone bill is paid by cheque and telephone account now appears as:

Dr		**Telephone account**		Cr
20-5	£	20-5		£
15 Jan Bank	100	1 Jan Balance b/d		100

The effect of the payment on 15 January is that telephone account now has a 'nil' balance and the bill received on 4 January will not be recorded as an expense in the income statement drawn up at the end of 20-5.

the effect of an accrual on profit

Taking note of the accrual of an expense has the effect of reducing profit for the year. As the expenses have been increased, profit is reduced. In this case the telephone bill due for the period reduces the profit of Tara Smith by £100 from £12,000 to £11,900.

PREPAYMENT OF EXPENSES

A prepayment is a payment made in advance, or the calculation of an amount paid in advance, of the accounting period to which it relates.

A prepayment is, therefore, the opposite of an accrual: with a prepayment of expenses, some part of the expense has been paid in advance.

In the financial statements, prepaid expenses are:

• deducted from the expense account shown in the trial balance before it is listed in the income statement

• shown as an asset in the year end statement of financial position

As with accruals, the reason for dealing with prepaid expenses in this way is to ensure that the income statement records the cost incurred for the year, and not the amount that has been paid – the income statement expense relates to the time period covered by the income statement. The year end statement of financial position shows an asset for the amount that has been prepaid.

journal entry

A journal entry – see Chapter 11 – is made at the end of the financial year for prepayments of expenses. The journal entry records the amounts of prepayments in a book of prime entry and gives the book-keeper the authority to record the transactions in the double-entry accounts.

Case Study

TARA SMITH: PREPAID EXPENSES

Tara Smith tells you that the trial balance figure for rent paid of £750 includes £75 of rent for January 20-5 paid in advance. An adjustment needs to be made to the financial statements for 20-4 to record this prepaid expense.

prepayments – the extended trial balance

The prepayment is shown in the extended trial balance as follows:

• in the adjustments columns

– record £75 on the credit side of the rent paid row

– record £75 on the debit side of the prepayments row

• on the debit side of the income statement column the total cost of rent paid is now £675 (ie £750 from the trial balance, less £75 prepaid)

• on the debit side of the statement of financial position column £75 from the prepayments row is shown as an asset of the business

The prepayment adjustment is shown on Tara Smith's extended trial balance (page 70), together with the accrual we have just dealt with – both are shaded for ease of reference.

prepayments – the double-entry book-keeping

In the double-entry accounts, the amount of the prepayment and the transfer of the year's expense to income statement are shown.

The rent paid account in the records of Tara Smith will appear as follows:

Dr			**Rent paid account**		Cr
20-4		£	20-4		£
31 Dec	Balance b/d	750	31 Dec	Income statement	675
			31 Dec	Balance c/d	75
		750			750
20-5		£	20-5		£
1 Jan	Balance b/d	75			

Notes:

• The trial balance total for rent paid is £750

• As £75 is prepaid at the end of the year, the transfer to the income statement is the expense that has been incurred for the year of £675

• The amount of the prepayment is carried down to the debit side of rent paid account; it is listed on the statement of financial position at 31 December 20-4 as an asset

• This now gives rent paid account a debit balance of £75 which will be included in the expense for rent paid for the year and will be transferred to the income statement on 31 December 20-5.

the effect of a prepayment on profit

Taking note of the prepayment of an expense has the effect of increasing a previously reported profit for the year – expenses have been reduced, so profit is greater.

TARA SMITH: ACCRUALS AND PREPAYMENTS IN THE FINANCIAL STATEMENTS

We will now focus on how the adjustments for accruals and prepayments are shown in the income statement and statement of financial position of Tara Smith. Remember that we are taking note of the following items at 31 December 20-4:

• telephone accrued £100

• rent prepaid £75

extended trial balance

The layout for the extended trial balance – see next page – includes rows for accruals and prepayments. The columns which are affected are adjustments, income statement and statement of financial position – the altered figures are shaded for illustrative purposes. Note that:

• the income statement columns show the net figure for each expense after allowing for the accrual or prepayment

• the statement of financial position columns show the accrual as a liability and the prepayment as an asset

The effect of taking note of accruals and prepayments is to alter profit for the year from that shown by the extended trial balance for Tara Smith, seen earlier (page 55):

	£
Profit for the year before adjustments	12,000
Less telephone accrued	100
	11,900
Add rent prepaid	75
Profit for the year after adjustments	11,975

EXTENDED TRIAL BALANCE   TARA SMITH TRADING AS "THE FASHION SHOP"   31 DECEMBER 20-4

Account name	Ledger balances		Adjustments		Income statement		Statement of financial position	
	Dr £	Cr £	Dr £	Cr £	Dr £	Cr £	Dr £	Cr £
Opening inventory	12,500				12,500			
Purchases	105,000				105,000			
Sales revenue		155,000				155,000		
Administration expenses	6,200				6,200			
Wages	23,500				23,500			
Rent paid	750			75	675			
Telephone	500		100		600			
Interest paid	4,500				4,500			
Travel expenses	550				550			
Premises at cost	100,000						100,000	
Shop fittings at cost	20,000						20,000	
Sales ledger control	10,500						10,500	
Bank	5,450						5,450	
Cash	50						50	
Capital		75,000						75,000
Drawings	7,000						7,000	
Loan from bank		50,000						50,000
Purchases ledger control		14,500						14,500
Value Added Tax		2,000						2,000
Closing inventory: income statement				10,500		10,500		
Closing inventory: statement of financial position			10,500				10,500	
Accruals				100				100
Prepayments			75				75	
Depreciation charge								
Irrecoverable debts								
Allowance for doubtful debts								
Allowance for doubtful debts:adjustment								
Profit/loss for the year					11,975			11,975
	296,500	296,500	10,675	10,675	165,500	165,500	153,575	153,575

ACCRUALS AND PREPAYMENTS OF INCOME

Just as expenses can be accrued or prepaid at the end of a financial year, income amounts can also be accrued or prepaid.

accrual of income

Here, income of a business is due but unpaid at the end of the financial year. For example, commission might have been earned, but the payment is received after the end of the financial year to which it relates. In the extended trial balance and financial statements, accrual of income is:

*   added to the income amount in the trial balance before it is listed in the income statement

*   shown as an asset in the year end statement of financial position

A journal entry – see Chapter 11 – is made at the end of the financial year for accruals of income.

prepayment of income

Here, the income of a business has been paid in advance by the payer. For example, the rent received account for this financial year could include an advance payment received from a tenant in respect of the next financial year. In the extended trial balance and financial statements, prepayment of income is:

*   deducted from the income amount in the trial balance before it is listed in the income statement

*   shown as a liability in the year end statement of financial position

As with expenses, the objective of taking note of accruals and prepayments of income is to ensure that the money amounts relate to the period covered by the income statement.

A journal entry – see Chapter 11 – is made at the end of the financial year for prepayments of income.

PRIVATE EXPENSES AND GOODS FOR OWN USE

Adjustments also have to be made in the final accounts for the amount of any business facilities that are used by the owner for private purposes. These adjustments are for private expenses and goods for own use.

private expenses

Sometimes the owner of a business uses business facilities for private purposes, eg telephone, or car. The owner will agree that part of the expense shall be charged to him or her as drawings, while the other part represents a business expense.

For example, the balance of the telephone account is £600 at the year-end, and the owner agrees that this should be split as one-quarter private use, and three-quarters to the business. The book-keeping entries to record such adjustments are:

- *debit* drawings account
- *credit* telephone account
- *debit* income statement
- *credit* telephone account

The telephone account will be completed at the end of the year as follows:

Dr		£	Telephone account		Cr
20-4		£	20-4		£
31 Dec	Balance b/d	600	31 Dec	Drawings	150
			31 Dec	Income statement	450
		600			600

When using a trial balance to produce the financial statements, private expenses should be adjusted by deducting from the expense account and adding to drawings.

A journal entry – see Chapter 11 – is made at the end of the financial year for private expenses.

goods for own use

When the owner of a business takes some of the goods in which the business trades for his or her own use, the double-entry book-keeping is:

- *debit* drawings account
- *credit* purchases account

Note that:

- Where a business is VAT-registered, VAT must be accounted for on goods taken by the owner.
- An alternative method of accounting for goods for own use is:
  - *debit* drawings account
  - *credit* sales revenue account

This method is preferred by HM Revenue and Customs for tax purposes; however, either is acceptable for the purpose of financial accounting – which method is used will depend on the custom and practice of the business.

When using a trial balance to produce the financial statements, goods for own use should be adjusted by adding to drawings and deducting from purchases (or adding to sales revenue).

A journal entry – see Chapter 11 – is made at the end of the financial year for goods for own use.

INCOME AND EXPENDITURE ACCOUNTING

In this chapter we have made adjustments for accruals and prepayments to ensure that the income statement shows the correct amount of income and expenses for the financial year, ie what should have been paid, instead of what has actually been paid. In doing this we are adopting the principle of *income and expenditure accounting*. If we simply used the trial balance figures, we would be following the principle of *receipts* and *payments accounting*, ie comparing money coming in, with money going out: this will usually give a false view of the profit for the year.

The principle of income and expenditure accounting is applied in the same way to purchases and sales, although no adjustments are needed because of the way in which these two are handled in the accounting records. For purchases, the amount is entered into the accounts when the supplier's invoice is received, although the agreement to buy will be contained in the legal contract which exists between buyer and seller. From the accounting viewpoint, it is receipt of the supplier's invoice that causes an accounting entry to be made; the subsequent payment is handled as a different accounting transaction. A business could have bought goods, not paid for them yet, but will have a purchases figure to enter into the income statement – the suppliers will soon be wanting payment!

Sales are recorded in a similar way – when the invoice for the goods is sent, rather than when payment is made. This applies the principle of income and expenditure accounting. In this way, a business could have made a large amount of sales, which will be entered in the income statement, but may not yet have received any payments.

accruals concept of accounting

The way in which financial statements are adjusted to take note of accruals and prepayments is recognised in the accruals (or matching) concept of accounting – this is discussed in more detail in Chapter 8.

Chapter Summary

■ Financial statements are prepared on the income and expenditure basis, rather than the receipts and payments basis.

■ Adjustments should be made at the end of the financial year in respect of accruals and prepayments.

■ In the financial statements, accrued expenses are:
 – added to the expense from the trial balance
 – shown as a liability in the statement of financial position

■ Prepaid expenses are:
 – deducted from the expense from the trial balance
 – shown as an asset in the statement of financial position

■ An accrual of income is:
 – added to the income amount from the trial balance
 – shown as an asset in the statement of financial position

■ A prepayment of income is:
 – deducted from the income amount from the trial balance
 – shown as a liability in the statement of financial position

■ Adjustments also need to be made in the financial statements for:
 – private expenses
 – goods for own use

■ A journal entry – see Chapter 11 – must be made for all adjustments for accruals and prepayments and for private expenses and goods for own use. The journal entry records the amounts in a book of prime entry and gives the book-keeper the authority to record the transactions in the double-entry accounts.

■ Accruals and prepayments are an application of the accruals (or matching) concept of accounting – see Chapter 8.

Key Terms		
	accrual of expenses	an amount due, or the calculation of an amount due, in an accounting period which is unpaid at the end of that period
	prepayment of expenses	a payment made in advance, or the calculation of an amount paid in advance, of the accounting period to which it relates
	accrual of income	income of a business due in an accounting period which is unpaid at the end of that period
	prepayment of income	income of a business which has been paid in advance of the accounting period to which it relates
	goods for own use	where the owner of a business takes some of the goods in which the business trades for his/her own use
	income and expenditure accounting	recording the amounts that should have been received and paid during an accounting period
	receipts and payments accounting	recording the actual amounts that have been received and paid during an accounting period, without taking note of accruals and prepayments

Activities

Extended trial balance format: a blank photocopiable pro-forma of the extended trial balance is included in the Appendix – it is advisable to enlarge it up to full A4 size.

5.1   Wages accrued are shown as:

(a)   an asset on the statement of financial position

(b)   a debit balance in wages account

(c)   income on the income statement

(d)   a credit balance in wages account

Answer (a) or (b) or (c) or (d)

5.2   Rates prepaid are shown as:

(a)   a liability on the statement of financial position

(b)   an expense on the income statement

(c)   debit balance in rates account

(d)   credit balance in rates account

Answer (a) or (b) or (c) or (d)

5.3   John Harrington runs an import/export business. At the end of his financial year, on 31 December 20-7, the vehicle expenses account is as follows:

Dr			Vehicle expenses account		Cr
20-7		£	20-7		£
31 Dec	Balance b/d	1,680			

John Harrington tells you that 25 per cent of vehicle expenses represents his private motoring expenses. He asks you to transfer the amount to his drawings account, before transferring the remainder to the income statement. Show the vehicle expenses account after these transactions have been entered.

5.4   Explain how the following would be dealt with in the income statement, and statement of financial position of a business with a financial year end of 31 December 20-1:

(a)   Wages and salaries paid to 31 December 20-1 amount to £55,640. However, at that date £1,120 is owing: this amount is paid on 4 January 20-2.

(b)   Rates totalling £3,565 have been paid to cover the period 1 January 20-1 to 31 March 20-2.

(c)   A computer is rented at a cost of £150 per month. The rental for January 20-2 was paid in December 20-1 and is included in the total payments during 20-1 which amount to £1,950.

5.5   This Activity is about accounting for accruals and prepayments and preparing a trial balance.

You are working on the accounts of a business for the year ended 31 March 20-7. In this Activity you can ignore VAT.

You have the following information:

Balances as at:	1 April 20-6
	£
Accrual for rent paid	750
Prepayment for administration expenses	250

The bank summary for the year shows payments for rent of £11,250. Included in this figure is £2,250 for the quarter ended 31 May 20-7.

(a) **You are to** prepare the rent paid account for the year ended 31 March 20-7 and close it off by showing the transfer to the income statement. Dates are not required.

Rent paid

	£		£

The bank summary for the year shows payments for administration expenses of £10,400. In April 20-7, £175 was paid for administration expenses incurred in March 20-7.

(b) **You are to** prepare the administration expenses account for the year ended 31 March 20-7 and close it off by showing the transfer to the income statement. Include dates.

Administration expenses

		£			£

You have the following extract of balances from the general ledger.

(c)   **Using your answers** to (a) and (b), and the figures given below, enter amounts in the appropriate debit or credit column for the accounts shown. Do not enter zeros in unused column cells.

Extract from trial balance as at 31 March 20-7

Account	**£**	**£ Dr**	**£ Cr**
Accruals			
Capital	75,000		
Discount received	680		
Drawings	10,000		
Interest received	200		
Machinery at cost	20,000		
Prepayments			
Sales revenue	115,000		

5.6   This Activity is about accounting for accruals and prepayments and preparing a trial balance.

You are working on the accounts of a business for the year ended 30 June 20-3. In this Activity you can ignore VAT.

You have the following information:

Balances as at:	**1 July 20-2** **£**
Prepayment for rent received	450
Accrual for vehicle expenses	220

The bank summary for the year shows rent received of £5,850. Included in this figure is £1,350 for the three months ended 31 August 20-3.

(a)   **You are to** prepare the rent received account for the year ended 30 June 20-3 and close it off by showing the transfer to the income statement. Dates are not required.

Rent received

	£		£

The bank summary for the year shows payments for vehicle expenses of £6,450. In July 20-3, £380 was paid for vehicle expenses incurred in June 20-3.

(b)   **You are to** prepare the vehicle expenses account for the year ended 30 June 20-3 and close it off by showing the transfer to the income statement. Include dates.

Vehicle expenses

		£			£

You have the following extract of balances from the general ledger.

(c) **Using your answers** to (a) and (b), and the figures given below, enter amounts in the appropriate debit or credit column for the accounts shown. Do not enter zeros in unused column cells.

Extract from trial balance as at 30 June 20-3

Account	£	£ Dr	£ Cr
Accruals			
Capital	30,000		
Cash	250		
Discount allowed	600		
Prepayments			
Purchases	15,500		
Sales returns	850		
Vehicles at cost	12,000		

5.7 The following trial balance has been extracted by the book-keeper of Don Smith, who runs a wholesale stationery business, at 31 December 20-2:

	Dr £	Cr £
Sales ledger control	24,325	
Purchases ledger control		15,408
Value Added Tax		4,276
Capital		30,000
Bank		1,083
Rent and rates	10,862	
Electricity	2,054	
Telephone	1,695	
Salaries	55,891	
Vehicles at cost	22,250	
Office equipment t cost	7,500	
Vehicle expenses	10,855	
Drawings	15,275	
Discount allowed	478	
Discount received		591
Purchases	138,960	
Sales revenue		257,258
Opening inventory	18,471	
	308,616	308,616

Notes at 31 December 20-2:
- closing inventory was valued at £14,075
- rates prepaid £250
- electricity owing £110
- salaries owing £365

You are to prepare the extended trial balance of Don Smith for the year ended 31 December 20-2.

5.8 The following trial balance has been extracted by the book-keeper of John Barclay at 30 June 20-3:

	Dr	Cr
	£	£
Sales revenue		864,321
Purchases	600,128	
Sales returns	2,746	
Purchases returns		3,894
Office expenses	33,947	
Salaries	122,611	
Vehicle expenses	36,894	
Discount allowed	3,187	
Discount received		4,951
Sales and purchases ledger control	74,328	52,919
Value Added Tax		10,497
Opening inventory	63,084	
Vehicles at cost	83,500	
Office equipment at cost	23,250	
Land and buildings at cost	100,000	
Bank loan		75,000
Bank	1,197	
Capital		155,000
Drawings	21,710	
	1,166,582	1,166,582

Notes at 30 June 20-3:
- closing inventory was valued at £66,941
- vehicle expenses owing £1,250
- office expenses prepaid £346
- goods costing £250 were taken by John Barclay for his own use

You are to prepare the extended trial balance of John Barclay for the year ended 30 June 20-3.

Depreciation of non-current assets

Non-current (fixed) assets, such as machinery and vehicles, lose value as time goes by, largely as a result of wear and tear. This loss in value is known as depreciation. In financial accounting it is necessary to record an estimate of depreciation in the accounting records. In this chapter we will:

- define depreciation and understand its purpose

- consider the main methods of calculating depreciation

- study the book-keeping entries for depreciation

- apply depreciation to the extended trial balance

- investigate the book-keeping entries involved when a non-current asset is sold

WHAT IS DEPRECIATION?

Depreciation is the estimate of the amount of the loss in value of a non-current asset over its useful life.

The purpose of depreciation is to spread the cost of a non-current asset over its useful life. Most non-current assets lose value over time and it is necessary, in order to present a realistic view of the business, to record the amount of the loss in value. This is done by

- showing an expense – depreciation charge – in the income statement
- showing the non-current asset at cost price and the amount of accumulated depreciation in the statement of financial position

Depreciation – which is linked to the cost price of the asset – *estimates* the loss in value and the time period over which the loss occurs.

The main factors which cause non-current assets to depreciate are:

- *wear and tear through use*, eg vehicles, machinery, etc
- *passage of time*, eg the lease on a building
- *depletion,* eg extraction of stone from a quarry
- *economic reasons*
  - obsolescence, eg a new design of machine which does the job better and faster, making the old machine obsolete
  - inadequacy, eg a machine such as a photocopier no longer has the volume capacity to meet the needs of the business

Non-current assets – including buildings – are depreciated over their useful life. The only exception is freehold land, which is a non-wasting asset that does not normally depreciate (unless it is a quarry or a mine, when it will have a known useful economic life).

Depreciation links directly to the non-current asset register (see Chapter 9) where a business keeps records of all the non-current assets it owns, together with the cost price of each, depreciation charge, and accumulated depreciation.

CALCULATING DEPRECIATION

There are several different ways in which we can allow for the loss in value of non-current assets. All of these are *estimates,* and it is only when disposal of the asset takes place that we will know the accuracy of the estimate. A business can use any acceptable depreciation method; however, once selected, the method would not be changed from one year to the next without good reason.

The two most common methods of calculating depreciation are:

- straight-line method
- reducing balance method (also called diminishing balance method)

To calculate the annual depreciation charge, we will use the following data:

DATA FOR DEPRECIATION OF MACHINE

Cost price (net of VAT)	£2,000
Useful life	4 years
Estimated residual value (net of VAT) at end of four years	£400

---

straight-line method of depreciation

With this method, a fixed percentage or fraction is written off the *original cost* of the asset each year. For this example, twenty-five per cent or one-quarter will be written off each year by the straight-line method. The depreciation charge (ignoring for the moment any residual value) for *each year* is:

$$£2,000 \times 25\% = £500 \text{ per year}$$

The depreciation percentage or fraction will be decided by a business on the basis of what it considers to be the useful life of the asset. Thus, twenty-five per cent each year gives a useful life of four years (assuming a nil residual value at the end of its life).

Different classes of non-current assets are often depreciated at different rates, eg vehicles may be depreciated at a different rate to office equipment. It is important that, once a particular method and rate of depreciation has been selected, depreciation should be applied consistently, ie methods and rates are not changed from year-to-year without good reason.

The method of calculating straight-line depreciation, taking into account the asset's estimated residual value at the end of its useful life, is:

$$\frac{\text{cost of asset} - \text{estimated residual (scrap or salvage) sale proceeds}}{\text{useful life of asset}}$$

For example, the machine is expected to have a residual (scrap or salvage) value of £400, so the depreciation charge will be:

$$\frac{£2,000 - £400}{4 \text{ years}} = £400 \text{ per year (ie 20\% per annum on cost)}$$

reducing (diminishing) balance method

With this method, a fixed percentage is written off the reduced balance – referred to as the 'carrying amount' – of the asset each year. The reduced balance is the cost of the asset less the accumulated depreciation. For example, the machine is to be depreciated by 33.3% (one-third) each year, using the reducing balance method. The depreciation charges for the four years of ownership are:

	£
Original cost	2,000
Year 1 depreciation: 33.3% of £2,000	667
Carrying amount at end of year 1	1,333
Year 2 depreciation: 33.3% of £1,333	444
Carrying amount at end of year 2	889
Year 3 depreciation: 33.3% of £889	296
Carrying amount at end of year 3	593
Year 4 depreciation: 33.3% of £593	193
Carrying amount at end of year 4	400

Note: the figures have been rounded to the nearest £, and year 4 depreciation has been adjusted by £5 to leave a residual value of £400.

The formula to calculate the percentage of reducing balance depreciation is:

$$r = 1 - \sqrt[n]{\frac{s}{c}}$$

where:

r = percentage rate of depreciation

n = number of years

s = scrap or salvage (residual) value

c = cost of asset

In the example above the 33.3% is calculated as:

$$r = 1 - \sqrt[4]{\frac{400}{2,000}}$$

$$r = 1 - \sqrt[4]{0.2}$$

(to find the fourth root press the square root key on the calculator twice)

$$r = 1 - 0.669$$

$$r = 0.331 \text{ or } 33.1\% \text{ (which is close to the 33.3\% used above)}$$

Note: you will not need to use this formula in AAT Assessments.

straight-line and reducing balance methods compared

The following tables use the depreciation amounts calculated above.

straight-line depreciation			
1	2	3	4
Year	Original cost	Depreciation charge	Accumulated depreciation	Carrying amount* (ie column 1-3)
	£	£	£	£
1	2,000	400	400	1,600
2	2,000	400	800	1,200
3	2,000	400	1,200	800
4	2,000	400	1,600	400

* Note: Carrying amount is cost less accumulated depreciation, ie column 1, less column 3.

reducing (diminishing) balance depreciation			
1	2	3	4
Year	Original cost	Depreciation charge	Accumulated depreciation	Carrying amount (ie column 1-3)
	£	£	£	£
1	2,000	667	667	1,333
2	2,000	444	1,111	889
3	2,000	296	1,407	593
4	2,000	193	1,600	400

Using these tables, we will now see how the two methods compare:

	straight-line method	reducing balance method
depreciation charge	Same money amount each year – see chart below	Different money amounts each year: more than straight-line in early years, less in later years – see chart below
depreciation percentage or fraction	Lower depreciation percentage or fraction required to achieve same residual value	Higher depreciation percentage required to achieve same residual value – but can never reach a nil value
suitability	Best used for non-current assets likely to be kept for the whole of their useful lives, eg machinery, office equipment, fixtures and fittings	Best used for non-current assets which depreciate more in early years and which are not kept for the whole of their useful lives, eg vehicles

The year-by-year depreciation charges of the machine in the example are shown on the following bar chart:

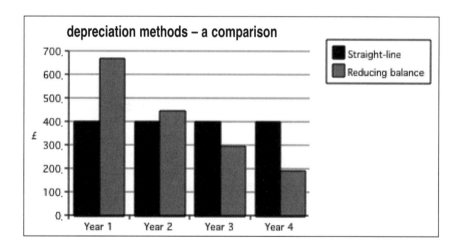

BOOK-KEEPING ENTRIES FOR DEPRECIATION

Once the depreciation charges have been calculated using the methods described in the previous section, they can be recorded in the non-current asset register (see Chapter 9) and in the book-keeping system. It is usual to separate out the main classes of non-current assets – premises, vehicles, machinery, computers, office equipment – and to record separately the financial information for each.

journal entry

A journal entry – see Chapter 11 – is made at the end of the financial year for the depreciation charge for each class of non-current asset. The journal entry records amounts of depreciation charges in a book of prime entry and gives the book-keeper the authority to record the transactions in the double-entry accounts.

book-keeping accounts

In the book-keeping, the usual procedure is to have three accounts in the general ledger:

- *non-current asset account* for each class of asset, which records the cost price of the asset (note that the value of the asset can include certain other capital costs, eg installation costs – see page 136)
- *depreciation charge account*, which records the amount of depreciation for the asset for the year
- *accumulated depreciation account* – also known as *provision for depreciation account* – which records the amount of depreciation to date for each class of non-current asset in separate accounts

Case Study

BOOK-KEEPING ENTRIES FOR DEPRECIATION

A machine is purchased for £2,000 net of VAT on 1 January 20-4. It is decided to depreciate it at twenty per cent each year, using the straight-line method. The firm's financial year runs from 1 January to 31 December. The general ledger accounting records for the first four years will be:

Dr		Machinery at cost account		Cr
20-4		£	20-4	£
1 Jan	Bank	2,000		

This account remains with the balance of £2,000, which is the cost price of the machine. (The other transactions on 1 January 20-4 are to bank account and VAT account – these have not been shown.)

Dr	Depreciation charge account		Cr
20-4	£	20-4	£
31 Dec Machinery: accumulated depreciation	400	31 Dec Income statement	400
20-5		20-5	
31 Dec Machinery: accumulated depreciation	400	31 Dec Income statement	400
20-6		20-6	
31 Dec Machinery: accumulated depreciation	400	31 Dec Income statement	400
20-7		20-7	
31 Dec Machinery: accumulated depreciation	400	31 Dec Income statement	400

The depreciation charge account acts as a 'holding' account for the year's depreciation. The amount is

- credited to depreciation charge account, and debited to income statement

- debited to depreciation charge account, and credited to accumulated depreciation account

Note that depreciation charge account may be credited with depreciation amounts for various classes of non-current assets (eg buildings, machinery, vehicles); the amounts are then debited out and credited to the accumulated depreciation account for each class of non-current asset.

Dr	Machinery: accumulated depreciation account		Cr
20-4	£	20-4	£
31 Dec Balance c/d	400	31 Dec Depreciation charge	400
20-5		20-5	
31 Dec Balance c/d	800	1 Jan Balance b/d	400
		31 Dec Depreciation charge	400
	800		800
20-6		20-6	
31 Dec Balance c/d	1,200	1 Jan Balance b/d	800
		31 Dec Depreciation charge	400
	1,200		1,200
20-7		20-7	
31 Dec Balance c/d	1,600	1 Jan Balance b/d	1,200
		31 Dec Depreciation charge	400
	1,600		1,600
20-8		20-8	
		1 Jan Balance b/d	1,600

The accumulated depreciation account – which is specific to each class of non-current asset – stores up the amounts of the depreciation charge year by year. Notice that, while the asset account of machinery has a debit balance, accumulated depreciation account has a credit balance. The difference between the two balances at any time will tell us the carrying amount of the asset, ie what it is worth according to our accounting records. For example, at 31 December 20-6, the carrying amount of the machine is £800 (£2,000 cost, less £1,200 accumulated depreciation).

When a business owns several non-current assets of the same class, eg several machines, it is usual practice to maintain only one asset at cost account and one accumulated depreciation account for that class. This does mean that the calculation of amounts of depreciation can become quite complex – particularly when assets are bought and sold during the year. It is good practice to calculate the separate depreciation amount for each machine, or asset, before amalgamating the figures as the year's depreciation charge. These amounts will be shown separately for each asset held in the non-current asset register – see Chapter 9.

DEPRECIATION AND FINANCIAL STATEMENTS

accruals and consistency concepts of accounting

The way in which financial statements are adjusted to take note of depreciation of non-current assets is recognised in the accruals and consistency concepts of accounting – these are discussed in more detail in chapter 8.

income statement

The depreciation amount calculated for each class of non-current asset is listed amongst the expenses in the income statement. For example, to consider the machine depreciated in the previous sections, the income statement will show 'depreciation charge: machinery £400' amongst the expenses. The double-entry book-keeping records the annual amount for depreciation as follows:

– *debit* income statement
– *credit* depreciation charge account

As we have seen earlier, amounts held in depreciation charge account are then debited out and credited to the appropriate accumulated depreciation accounts.

statement of financial position

Each class of non-current asset is shown:

– at cost price in the debit column
– with accumulated depreciation (often on the line below cost price – see page 92) in the credit column

Note that the net amount of these two shows the carrying amount of the asset at the date of the statement of financial position.

The table below shows how the depreciation on the machine in the Case Study (book-keeping entries on page 89) will be shown in the extended trial balances.

Year	Income statement		Statement of financial position	
	Dr	Cr	Dr	Cr
	Expense	*Income*	*Cost*	*Accumulated depreciation*
	£	£	£	£
20-4	400	–	2,000	400
20-5	400	–	2,000	800
20-6	400	–	2,000	1,200
20-7	400	–	2,000	1,600

depreciation policies of a business

In Activities and Assessments, information will be given – where it is needed – on the accounting policy for depreciation of the business whose accounts are being prepared. In particular, information will be given on what to do when a non-current asset is bought part of the way through a firm's financial year. The choices here will be to depreciate for the part of the year that it is owned; alternatively the firm may choose to depreciate for the whole year on assets held at the end of the year.

Note: In AAT Assessments you may be required to make pro-rata calculations for part of a year for the straight-line depreciation method only (not the diminishing balance method).

Case Study

TARA SMITH:
DEPRECIATION IN THE FINANCIAL STATEMENTS

We will now focus on how the depreciation amounts are shown in the income statement and the statement of financial position. We will continue with the trial balance of Tara Smith and include depreciation adjustments for the year of:

• premises: 2 per cent straight-line, ie £2,000
• shop fittings: 25 per cent reducing balance, ie £5,000

extended trial balance

The layout for the extended trial balance – see next page – includes a pre-printed row for depreciation. Study the extended trial balance on the next page and read the notes that follow.

EXTENDED TRIAL BALANCE   TARA SMITH TRADING AS "THE FASHION SHOP"   31 DECEMBER 20-4

Account name	Ledger balances Dr £	Ledger balances Cr £	Adjustments Dr £	Adjustments Cr £	Income statement Dr £	Income statement Cr £	Statement of financial position Dr £	Statement of financial position Cr £
Opening inventory	12,500				12,500			
Purchases	105,000				105,000			
Sales revenue		155,000				155,000		
Administration expenses	6,200				6,200			
Wages	23,500				23,500			
Rent paid	750			75	675			
Telephone	500		100		600			
Interest paid	4,500				4,500			
Travel expenses	550				550			
Premises at cost	100,000						100,000	
Premises: accumulated depreciation				2,000				2,000
Shop fittings at cost	20,000						20,000	
Shop fittings: accumulated depreciation				5,000				5,000
Sales ledger control	10,500						10,500	
Bank	5,450						5,450	
Cash	50						50	
Capital		75,000						75,000
Drawings	7,000						7,000	
Loan from bank		50,000						50,000
Purchases ledger control		14,500						14,500
Value Added Tax		2,000						2,000
Closing inventory: income statement				10,500		10,500		
Closing inventory: statement of financial position			10,500				10,500	
Accruals				100				100
Prepayments			75				75	
Depreciation charge			7,000		7,000			
Irrecoverable debts								
Allowance for doubtful debts								
Allowance for doubtful debts:adjustment								
Profit/loss for the year					4,975			4,975
	296,500	296,500	17,675	17,675	165,500	165,500	153,575	153,575

The depreciation is shown in the extended trial balance as follows:

- in the account name column
  - on the blank line below premises write in 'premises: accumulated depreciation'
  - on the blank line below shop fittings write in 'shop fittings: accumulated depreciation'
- in the adjustments columns
  - record £7,000 (ie £2,000 + £5,000) on the debit side of the depreciation charge row
  - record £2,000 on the credit side of the premises: accumulated depreciation row
  - record £5,000 on the credit side of the shop fittings: accumulated depreciation row
- on the debit side of the income statement column record the depreciation charge for the year of £7,000
- on the credit side of the statement of financial position column record the £2,000 and £5,000 accumulated depreciation on the two classes of assets

Remember that:

- depreciation charge is the annual amount of depreciation
- accumulated depreciation is the total depreciation to date for each class of non-current asset

As this is the first year that Tara Smith has recorded depreciation, both depreciation charge and accumulated depreciation amounts are the same. The figures for depreciation are shaded for ease of reference (note that the extended trial balance already incorporates adjustments for accruals and prepayments of expenses). As a result of the depreciation charge, profit for the year is reduced by £7,000 (ie £2,000 + £5,000) to £4,975.

DEPRECIATION: A NON-CASH EXPENSE

It is very important to realise that depreciation is a non-cash expense: unlike the other expenses in the income statement, no cheque is written out, or cash paid, for depreciation. In cash terms, depreciation causes no outflow of money. Nevertheless, it is correct, in the financial statements of a business, to show an allowance for depreciation in the income statement, and the accumulated depreciation in the statement of financial position. This is because the business has had the use of the asset, and needs to record the fall in value as an expense to present a true picture of its financial state. Thus we are led back to the definition of depreciation as "the estimate of the amount of the loss in value of a non-current asset over its useful life, ie it is an accounting adjustment.

As depreciation is a non-cash expense, it should be noted that depreciation is not a method of providing a fund of cash which can be used to replace the asset at the end of its life. In order to do this, it is necessary to create a separate fund into which cash is transferred at regular intervals. This technique is often known as a sinking fund, and it needs to be represented by a separate bank account, eg a deposit account, which can be drawn against when the new non-current asset is to be purchased.

DISPOSAL OF NON-CURRENT ASSETS

When a non-current asset is sold or disposed, it is necessary to bring together:

- the original cost of the asset
- accumulated depreciation over the life of the asset
- disposal proceeds

In the non-current asset register (see Chapter 9) it is necessary to identify the correct asset which is being disposed and to remove it from the non-current asset register. At the same time, amounts for original cost, accumulated depreciation and disposal proceeds are transferred from the appropriate accounts in the general ledger of the double-entry system to an asset disposal account. The disposals account will enable us to calculate the profit or loss on disposal of the asset caused by over or under depreciation (over depreciation = profit on disposal; under depreciation = loss on disposal).

The double-entry transactions are:

- original cost of the asset
  - *debit* asset disposals account
  - *credit* non-current asset account
- depreciation to date
  - *debit* accumulated depreciation account
  - *credit* asset disposals account

Note:
The depreciation charge for the current accounting period may need to be calculated, eg if disposal takes place part of the way through a financial year and the firm's policy is to charge for part-years.

- disposal proceeds
  - *debit* bank/cash account
  - *credit* asset disposals account

- loss on disposal
  - *debit* income statement
  - *credit* asset disposals account
- profit on disposal
  - *debit* asset disposals account
  - *credit* income statement

Small adjustments for profits or losses on disposals – caused by over or under depreciation respectively – will usually be needed because it is impossible, at the start of an asset's life, to predict exactly what it will sell for in a number of years' time.

journal entries

A journal entry – see Chapter 11 – is made to record all general ledger transfers in connection with the disposal of non-current assets. This journal entry records in a book of prime entry:

- the original cost of the asset being debited to asset disposals account
- the accumulated depreciation being credited to asset disposals account
- the disposal proceeds being credited to asset disposals account
- the amount of over or under depreciation being credited or debited to the income statement

The journal entry gives the book-keeper the authority to record the transactions in the double-entry accounts.

We will see the journal entries for the following Case Study when we study journals in detail in Chapter 11.

Case Study

DISPOSAL OF NON-CURRENT ASSETS

To illustrate the transactions to record the disposal of non-current assets, we will use the machine purchased for £2,000 (net of VAT) on 1 January 20-4, which is depreciated at twenty per cent each year, using the straight-line depreciation method. On 31 December 20-6, the machine is sold for £600 (net of VAT) received into the bank; the company's accounting policy is to depreciate assets in the year of sale. The calculations are:

	£
cost price of machine (net of VAT)	2,000
less accumulated depreciation to date	1,200
carrying amount at date of sale	800
disposal price (net of VAT)	600
loss on disposal	200

The book-keeping entries (excluding bank account and VAT account) are:

Dr	Machinery at cost account			Cr
20-4		£	20-6	£
1 Jan Bank		2,000	31 Dec Disposals	2,000

Dr	Machinery: accumulated depreciation account			Cr
20-4		£	20-4	£
31 Dec Balance c/d		400	31 Dec Depreciation charge	400
20-5			20-5	
31 Dec Balance c/d		800	1 Jan Balance b/d	400
			31 Dec Depreciation charge	400
		800		800
20-6			20-6	
31 Dec Disposals		1,200	1 Jan Balance b/d	800
			31 Dec Depreciation charge	400
		1,200		1,200

Dr	Machinery: disposals account			Cr
20-6		£	20-6	£
31 Dec Machinery at cost		2,000	31 Dec Accumulated depreciation	1,200
			31 Dec Bank	600
			31 Dec Income statement	
			(loss on disposal)	200
		2,000		2,000

Income statement for the year ended 31 December 20-6		
	Dr *Expense* £	Cr *Income* £
Depreciation charge*: machinery	400	–
Loss on disposal of machinery	200	–
* depreciation charge account is on page 89		

Notes:

• In the machinery account, which is always kept 'at cost', the original price of the asset is transferred at the date of disposal to disposals account. In this example, a nil balance remains on machinery account; however it is quite likely that the machinery account includes several machines, only one of which is being sold – in this case, there would be a balance on machinery account comprising the cost prices of the remaining machines.

- In accumulated depreciation account, the amount of depreciation relating to the machine disposed is transferred to disposals account. In this example, as only one machine is owned, the whole balance is transferred. However, if there were machines remaining, only part of the balance would be transferred – the amount left on the account comprising the accumulated depreciation of the remaining machines.

- Disposals account would balance without the need for an income statement transfer if the depreciation rate used reflected exactly the fall in value of the machine. In practice, this is unlikely to happen, so a transfer to income statement must be made. In this example, it is an under-depreciation (loss on disposal), and the income statement lists an extra expense. If there had been an over-depreciation (profit on disposal), an item of additional income would be shown in the income statement.

- In an extended trial balance the disposal of a non-current asset will show as either a debit balance (loss on disposal) or a credit balance (profit on disposal). In this Case Study it will be a debit balance of £200. All that has to be done in the ETB is to transfer the disposal amount to the same – debit or credit – column of the income statement.

The journal entries for the accounting entries in this Case Study are shown on page 205.

PART-EXCHANGE OF NON-CURRENT ASSETS

Instead of disposing of an old non-current asset for cash, it is quite common to part-exchange it for a new asset. This is exactly the same as if a person trades in their old car for a new (or newer) one.

Once the part-exchange allowance has been agreed, the book-keeping entries for disposal are as detailed earlier except that, instead of disposal proceeds, there will be:

- *debit* non-current asset account with the amount of the part-exchange allowance

- *credit* asset disposals account with the amount of the part-exchange allowance

The remainder of the purchase cost of the new non-current asset paid from the bank is debited to non-current asset account and credited to bank account in the usual way. For a VAT-registered business there will also be amounts to record on the VAT account.

For example, the machine referred to earlier in this section is part-exchanged on 31 December 20-6 at an agreed value of £600 (net of VAT) for a new machine costing £2,500 (net of VAT). The balance is paid from the bank.

Machinery at cost account is now be shown as:

Dr			Machinery at cost account		Cr
20-4		£	20-6		£
1 Jan	Bank	2,000	31 Dec	Disposals	2,000
20-6					
31 Dec	Disposals (part-exchange allowance)	600	31 Dec	Balance c/d	2,500
31 Dec	Bank (balance paid)	1,900			
		2,500			2,500
20-7					
1 Jan	Balance b/d	2,500			

Notes:
- This gives two debits (£600 and £1,900) in machinery account for a single machine.
- Disposals account is unchanged, except that the description for the credit transaction of £600 is machinery at cost account, instead of bank. The account is as follows:

Dr			Machinery: disposals account		Cr
20-6		£	20-6		£
31 Dec	Machinery at cost	2,000	31 Dec	Accumulated depreciation	1,200
			31 Dec	Machinery at cost	600
			31 Dec	Income statement (loss on disposal)	200
		2,000			2,000

IAS 16: PROPERTY, PLANT AND EQUIPMENT

International Accounting Standard (IAS) No 16, entitled *Property, Plant and Equipment,* is the accounting standard (see also Chapters 8 and 9) which includes the rules for dealing with depreciation in financial statements.

IAS 16 states that:

- all non-current assets having a known useful life are to be depreciated
- depreciation methods that can be used include straight-line and reducing (diminishing) balance
- depreciation amounts are normally based on the cost of the non-current assets (where assets are revalued, depreciation is based on the revalued amount)

Chapter Summary

■ Non-current assets lose value – depreciation – as time goes by as a result of:

- – wear and tear
- – passage of time
- – depletion
- – economic reasons, such as obsolescence and inadequacy

■ The purpose of depreciation is to spread the cost of a non-current asset over its useful life.

■ Two common methods of calculating depreciation are the straight-line method and the reducing balance method.

■ In terms of book-keeping, the accounts used to record depreciation are:

- – depreciation charge account, which records the amount of depreciation for the asset for the year
- – accumulated depreciation account, which records the amount of depreciation to date for each class of non-current asset

■ The depreciation charge for each class of non-current asset is included amongst the expenses in the income statement, while the cost of the asset is shown in the statement of financial position together with accumulated depreciation.

■ Depreciation is a non-cash expense.

■ When a non-current asset is disposed, it is necessary to make an adjustment in respect of any under depreciation (loss on disposal) or over depreciation (profit on disposal) during the life of the asset. The amount is calculated by means of a disposals account, and is then transferred to the income statement.

■ Journal entries – see Chapter 11 – must be made for all year end depreciation charges and for all accounting transactions relating to the disposal of non-current assets. The journal entries record amounts in a book of prime entry and give the book-keeper the authority to record the transactions in the double-entry accounts.

■ IAS 16, *Property, Plant and Equipment*, is the international accounting standard which includes depreciation.

Key Terms		
	depreciation	the estimate of the amount of the loss in value of a non-current asset over its useful life
	straight-line depreciation	a fixed percentage or fraction is written off the original cost (less any residual or scrap value) of the asset each year
	reducing (diminishing) balance depreciation	a fixed percentage is written off the reduced balance of the asset each year
	depreciation charge account	used to record the annual depreciation charge, which is debited to the income statement, for one or more classes of non-current assets
	accumulated depreciation account	used to record the amount of accumulated depreciation for an asset or class of non-current asset
	depreciation policy	the method and rate of depreciation used by a business for each class of non-current asset
	asset disposal account	used to calculate any profit or loss on disposal of non-current assets

Activities

6.1   A machine costs £5,000 net of VAT and is expected to last for five years. At the end of this time, it is estimated that it will have a residual (scrap) value of £500 net of VAT. The annual depreciation charge for a VAT-registered business which uses the straight-line method will be:

(a)   £900

(b)   £1,000

(c)   £1,100

(d)   £1,250

Answer (a) or (b) or (c) or (d)

6.2 The business for which you work depreciates its delivery vans on the reducing balance method. Why do you think this method is used?

6.3 On 1 January 20-2, Martin Jackson bought a car for £12,000. In his financial statements, which have a year end of 31 December, he has been depreciating it at 25 per cent per annum using the reducing balance method. On 31 December 20-4, he sells the car for £5,500 (cheque received); his accounting policy is to depreciate assets in the year of sale.

You are to show:

(a) accumulated depreciation account for 20-2, 20-3 and 20-4

(b) statement of financial position extract, showing cost and accumulated depreciation, at 31 December 20-2 and 20-3

(c) asset disposals account

Round your answers down to whole £s where appropriate.

6.4 This Activity is about recording non-current asset information in the general ledger.

- You are working on the accounts of a business that is registered for VAT.

- A new machine has been acquired. VAT can be reclaimed on this machine.

- The cost excluding VAT was £8,000; this was paid from the bank.

- The residual value is expected to be £3,000 excluding VAT.

- The depreciation policy for machines is that they are depreciated on a straight line basis over four years.

- Depreciation has already been entered into the accounts for the existing machines.

You are to make entries to account for:

- the purchase of the new machine

- the depreciation on the new machine

On each account, show clearly the balance carried down or transferred to the income statement. (Note that dates are not required in the accounts.)

Machinery at cost

Balance b/d	£20,000		

Machinery: accumulated depreciation

		Balance b/d	£6,000

Machinery: depreciation charge

Balance b/d	£2,000		

6.5   This Activity is about recording non-current asset information in the general ledger.

- You are working on the accounts of a business that is registered for VAT.
- During the year an old vehicle was disposed.
- The vehicle had been bought for £12,000 plus VAT (the VAT was reclaimed).
- Two years' depreciation has been applied.
- Depreciation is provided at 25 per cent per year on a reducing balance basis.
- The vehicle was sold for £7,000 plus VAT (at 20%), with payment being received into the bank.

You are to:

(a)   Calculate the accumulated depreciation on the vehicle now sold:

year 1	£
year 2	£
total	£

(b)   Make entries in the accounts which follow to record the disposal of the vehicle, showing clearly any balance carried down or transferred to the income statement (note that dates are not required in the accounts)

Vehicle at cost

Balance b/d	£12,000		

Vehicle: disposals

Bank/cash

(c)   Tick the relevant box to show whether there is a profit or loss on disposal of the vehicle

profit	
loss	

6.6   This Activity is about recording non-current asset information in the general ledger.

- You are working on the accounts of a business that is registered for VAT.

- The business has part-exchanged a machine during the year, but no entries have been made in the general ledger for this transaction.

- The original cost of the machine that was part-exchanged was £4,200 plus VAT (the VAT was reclaimed).

- The accumulated depreciation on the machine that was part-exchanged was £3,150.

- A part-exchange allowance of £1,200 plus VAT (which can be reclaimed) was given against the new machine.

- The £4,800, plus VAT, balance owing for the new machine was paid from the bank during the year. The VAT can be reclaimed.

- A full year's depreciation charge needs to be made on the new machine on a 25 per cent straight-line basis. It is assumed that there will be no residual value. No other depreciation charge needs to be made.

You are to make entries to account for:

- the disposal of the old machine

- the purchase of the new machine

- the depreciation on the new machine

On each account, show clearly the balance carried down or transferred to the income statement. (Note that dates are not required in the accounts.)

Machinery at cost

Balance b/d	£4,200		

Machinery: accumulated depreciation

		Balance b/d	£3,150

Machinery: depreciation charge

Machinery: disposals

6.7   You are given the following extract of balances from the general ledger of a business.

You are to enter the amounts in the appropriate column for the accounts shown. Do not enter zeros in unused column cells.

Extract from trial balance as at 31 December 20-4

Account	£	£ Dr	£ Cr
Accrual of expenses	680		
Capital	25,000		
Depreciation charge	1,200		
Drawings	8,000		
Interest received	200		
Machinery at cost	6,500		
Machinery: accumulated depreciation	2,400		
Prepayment of expenses	210		

6.8   The following list of balances has been extracted from the books of John Henson at 31 December 20-1:

	£
Purchases	71,600
Sales revenue	121,750
Opening inventory	6,250
Vehicle running expenses	1,480
Rent and rates	5,650
Office expenses	2,220
Discount received	285
Wages and salaries	18,950
Office equipment at cost	10,000
Vehicle at cost	12,000
Sales ledger control	5,225
Purchases ledger control	3,190
Value Added Tax (owing to HMRC)	1,720
Capital	20,000
Drawings for the year	13,095
Bank	725
Profit on disposal of non-current asset	250

Notes at 31 December 20-1:

- inventory was valued at £8,500
- depreciation charge for office equipment for the year £1,000
- depreciation charge for vehicle for the year £3,000

You are to prepare the extended trial balance of John Henson for the year ended 31 December 20-1.

6.9 A friend of yours has recently started in business: knowing that you are studying financial accounting, she seeks your assistance. She has just bought a machine at a cost of £1,000 net of VAT and asks you to advise on depreciation methods. The machine is expected to last for five years after which it will be valueless. She tells you that, if there is a choice of depreciation methods, she would like to use the one "that gives the larger net profit in the early years because the business could make good use of the extra cash". Advise your friend by means of a letter.

6.10 The following trial balance has been extracted by the book-keeper of Hazel Harris at 31 December 20-8:

	Dr £	Cr £
Bank loan		75,000
Capital		125,000
Purchases and sales revenue	465,000	614,000
Building repairs	8,480	
Vehicle at cost	12,000	
Vehicles: accumulated depreciation		2,400
Vehicle expenses	2,680	
Premises at cost	100,000	
Premises: accumulated depreciation		4,000
Bank overdraft		2,000
Furniture at cost	25,000	
Furniture: accumulated depreciation		2,500
Wages and salaries	86,060	
Discounts	10,610	8,140
Drawings	24,000	
Rates and insurance	6,070	
Sales and purchases ledger control	52,130	32,600
Value Added Tax		5,250
Administration expenses	15,460	
Opening inventory	63,000	
Disposal of non-current asset	400	
	870,890	870,890

Notes at 31 December 20-8:

- inventory was valued at £88,000
- wages and salaries outstanding: £3,180
- rates and insurance paid in advance: £450
- depreciate premises at 2 per cent using the straight-line method
- depreciate the vehicle at 20 per cent using the reducing balance method
- depreciate furniture at 10 per cent using the straight-line method

You are to prepare the extended trial balance of Hazel Harris for the year ended 31 December 20-8.

7 Irrecoverable debts and allowance for doubtful debts

this chapter covers...

Most businesses selling their goods and services to other businesses do not receive payment immediately. Instead, they often have to allow a period of credit and, until the payment is received, they have an asset of trade receivables (in sales ledger control account).

Unfortunately, it is likely that not all receivables will eventually settle the amounts they owe, ie the amounts are irrecoverable debts which have to be written off.

At the same time a business needs to make an allowance for doubtful debts, which allows for receivables who may not pay.

In this chapter we will:

- *distinguish between irrecoverable debts and allowance for doubtful debts*

- *prepare the accounting entries for irrecoverable debts, and consider the effect on the financial statements*

- *prepare the accounting entries to make an allowance for doubtful debts, and consider the effect on the financial statements*

IRRECOVERABLE DEBTS AND ALLOWANCE FOR DOUBTFUL DEBTS

irrecoverable debts

Irrecoverable debts (sometimes called bad debts) are debts owing to a business which it considers will never be paid.

Let us consider a business with receivables of £10,000, made up of a number of customers' accounts. At any one time, a few of these accounts will be irrecoverable, and therefore the amount is uncollectable: they need to be written off as irrecoverable debts, ie the business will give up trying to collect the debt and will accept the loss.

allowance for doubtful debts

Allowance for doubtful debts (sometimes called provision for bad debts) is the estimate by a business of the likely percentage of its receivables which may become irrecoverable during any one accounting period.

There are likely to be some receivables accounts which, although they are not yet irrecoverable, may be giving some concern as to their ability to pay: An allowance for doubtful debts needs to be made in respect of these. The one thing the business with receivables of £10,000 cannot do is to show this amount as an asset in the statement of financial position: to do so would be to imply that the full £10,000 is recoverable. Instead, this receivables figure might be reduced in two stages, for example:

- accounts with balances totalling £200 are to be written off as **irrecoverable debts**
- an **allowance for doubtful debts** is to be made amounting to 2% of remaining receivables after the £200 has been written off

The receivables figure then becomes:	£
Gross receivables	10,000
Less: irrecoverable debts written off	200
	9,800
Less: allowance for doubtful debts at 2%	196
Net receivables	9,604

*   Note: the level of percentage is likely to reflect the level of risk of the doubtful debt

general and specific allowances

A **general allowance** for doubtful debts is an allowance applied (as in the above example) to the total receivables after writing off irrecoverable debts.

A **specific allowance** is an allowance applied to one or more specific debts. If the risk of default is higher, for example, the percentage will be higher.

prudence concept of accounting

Irrecoverable debts and allowance for doubtful debts is an application of the accounting concept of prudence (see Chapter 8). By reducing the receivables figure, a more realistic figure is shown in the statement of financial position of the amount that the business can expect to receive.

TREATMENT OF IRRECOVERABLE DEBTS

Irrecoverable debts are written off when they become uncollectable. This means that all reasonable efforts to recover the amount owing have been exhausted, ie statements, letters and emails have been sent to the customer requesting payment and legal action, where appropriate, or the threat of legal action has failed to obtain payment.

In writing off a receivable's account as irrecoverable, the business is bearing the cost of the amount due. The account is closed and the amount (or amounts, where a number of accounts are dealt with in this way) is debited to *irrecoverable debts* account in the general ledger. This account stores up the amounts of account balances written off during the year (in much the same way as an expense account). At the end of the financial year, the balance of the account is transferred to the income statement as an expense, where it is described as *irrecoverable debts*.

In terms of double-entry book-keeping, the transactions are:

– *debit* irrecoverable debts

– *credit* receivable's account

At the end of the financial year, irrecoverable debts account is transferred to the income statement as an expense:

– *debit* income statement

– *credit* irrecoverable debts

For example, the following customer's account is in the sales ledger:

Dr			**T Hughes**		Cr
20-7		£	20-7		£
5 Jan	Sales	55	8 May	Bank	25
			6 Jul	Cash	5

It is now 15 December 20-7 and you are reviewing the customers' accounts before the end of the financial year on 31 December. Your business has sent statements and 'chaser' letters to T Hughes – the last letter was dated 30 September, and was returned marked 'gone away, not known at this address'. Nothing further has been heard from T Hughes. You take the decision to write off this account as an irrecoverable debt; the account will be closed off as shown below:

Dr			**T Hughes**		Cr
20-7		£	20-7		£
5 Jan	Sales	55	8 May	Bank	25
			6 Jul	Cash	5
			15 Dec	Irrecoverable debts	25
		55			55

The balance is transferred to the 'holding' account, *irrecoverable debts,* together with other accounts written off. At the end of the financial year, the total of this account is transferred to the income statement:

Dr			**Irrecoverable debts account**		Cr
20-7		£	20-7		£
15 Dec	Sales ledger control (T Hughes)	25	31 Dec	Income statement	200
15 Dec	Sales ledger control (Lane & Co)	85			
15 Dec	Sales ledger control (A Harvey)	90			
		200			200

Tutorial note: irrecoverable debts must be recorded in sales ledger control account – see Chapter 10.

In financial statements, the effect of writing off debts as irrecoverable is to reduce the previously reported profit for the year – in the example above, by £200.

Notes:
• If you are preparing financial statements and the figure for irrecoverable debts is shown in the trial balance (debit side), simply record the amount as an expense in income statement – the receivables (sales ledger control) figure has been reduced already.

• If the irrecoverable debts figure is not already shown in the trial balance, and a note tells you to write off a particular account as bad, you need to list the amount as an expense in the income statement and reduce the receivables (sales ledger control) figure for the statement of financial position. In an extended trial balance, use the adjustments columns, debit irrecoverable debts, and credit the sales ledger control figure (in the statement of financial position columns show a net amount for sales ledger control, ie less adjustment).

- In sales ledger control account (see Chapter 10) the amount of irrecoverable debts must be recorded on the credit side of the control account.

journal entries

A journal entry – see Chapter 11 – must be made for all irrecoverable debts which are written off. The journal entry records the amounts being written off in a book of prime entry and gives the book-keeper the authority to record the transactions in the double-entry accounts.

RECOVERY OF A DEBT

This topic is discussed on page 404.

TREATMENT OF ALLOWANCE FOR DOUBTFUL DEBTS

Allowance for doubtful debts is different from writing off an irrecoverable debt because there is only the possibility – not the certainty – of future irrecoverable debts. The receivables figure (after writing off irrecoverable debts) is reduced either by totalling the balances of the accounts that may not pay or, more likely, by applying a percentage to the total figure for receivables. The percentage chosen is based on past experience and varies from business to business – for example, a hire purchase company may well use a higher percentage than a bank.

The usual procedure is to have two accounts in the general ledger:

- *allowance for doubtful debts: adjustment account*, which records the amount to create, increase or decrease the allowance each year
- *allowance for doubtful debts account,* which records the accumulated total of the allowance

initial creation of an allowance for doubtful debts

Making an allowance for doubtful debts comes *after* writing off irrecoverable debts (if any). The steps are:

step 1   A business, at the end of its financial year in 20-1, estimates the percentage of its receivables which are doubtful and may become irrecoverable, say two per cent.

step 2   The allowance is calculated (eg £9,800 x 2% = £196)

step 3   The allowance is recorded in the double-entry system:

- *debit* income statement (as an expense)
- *credit* allowance for doubtful debts: adjustment
- *debit* allowance for doubtful debts: adjustment
- *credit* allowance for doubtful debts

The allowance for doubtful debts: adjustment account acts as a 'holding' account, through which transfers to and from the income statement are made. The allowance for doubtful debts account holds the accumulated total of the allowance, which is shown on the opposite side from sales ledger control in the statement of financial position (see below).

step 4   In financial statements, the amount of the allowance for doubtful debts is shown as:

- a debit in the income statement columns
- a credit in the statement of financial position columns

The amounts are as follows:

Year	Income statement		Statement of financial position	
	Dr	Cr	Dr	Cr
	Expense	*Income*	*Sales ledger control*	*Allowance for doubtful debts*
	£	£	£	£
	196	–	9,800	196

Note that the business, in creating an allowance for doubtful debts, is presenting a realistic and prudent estimate of its trade receivables – this follows the prudence concept of accounting (see Chapter 8).

adjustments to allowance for doubtful debts

Once an allowance for doubtful debts has been created, the only adjustments that need to be made are as a result of:

- a *policy change* in the allowance, eg an increase in the fixed percentage from 2% to 5%
- an *arithmetical adjustment* in the allowance as a result of a change in the total of receivables, eg increase in receivables of £5,000 will require a proportionally higher allowance

If, or when, either of these two situations arises, the adjustment to the existing allowance will be:

- either *upwards* (increase in allowance percentage, or increase in receivables figure)
- or *downwards* (decrease in allowance percentage, or decrease in receivables figure)

increasing the allowance

The *increase in the allowance* is recorded in the double-entry system as follows:

– *debit* income statement (as an expense)

– *credit* allowance for doubtful debts: adjustment account

– *debit* allowance for doubtful debts: adjustment account

– *credit* allowance for doubtful debts account

For the statement of financial position, the balance of allowance for doubtful debts account is shown on the opposite side to sales ledger control.

decreasing the allowance

The *decrease in the allowance* is recorded as:

– *debit* allowance for doubtful debts: adjustment account

– *credit* income statement (ie income)

– *debit* allowance for doubtful debts account

– *credit* allowance for doubtful debts: adjustment account

Again, the statement of financial position shows the balance of allowance for doubtful debts account in the credit column.

Note that allowance for doubtful debts and irrecoverable debts are completely separate adjustments: the two should not be confused. It is quite usual to see, in an income statement, entries for both irrecoverable debts and allowance for doubtful debts.

journal entries

A journal entry – see Chapter 11 – must be made for the creation of, and any subsequent adjustments to, the allowance for doubtful debts. The journal entry records the amount in a book of prime entry and gives the book-keeper the authority to record the transaction in the double-entry accounts.

BOOK-KEEPING FOR ALLOWANCE FOR DOUBTFUL DEBTS

A business decides to create an allowance for doubtful debts of five per cent of its trade receivables. After writing off irrecoverable debts, the receivables figures at the end of each of three years are:

    20-6 £10,000

    20-7 £15,000

    20-8 £12,000

book-keeping entries

creating the allowance (year 20-6):
£10,000 x 5% = £500

– *debit* income statement

– *credit* allowance for doubtful debts: adjustment

– *debit* allowance for doubtful debts: adjustment

– *credit* allowance for doubtful debts

increasing the allowance (year 20-7):
£5,000 (increase in receivables) x 5% = £250

– *debit* income statement

– *credit* allowance for doubtful debts: adjustment

– *debit* allowance for doubtful debts: adjustment

– *credit* allowance for doubtful debts

decreasing the allowance (year 20-8):
£3,000 (decrease in receivables) x 5% = £150

– *debit* allowance for doubtful debts: adjustment

– *credit* income statement

– *debit* allowance for doubtful debts

– *credit* allowance for doubtful debts: adjustment

The book-keeping entries in the general ledger for

• allowance for doubtful debts: adjustment

• allowance for doubtful debts

are as follows (on the next page):

116 sole trader and partnership accounts tutorial

Dr	Allowance for doubtful debts: adjustment account		Cr

20-6		£	20-6		£
31 Dec	Allowance for doubtful debts	500	31 Dec	Income statement	500
20-7			20-7		
31 Dec	Allowance for doubtful debts	250	31 Dec	Income statement	250
20-8			20-8		
31 Dec	Income statement	150	31 Dec	Allowance for doubtful debts	150

Dr	Allowance for doubtful debts account		Cr

20-6		£	20-6		£
			31 Dec	Allowance for doubtful debts: adjustment	500
31 Dec	Balance c/d	500			
20-7			20-7		
31 Dec	Balance c/d	750	1 Jan	Balance b/d	500
			31 Dec	Allowance for doubtful debts: adjustment (increase in allowance)	250
		750			750
20-8			20-8		
31 Dec	Allowance for doubtful debts: adjustment (decrease in allowance)	150	1 Jan	Balance b/d	750
31 Dec	Balance c/d	600			
		750			750
20-9			20-9		
			1 Jan	Balance b/d	600

the financial statements

The effect of the above transactions on the financial statements is shown as follows:

Year	Income statement		Statement of financial position	
	Dr	Cr	Dr	Cr
	Expense	Income	Sales ledger control	Allowance for doubtful debts
	£	£	£	£
20-6	500	–	10,000	500
20-7	250	–	15,000	750
20-8	–	150	12,000	600

Note:

When preparing financial statements in Activities and Assessments, there will be a note to the trial balance telling you to make an adjustment to the allowance for doubtful debts. Sometimes you will be told a percentage figure, eg 'allowance for doubtful debts is to be maintained at five per cent of receivables'; alternatively, you may be told the new allowance figure (be careful of the wording – distinguish between 'increase the allowance to £750' and 'increase the allowance by £750').

IRRECOVERABLE DEBTS AND ALLOWANCE FOR DOUBTFUL DEBTS IN THE EXTENDED TRIAL BALANCE

irrecoverable debts

If irrecoverable debts already appear in the trial balance, simply show the amount in the income statement debit column: this will have the effect of reducing profit for the year. Do not alter the figure for sales ledger control, as it will have been reduced already by the amount written off.

If a note to the trial balance tells you to write off, say, £100 of irrecoverable debts, then you will need to include a row in the extended trial balance for irrecoverable debts. In the adjustments column, show £100 as a debit to this row, and credit the sales ledger control row. This will give an expense of £100 for the income statement, and will reduce sales ledger control for the statement of financial position by £100 (show a net figure for sales ledger control in the statement of financial position column).

recovery of a debt

If a trial balance shows a credit balance for recovery of a debt, simply show the amount in the income statement credit column: this will have the effect of increasing profit for the year.

allowance for doubtful debts

In the extended trial balance layout you will see that, towards the bottom, a row is preprinted for allowance for doubtful debts: adjustment. Use this as the 'holding' account to create, or increase, or decrease the allowance.

For example, to increase an existing allowance of £500 (which will be shown in the trial balance) by, say, £250, record the following in the extended trial balance:

- in the adjustments column
    - *debit* allowance for doubtful debts: adjustment
    - *credit* allowance for doubtful debts

- in the income statement column record the £250 amount of the allowance for doubtful debts: adjustment as an expense in the debit column

- in the statement of financial position column record the allowance for doubtful debts as £750, ie the trial balance figure of £500 and the amount of £250 shown in the adjustments column

Where a new allowance is to be created the above principles are followed; to reduce an existing allowance, then the reverse of the above will be followed.

Remember that, in the extended trial balance:

- allowance for doubtful debts: adjustment is shown in the income statement and records the amount to create, increase or decrease the allowance each year

- allowance for doubtful debts is shown in the credit column of the statement of financial position and is the accumulated total of the allowance

Case Study

TARA SMITH: IRRECOVERABLE DEBTS AND ALLOWANCE FOR DOUBTFUL DEBTS

We will now focus on how the irrecoverable debt and allowance for doubtful debts amounts are shown in the income statement and statement of financial position. We will continue with the trial balance of Tara Smith and include adjustments for the year for:

- irrecoverable debts of £100 written off
- allowance for doubtful debts of £250 created (note that there is no existing allowance)

extended trial balance (see next page)

The columns which are affected are adjustments, income statement, and statement of financial position – the altered figures are shaded for illustrative purposes.

EXTENDED TRIAL BALANCE   **TARA SMITH TRADING AS "THE FASHION SHOP"**   **31 DECEMBER 20-4**

Account name	Ledger balances		Adjustments		Income statement		Statement of financial position	
	Dr £	Cr £	Dr £	Cr £	Dr £	Cr £	Dr £	Cr £
Opening inventory	12,500				12,500			
Purchases	105,000				105,000			
Sales revenue		155,000				155,000		
Administration expenses	6,200				6,200			
Wages	23,500				23,500			
Rent paid	750			75	675			
Telephone	500		100		600			
Interest paid	4,500				4,500			
Travel expenses	550				550			
Premises	100,000						100,000	
Premises: accumulated depreciation				2,000				2,000
Shop fittings	20,000						20,000	
Shop fittings: accumulated depreciation				5,000				5,000
Sales ledger control	10,500			100			10,400	
Bank	5,450						5,450	
Cash	50						50	
Capital		75,000						75,000
Drawings	7,000						7,000	
Loan from bank		50,000						50,000
Purchases ledger control		14,500						14,500
Value Added Tax		2,000						2,000
Closing inventory: income statement				10,500		10,500		
Closing inventory: statement of financial position			10,500				10,500	
Accruals				100				100
Prepayments			75				75	
Depreciation charge			7,000		7,000			
Irrecoverable debts			100		100			
Allowance for doubtful debts				250				250
Allowance for doubtful debts:adjustment			250		250			
Profit/loss for the year					4,625			4,625
	296,500	296,500	18,025	18,025	165,500	165,500	153,475	153,475

Chapter Summary

■ Not all receivables of a business will eventually settle the amounts they owe: such amounts are *irrecoverable debts* which have to be written off.

■ *An allowance for doubtful debts* is made for receivables who may not pay.

■ This sequence should be followed:
  – write off irrecoverable debts (if any)
  – create (or adjust) allowance for doubtful debts

■ To write off an irrecoverable debt:
  – *debit* irrecoverable debts account
  – *credit* receivables account

  At the end of the financial year irrecoverable debts account is transferred, as an expense, to the debit column of the income statement.

■ An allowance for doubtful debts is often based on a fixed percentage of receivables at the year-end.

■ For book-keeping purposes, two accounts are used to create, increase or decrease an allowance for doubtful debts:

  – allowance for doubtful debts: adjustment account, to record the annual change

  – allowance for doubtful debts account, to record the accumulated total

■ Having created an allowance for doubtful debts, it will usually be adjusted either upwards or downwards in subsequent years in line with the change in the level of receivables.

■ A journal entry – see Chapter 11 – must be made for all irrecoverable debts which are written off and for the creation of, and any subsequent adjustments to, the allowance for doubtful debts. The journal entries record the amounts in a book of prime entry and give the book-keeper the authority to record the transactions in the double-entry accounts.

Key Terms

irrecoverable debts	debts owing to a business which it considers will never be paid
irrecoverable debts account	the account to which the amounts of account balances written off as irrecoverable are transferred
allowance for doubtful debts	an estimate by a business of the likely percentage of its receivables which are doubtful and may become irrecoverable during any one accounting period
allowance for doubtful debts: adjustment account	used to record the annual change in the allowance for doubtful debts
allowance for doubtful debts account	used to record the accumulated total of the allowance for doubtful debts

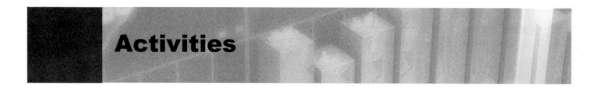

Activities

7.1 Ken Shah, a customer of the business where you work, is unable to pay the amount owing and the accounts supervisor has decided to write off his account as irrecoverable. How will this be recorded in the double-entry accounts (assume that the business does not use control accounts)?

	Debit	Credit
(a)	irrecoverable debts	K Shah's account
(b)	K Shah's account	irrecoverable debts
(c)	cash account	K Shah's account
(d)	sales revenue account	K Shah's account

Answer (a) or (b) or (c) or (d)
(Ignore VAT)

7.2 A trial balance shows trade receivables of £48,000 and an allowance for doubtful debts of £2,200. It is decided to make the allowance for doubtful debts equal to five per cent of receivables. What book-keeping entry will be made on the allowance for doubtful debts account?

(a) debit £200
(b) debit £2,400
(c) credit £200
(d) credit £2,200

Answer (a) or (b) or (c) or (d)

7.3 You are the book-keeper at Waterston Plant Hire. At 31 December 20-2, the end of the financial year, the business has trade receivables of £20,210. The owner decides to:

(a) write off, as irrecoverable debts, the accounts of:

P Ross	£55
J Ball	£105
L Jones	£50

(b) make an allowance for doubtful debts of 2.5% of receivables (after writing off the above debts)

You are to explain how these transactions will be recorded in the financial statements at the end of the year.

7.4 Ross Engineering has an existing allowance for doubtful debts of £300, based on 5 per cent of receivables. After writing off irrecoverable debts, the amounts of receivables at the end of the next two financial years are found to be:

31 December 20-5	£8,000
31 December 20-6	£7,000

The business continues to keep the allowance for doubtful debts equal to 5 per cent of receivables.

As an accounts assistant at Ross Engineering, you are to show how the allowance for doubtful debts account will be adjusted at the end of the financial years ended 31 December 20-5 and 31 December 20-6, and how it will be recorded in the appropriate financial statements.

7.5 This Activity is about accounting for irrecoverable debts and allowance for doubtful debts and preparing a trial balance.

You are working on the financial statements of a business for the year ended 31 December 20-8. In this task you can ignore VAT.

You have the following information:

Irrecoverable debts to be written off:	£
Thompson & Co	110
T Aziz	65
Wyvern Traders	80
Allowance for doubtful debts at 1 January 20-8	600

The balance of trade receivables (sales ledger control account) before irrecoverable debts are written off is £28,255. The allowance for doubtful debts is to be 2.5% of trade receivables after irrecoverable debts.

(a) **You are to** prepare the irrecoverable debts account for the year ended 31 December 20-8 and close it off by showing the transfer to the income statement. Dates are not required.

Irrecoverable debts

	£		£

(b)   **You are to** prepare the allowance for doubtful debts account for the year ended 31 December 20-8 and to show clearly the balance carried down. Include dates.

Allowance for doubtful debts

		£			£

You have the following extract of balances from the general ledger.

(c)   **Using your answers** from (a) and (b), record the adjustments on the extract from the extended trial balance. Do not enter zeros in unused column cells.

Extract from trial balance as at 31 December 20-8

Account	Ledger balances		Adjustments	
	Dr £	Cr £	Dr £	Cr £
Allowance for doubtful debts		600		
Allowance for doubtful debts: adjustment				
Irrecoverable debts				
Loan interest	790			
Sales ledger control	28,255			
Vehicles at cost	12,000			
Vehicles: accumulated depreciation		6,400		
Wages	35,470			

7.6 The following trial balance has been extracted by the book-keeper of Paul Sanders, who runs an office supplies business, as at 31 December 20-4:

	Dr £	Cr £
Purchases and sales revenue	51,225	81,762
Sales and purchases returns	186	254
Opening inventory	6,031	
Discounts allowed and received	324	238
Vehicle expenses	1,086	
Wages and salaries	20,379	
Electricity	876	
Telephone	1,241	
Rent and rates	4,565	
Sundry expenses	732	
Irrecoverable debts	219	
Sales and purchases ledger control	1,040	7,671
Value Added Tax		1,301
Bank	3,501	
Cash	21	
Vehicles at cost	15,000	
Vehicles: accumulated depreciation		3,000
Office equipment at cost	10,000	
Office equipment: accumulated depreciation		5,000
Capital		25,000
Drawings	8,000	
Disposal of non-current asset		200
	124,426	124,426

Notes at 31 December 20-4:

- inventory was valued at £8,210

- electricity owing £102

- rent prepaid £251

- depreciate vehicles at 20 per cent and office equipment at 10 per cent per annum, using the straight-line method

- create an allowance for doubtful debts of 5 per cent of receivables

You are to prepare the extended trial balance of Paul Sanders for the year ended 31 December 20-4.

7.7 The following trial balance has been extracted by the book-keeper of James Jenkins, who owns a patisserie and coffee lounge, as at 30 June 20-5:

	Dr	Cr
	£	£
Capital		36,175
Drawings	19,050	
Purchases and sales revenue	105,240	168,432
Opening inventory	9,427	
Sales and purchases ledger control	3,840	5,294
Value Added Tax		1,492
Sales and purchases returns	975	1,237
Discounts allowed and received	127	643
Wages and salaries	30,841	
Vehicle expenses	1,021	
Rent and rates	8,796	
Heating and lighting	1,840	
Telephone	355	
General expenses	1,752	
Irrecoverable debts	85	
Vehicle at cost	8,000	
Vehicle: accumulated depreciation		3,500
Shop fittings at cost	6,000	
Shop fittings: accumulated depreciation		2,000
Allowance for doubtful debts		150
Cash	155	
Bank	21,419	
	218,923	218,923

Notes at 30 June 20-5:
- inventory was valued at £11,517
- vehicle expenses owing £55
- rent prepaid £275
- depreciate the vehicle at 25 per cent per annum, using the reducing balance method
- depreciate shop fittings at 10 per cent per annum, using the straight-line method
- the allowance for doubtful debts is to be equal to 2.5 per cent of receivables

You are to prepare the extended trial balance of James Jenkins for the year ended 30 June 20-5.

The rules of accounting

In this chapter we will explain the rules of accounting to be followed when preparing financial statements. These rules take the form of

- *accounting concepts*

- *accounting standards*

If the same rules have been followed, then broad comparisons can be made between the financial statements of different businesses.

We will see the accounting rules relating to:

- *the accounting treatment for non-current assets, including depreciation (IAS 16, Property, plant and equipment)*

- *the valuation of inventory (IAS 2, Inventories)*

Later in the chapter we focus on the importance of the distinction between capital expenditure and revenue expenditure.

ACCOUNTING CONCEPTS

Accounting concepts underlie the maintaining of financial records and the preparation of financial statements. Accounting concepts help to ensure that the records and statements we prepare are relevant and reliable to users, and that they are comparable and understandable. In particular, concepts help to ensure that records and statements are fit to be used for:

- *internal control* – within the business to ensure that financial records are accurate and that financial statements show the true position of the business

- *measuring business performance* – both internally and externally – so that financial reports and statements can be compared

- *obtaining credit/financing* – providing lenders with the current financial position of the business

- *statutory requirements* – providing information for tax and other purposes when required to do so by law

The diagram below illustrates the more important accounting concepts – we will look in more detail at these concepts over the next few pages.

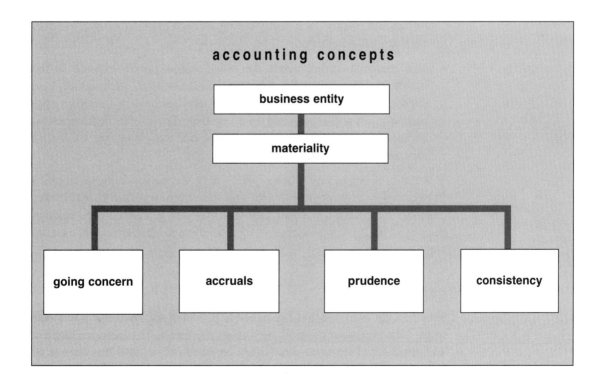

business entity

This refers to the fact that financial statements record and report on the activities of one particular business. They do not include the assets and liabilities of those who play a part in owning or running the business. Thus the personal assets and liabilities of the owner/owners are kept separate from those of the business: the main links between the business and the personal funds of the owner/owners are capital and drawings.

materiality

Some items in accounts are of such low value that it is not worthwhile recording them separately, ie they are not 'material'.

Examples include:

- Small expense items, such as donations to charities, the purchase of plants for the office, window cleaning, etc, do not justify their own separate expense account; instead they are grouped together in a sundry expenses account.

- End-of-year unused office stationery, eg paper clips, staples, photocopying paper, etc, is often not valued for the purpose of financial statements, because the amount is not material and does not justify the time and effort involved. This does mean, however, that the cost of all stationery purchased during the year is charged as an expense to the income statement – technically wrong, but not material enough to affect the financial statements.

- Low-cost non-current assets are often charged as an expense in the income statement, instead of being classed as capital expenditure, eg a stapler, waste-paper basket, etc. Strictly, these should be treated as non-current assets and depreciated each year over their useful life; in practice, because the amounts involved are not material, they are treated as expenses in the income statement.

Materiality depends very much on the size of the business. For example, a large company may consider that the cost of items of less than £1,000 are not material; by contrast, a small business may use a much lower amount, perhaps £100. It is for a business to set a policy as to what amount is material and what is not.

going concern

This concept assumes that the business to which the financial statements relate will continue to trade in the foreseeable future. The income statement and statement of financial position are prepared on the basis that there is no intention to reduce significantly the size of the business or to liquidate the business. If the business is no longer a going concern, assets will have very different values, and the statement of financial position will be affected considerably. For example, a large, purpose-built factory has considerable value to a going concern business but, if the factory had to be sold, it is likely to have a limited use for other industries, and therefore will have a lower market value. Values based on liquidation amounts are the opposite of the going concern concept and require extra depreciation to be charged as an expense to the income statement to allow for the reduced value of non-current assets. In a similar way, inventory that is to be sold in a clearance sale will be reduced in value.

accruals (or matching)

This means that expenses and revenues must be matched so that they concern the same goods or services and the same time period. We have already put this concept into practice in Chapter 5, where expenses and revenues were adjusted to take note of prepayments and accruals. The income statement should always show the amount of the expense that should have been incurred, and the amount of income that should have been received. This is the principle of income and expenditure accounting, rather than using receipts and payments as and when they fall due. Other examples of the accruals concept are accounting for:

- trade receivables
- trade payables
- depreciation
- irrecoverable debts
- allowance for doubtful debts
- opening and closing inventory adjustments

prudence

This concept, also known as conservatism in accounting, requires that financial statements should, where there is any doubt, report a conservative figure for profit or the valuation of assets. To this end, profits are not to be anticipated and should only be recognised when it is reasonably certain that they will be realised; at the same time all known liabilities should be provided for. A good example of the prudence concept is where an allowance is made for doubtful debts (see Chapter 7) – the receivables are not yet irrecoverable, but it is expected, from experience, that a certain percentage will eventually need to be written off. The valuation of inventory (see later in this chapter) also follows the prudence concept. 'Anticipate no profit, but anticipate all losses' is a summary of the concept which, in its application, prevents an over-optimistic presentation of a business through the financial statements.

consistency

This requires that, when a business adopts particular accounting methods, it should continue to use such methods consistently. For example, a business that decides to make a depreciation charge on machinery at ten per cent per annum, using the straight-line method, should continue to use that percentage and method for future financial statements for this asset. Of course, having once chosen a particular method, a business is entitled to make changes provided there are good reasons for so doing, and a note to the financial statements would explain what has happened. By applying the consistency concept, direct comparison between the financial statements of different years can be made. Further examples of the use of the consistency concept are:

- inventory valuation (see later in this chapter)
- the application of the materiality concept

other accounting concepts

Other concepts followed when preparing financial statements include:

- **money measurement** – all items are expressed in the common denominator of money; only by using money can items be added together to give, for example, profit for the year or a total for the statement of financial position

- **historical cost** – assets and liabilities are initially recorded in the financial statements at historical cost, ie the actual amount of the transaction (note that some businesses may adopt a policy of regular revaluation of assets)

- **dual aspect** – each business transaction is recorded by means of two opposite accounting entries (debit and credit), but of equal values; note that double-entry book-keeping is an example of the dual aspect concept in practice

- **realisation** – business transactions are recorded in the financial statements when the legal title passes between buyer and seller; this may well not be at the same time as payment is made, eg credit sales are recorded when the sale is made, but payment will be made at a later date

- **objectivity** – the presentation of financial statements should be objective, rather than subjective, and should not be influenced by the opinions or personal expectations of the owner/owners of the business concerned, or the accountant preparing the accounts

ACCOUNTING STANDARDS

Accounting standards – which form part of the rules of accounting – have been developed to provide a framework for accounting and to reduce the variety of accounting treatments used in financial statements.

Accounting standards take the form of:

*   International Accounting Standards (IASs)
*   International Financial Reporting Standards (IFRSs)

International standards are widely used in the UK.

There are two accounting standards relevant to your studies from this book – one deals with inventories, and the other with non-current assets.

IAS 2 Inventories

The purpose of this standard is to set out the accounting techniques to be used when valuing inventories. The broad rule is that inventories are to be valued at the lower of cost and net realisable value – see the following section.

IAS 16 Property, plant and equipment

This standard sets out the accounting treatment for non-current assets – such as land and buildings, machinery, office equipment, shop fittings and vehicles.

A key feature of the IAS is depreciation and, as we have already seen in Chapter 6, most non-current assets lose value over time. Therefore it is necessary, in order to present a realistic view of the business, to record the amount of the loss in value. The standard defines the following terms:

*   *useful life* – the length of time, or the number of units of production, for which an asset is expected to be used
*   *residual value* – the net amount the business expects to obtain for an asset at the end of its useful life after deducting the expected costs of disposal
*   *carrying amount* (or *net book value*) – the amount at which an asset is shown in the statement of financial position, after deducting accumulated depreciation

The purpose of depreciation is to spread the cost of a non-current asset over its useful life. This is an application of the accruals concept – seen earlier in this chapter – where the depreciation charge is matched to the accounting periods over which it is used.

IAS 16 requires that depreciation is to be charged on all non-current assets, with the exception of freehold land. Depreciation methods to be used include the straight-line and reducing (diminishing) balance methods (see Chapter 6):

- straight-line depreciation results in a constant depreciation charge over the asset's useful life

- reducing balance depreciation results in a decreasing depreciation charge over the useful life (ie the depreciation charge in the early years is greater than in later years)

A business chooses the depreciation method which best reflects the way in which the benefits of the asset are used. IAS 16 requires that the depreciation method used should be reviewed at least annually in order to consider if the method used is still the most appropriate one.

IAS 2: VALUATION OF INVENTORIES

The control and valuation of inventory is an important aspect in the efficient management of a business. Manual or computer records are used to show the amount of inventory held and its value at any time during the year. However, at the end of the financial year it is essential for a business to make a physical *inventory-take* for use in the financial statements. This involves inventory control personnel going into the stores, the shop, or the warehouse and counting each item. The counted inventory is then valued as follows:

number of items held x inventory valuation per item = inventory value

The auditors of a business may make random checks to ensure that the inventory value is correct.

The value of inventory at the beginning and end of the financial year is used as an adjustment to the financial statements – see Chapter 4. Therefore, the inventory value has an effect on profit for the year.

IAS 2 applies to all types of inventories – raw materials, work-in-progress (partly manufactured goods), finished goods, products bought in for resale by a retailer and service items, such as stationery, bought for use within a business.

The overriding principle of inventory valuation, as set out in IAS 2, is that inventories are to be valued at *'the lower of cost and net realisable value'*. This means that two different inventory values are compared:

- cost, which means the purchase price, plus any other costs incurred to bring the product to its present location and condition (eg delivery charges)

- net realisable value, which is the estimated selling price less the estimated costs to get the product into a condition necessary to complete the sale

This inventory valuation – the lower of cost and net realisable value – is an application of the *prudence concept*. The valuation is illustrated as follows:

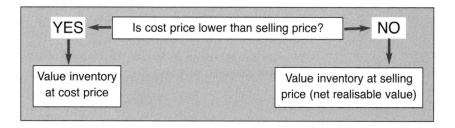

As the diagram shows, the lower of cost and net realisable value is taken; note that *different items or groups of inventory are compared separately*. The principles are illustrated in the two Case Studies which follow.

Case Study

THE CLOTHING STORE: INVENTORY VALUATION

situation

The Clothing Store bought in a range of 'designer' beachwear in the spring, with each item costing £15 and retailing for £30. Most of the goods sell well but, by autumn, ten items remain unsold. These are put on the 'bargain rail' at £18 each. On 31 December, at the end of the store's financial year, five items remain unsold. At what price will they be included in the year end inventory valuation?

Twelve months later, three items still remain unsold and have been reduced further to £10 each. At what price will they now be valued in the year end inventory valuation?

solution

- At 31 December, the five items will be valued at a cost of £15 each, ie 5 x £15 = £75.

- Twelve months later, the three items remaining unsold will be valued at a net realisable value of £10 each, ie 3 x £10 = £30.

Important note: Inventory is *never* valued at selling price when selling price is above cost price. The reason for this is that selling price includes profit, and to value inventory in this way would bring the profit into the financial statements before it has been earned.

Case Study

PAINT AND WALLPAPER SUPPLIES: INVENTORY VALUATION

situation

The year end valuations for the two main groups of inventory held by the business 'Paint and Wallpaper Supplies' are found to be:

	Cost	Net Realisable Value
	£	£
Paints	2,500	2,300
Wallpapers	5,000	7,500
	7,500	9,800

Which of the following inventory valuations do you think is correct?

(a)   £7,500

(b)   £9,800

(c)   £7,300

(d)   £10,000

solution

Inventory valuation (c) is correct, because it has taken the 'lower of cost and net realisable value' for each *group* of inventory, ie

Paints (at net realisable value)	£2,300
Wallpapers (at cost)	£5,000
	£7,300

You will also note that this valuation is the lowest of the four possible choices, indicating that inventory valuation follows the *prudence concept.*

inventory valuation methods

IAS 2 allows two different methods to be used to calculate the cost price of inventories.

- **FIFO** (first in, first out) – this method assumes that the first items received are the first to be used, so that the valuation of inventory on hand at any time consists of the most recently acquired items.

- **AVCO** (average cost), or **weighted average cost** – here the average cost of items held at the beginning of the period is calculated; as new inventory is received a new average cost is calculated (usually based on a weighted average, using the number of units bought as the weighting).

A further method of inventory valuation but which cannot be used under IAS 2 is:

- **LIFO** (last in, first out) – this method assumes that the last items received are the first to be used, so that the inventory on hand is made up of earlier purchases.

LIFO is sometimes used by businesses for their internal purposes – such as working out the cost of a product to the customer. However, for financial accounting, it cannot be used in financial statements.

The use of a particular method does not necessarily correspond with the method of physical distribution adopted in a firm's stores. For example, in a car factory one car battery of type X is the same as another, and no-one will be concerned if the storekeeper issues one from the latest batch received, even if the FIFO method has been adopted. However, perishable goods are always physically handled on the basis of first in, first out, even if the accounting inventory records use the AVCO method.

Having chosen a suitable inventory valuation method, a business would continue to use that method unless there were good reasons for making the change. This is in line with the *consistency concept* of accounting.

effect on profit

As the inventory valuation methods can give different values for closing inventory, this will have an effect on profit. In times of rising prices, FIFO gives the highest profit (because the closing inventory is higher, being based on the latest prices); LIFO gives the lowest profit (closing inventory is lower, being based on older prices); AVCO is in between. In times of falling prices, the reverse will be true. However, over the life of a business, total profit is the same in total, whichever method is chosen: the profit is allocated to different years depending on which method is selected.

The 'rules' to remember for closing inventory are:

- higher closing inventory = higher profit
- lower closing inventory = lower profit

For opening inventory, the 'rules' are:

- higher opening inventory = lower profit
- lower opening inventory = higher profit

CAPITAL EXPENDITURE AND REVENUE EXPENDITURE

When preparing financial statements it is important to distinguish between *capital expenditure* and *revenue expenditure*.

capital expenditure

Capital expenditure is expenditure incurred on the purchase, alteration or improvement of non-current assets.

Included in capital expenditure are directly attributable costs, such as:

- delivery of non-current assets
- installation of non-current assets
- improvement (but not repair) of non-current assets
- legal costs of buying property

An example of capital expenditure is the purchase of a car for use in the business.

Note that we use the word 'capitalised' to mean that an item has been treated as capital expenditure.

Capital expenditure is always subject to the application of the materiality concept – when items have a low monetary value it is not worth recording them separately.

revenue expenditure

Revenue expenditure is expenditure incurred on running expenses.

Included in revenue expenditure are the costs of:

- maintenance and repair of non-current assets
- administration of the business
- selling and distributing the goods or products in which the business trades

An example of revenue expenditure is the cost of petrol or diesel for the car (above) used in the business.

capital and revenue expenditure – the differences

Capital expenditure is shown on the statement of financial position, while revenue expenditure is an expense in the income statement. It is important to classify these types of expenditure correctly in the accounting system. For example, if the cost of the car was shown as an expense in the income statement, then profit for the year would be reduced considerably, or a loss recorded; meanwhile, the statement of financial position would not show the car as a non-current asset – clearly this is incorrect as the business owns the asset. Note, however, that there is a link between capital expenditure and the income statement: as non-current assets are depreciated, the depreciation charge is shown as an expense in the income statement. This is an application of the *accruals concept*, ie the depreciation charge relates to the useful life of the asset.

A business will always have a policy as to the value at which non-current assets are capitalised. A large business may consider that £1,000 (or higher) is the value; a small business may use a lower figure.

In some circumstances we must take care to distinguish between capital and revenue expenditure. For example:

- *cost of building an extension to the factory £30,000, which includes £1,000 for repairs to the existing factory*

  - capital expenditure, £29,000

  - revenue expenditure, £1,000 (because it is for repairs to an existing non-current asset)

- *a plot of land has been bought for £20,000, the legal costs are £750*

  - capital expenditure £20,750 (the legal costs are included in the capital expenditure, because they are the cost of acquiring the non-current asset, ie the legal costs are capitalised)

- *the business' own employees are used to install a new air conditioning system: wages £1,000, materials £1,500*

  - capital expenditure £2,500 (an addition to the property). Note that, in cases such as this, revenue expenditure, ie wages and materials purchases, will need to be reduced to allow for the transfer to capital expenditure

- *own employees used to repair and redecorate the premises: wages £500, materials £750*

  - revenue expenditure £1,250 (repairs and redecoration are running expenses)

- *purchase of a new machine £10,000, payment for installation and setting up £250*

  – capital expenditure £10,250 (costs of installation of a non-current asset are capitalised)

Only by allocating capital expenditure and revenue expenditure correctly between the statement of financial position and the income statement can the financial statements provide a realistic view of the business. The chart below shows the main items of capital expenditure and revenue expenditure associated with the major classes of non-current assets – premises, vehicles, machinery, computers and office equipment.

classes of non-current assets	capital expenditure	revenue expenditure
premises	• cost of building • cost of extension • carriage on raw materials used • legal fees • labour cost of own employees used on building • installation of utilities, eg gas, water, electricity	• insurance of building • general maintenance • repairs • redecoration • depreciation charge
vehicles	• cost of vehicle, including any optional extras • delivery costs • number plates • changes to the vehicle	• fuel • tax disc • extended warranty • painting company logo • insurance • servicing and repairs • depreciation charge
machinery/ computers/ office equipment	• cost of asset • installation and testing • modifications to meet specific needs of business • installation of special wiring, etc • computer programs (but can be classified as revenue expenditure if cost is low and will have little impact on financial statements – the accounting concept of materiality)	• insurance of asset • servicing and repairs • consumables – such as paper, ink, cartridges, etc • staff training • computer programs (or can be classified as capital expenditure if cost is high and will have a large impact on financial statements) • depreciation charge

Chapter Summary

- The accounting concepts of business entity, materiality, going concern, accruals, prudence and consistency are fundamental to the relevance and reliability of financial records and statements.

- Accounting standards comprise IASs and IFRSs. International standards are now widely used in the UK.

- IAS 16, *Property, plant and equipment*, sets out the accounting treatment for non-current assets; a key feature of the IAS is depreciation.

- The purpose of depreciation is to spread the cost of a non-current asset over its useful life.

- The usual valuation for inventory is at the lower of cost and net realisable value – IAS 2, *Inventories*.

- Inventory valuation methods include:
  - FIFO (first in, first out)
  - LIFO (last in, first out)
  - AVCO (average cost, based on a weighted average)

- Having chosen one inventory valuation method, a business should apply it consistently.

- It is important to allocate capital expenditure and revenue expenditure correctly between the statement of financial position and income statement so that the financial statements provide a realistic view of the business.

Key Terms

accounting concepts	part of the rules of accounting
business entity concept	financial statements record and report on the activities of one particular business
materiality concept	items with a low monetary value are not worthwhile recording in the accounts separately
going concern concept	the presumption that the business to which the financial statements relate will continue to trade in the foreseeable future
accruals concept	expenses and revenues are matched so that they concern the same goods or services and the same time period
prudence concept	financial statements should always, where there is any doubt, report a conservative figure for profit or the valuation of assets

consistency concept	when a business adopts particular accounting methods, it should continue to use such methods consistently
accounting standard	provide a framework for accounting and reduce the variety of accounting treatments used in financial statements
inventory valuation	inventory is valued 'at the lower of cost and net realisable value' (IAS 2)
capital expenditure	expenditure incurred on the purchase, alteration or improvement of non-current assets
revenue expenditure	expenditure incurred on running expenses

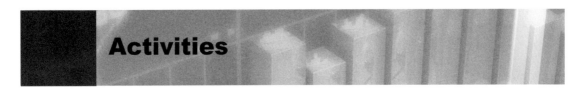

Activities

8.1   A business should not change its basis of valuing inventory without good reason. This follows the concept of:

(a)   money measurement

(b)   going concern

(c)   prudence

(d)   consistency

Answer (a) or (b) or (c) or (d)

8.2   Explain the appropriate accounting concept in each of the following circumstances.

(a)   A business has a customer who owes £1,000. Despite sending numerous statements of account, payment has not been received. It has been decided to make an allowance for doubtful debts in respect of this customer.

(b)   From time-to-time a business buys a pack of recordable discs in order to record business meetings. The discs are re-used over a number of years and are sometimes kept as a permanent record of meetings. Accounting policy is to charge the cost of the discs – £10 for a pack of five discs – as an expense in the income statement.

(c)   As an accounting trainee you are instructed to prepare two sets of a business' financial statements for a particular year, one of which uses straight-line depreciation while the other uses reducing balance depreciation. The owner of the business says that he will use the set which shows the lower profit.

(d)   A business has a financial year end of 31 December 20-4. In early February 20-5, an electricity bill is received covering the period November 20-4 to January 20-5. It is decided to apportion two-thirds of the bill to the income statement for 20-4 and one-third to the income statement for 20-5.

8.3 A discussion is taking place between Jane Smith, a sole trader, who owns a furniture shop, and her husband, John, who solely owns an engineering business. The following points are made:

(a) John says that, having depreciated his firm's machinery last year on the reducing balance method, for this year he intends to use the straight-line method. By doing this he says that he will deduct less depreciation from the income statement, so his profit for the year will be higher and his bank manager will be impressed. He says he might revert back to reducing balance method next year.

(b) At the end of her financial year, Jane comments that the inventory of her shop had cost £10,000. She says that, as she normally adds 50 per cent to cost price to give the selling price, she intends to put a value of £15,000 for closing inventory in the financial statements.

(c) John's car is owned by his business but he keeps referring to it as my car. Jane reminds him that it does not belong to him, but to the firm. He replies that of course it belongs to him and, furthermore, if the firm went bankrupt, he would be able to keep the car.

(d) John's business has trade receivables of £30,000. He knows that, included in this figure is an irrecoverable debt of £2,500. He wants to show £30,000 as trade receivables in the year-end statement of financial position in order to have a high figure for assets.

(e) On the last day of her financial year, Jane sold a large order of furniture, totalling £3,000, to a local hotel. The furniture was invoiced and delivered that day, before the year-end inventory-take commenced. The payment was received early in the new financial year and Jane now asks John if she will be able to put this sale through the accounts for the new year, instead of the old, but without altering the figures for purchases and closing inventory for the old year.

(f) John says that his accountant talks of preparing his financial statements on a going concern basis. He asks Jane if she knows of any other basis that can be used, and which it is usual to follow.

You are to take each of the points and state the correct accounting treatment, referring to appropriate accounting concepts.

8.4 (a) Explain briefly the purpose of depreciation of non-current assets.

(b) A business is going to buy some office furniture. The furniture is expected to be of equal use to the business for each of the next four years, at the end of which it will have no value.

Which method of depreciation do you recommend them to use?

A   20% reducing balance method

B   20% straight line method

C   25% reducing balance method

D   25% straight line method

Answer A or B or C or D

8.5 Inventory is valued at:

(a) cost price

(b) net realisable value

(c) lower of cost and net realisable value

(d) selling price

Answer (a) or (b) or (c) or (d)

8.6 A furniture shop sells coffee tables amongst the lines that it sells. The inventory movements for coffee tables in February 20-6 were:

1 February   10 tables brought forward at a cost of £30 each

4 February   Sold 2 tables

7 February   Sold 5 tables

10 February   Bought 12 tables at £32 each

12 February   Sold 6 tables

17 February   Sold 4 tables

20 February   Bought 8 tables at £31 each

24 February   Sold 4 tables

27 February   Sold 3 tables

Each table sells at £50.

Inventory is valued on the FIFO (first in, first out) basis.

You are to calculate the value of:

(a) sales revenue for February

(b) closing inventory valuation at 28 February

8.7   A garden supplies shop has the following valuations for each group of inventory at the end of its financial year:

	cost £	selling price £
seeds	1,550	1,450
fertilisers and insecticides	2,270	3,560
tools	4,390	6,920

What valuation for closing inventory will be used in its financial statements?

8.8   A business has, in error, overvalued of its closing inventory by £1,000. Before the error is corrected, what is the effect

(a)   on this year's profit?

(b)   on next year's profit?

8.9   (a)   Describe the basis of inventory valuation according to IAS 2, *Inventories.*

<table>
<tr><td>

</td></tr>
<tr><td>

</td></tr>
</table>

(b)   You are an accounts assistant at Canley Cakes, a business that bakes and sells speciality cakes for birthdays, Christmas and Easter. The financial year end is 30 June.

The policy of the business is that if cakes are unsold after five days from baking they are reduced to half of the normal selling price.

You are helping with the inventory-take at 30 June 20-4 and have the following information:

	number of cakes	220
of which:	up to 5 days old	160
	over 5 days old	60
	normal selling price	£10
	cost price	£6

What is the inventory valuation for the 220 cakes held at 30 June 20-4?

A   £1,100

B   £1,260

C   £1,320

D   £2,200

Answer A or B or C or D

(c)   An error in the date stamping of cakes has been found and this means that, of the 220 cakes, 100 cakes are now found to be over five days old. By how much will the inventory valuation change?

A   £500 decrease

B   £400 decrease

C   £40 increase

D   £40 decrease

Answer A or B or C or D

(d)   Will the change in inventory valuation from (c) cause the profit for the year to 30 June 20-4 to increase, decrease or stay the same? Tick one box.

☐   increase

☐   decrease

☐   stay the same

8.10   A business has bought an accounting program for its computer system. The cost of the software is £99. Will this be treated as capital expenditure or revenue expenditure? Give reasons for your answer in the form of an email to the owner of the business.

8.11   "Capital expenditure is money spent on non-current assets. As these are recorded on the statement of financial position, then it is true to say that capital expenditure has no effect on the income statement."

Discuss this statement, saying whether or not you agree with it and giving reasons for your answer.

8.12   Classify the following costs (tick the appropriate column):

		capital expenditure	revenue expenditure
(a)	purchase of machinery		
(b)	installation of machinery		
(c)	depreciation of machinery		
(d)	purchase of property		
(e)	legal fees relating to the purchase of property		
(f)	repairs to property		
(g)	insurance of property		
(h)	labour costs of own employees used to build extension to property		
(i)	repainting and redecoration of property		

9 Accounting for capital transactions

this chapter covers...

Capital transactions concern all aspects of the acquisition and disposal of non-current assets. Because of the nature of capital transactions – their high cost and long-term use within the business – management keeps careful control over them.

In this chapter we will examine:

- accounting entries to record acquisition, depreciation, and disposal of non-current assets

- the importance of distinguishing between capital expenditure and revenue expenditure

- acquisition and control of non-current assets, including the use of a non-current asset register

- methods of funding capital expenditure; cash purchase, part exchange, borrowing (loans, hire purchase and finance leases)

CAPITAL TRANSACTIONS

Capital transactions concern all aspects of non-current assets – through purchasing, control and final disposal.

Non-current assets are tangible items that are:

- held for use in the production or supply of goods or services

- are expected to have a life span of more than one year

Examples of non-current assets include land, premises, vehicles, machinery, computers and office equipment. Tangible non-current assets have a physical existence, ie they can be touched and felt. By contrast, assets which have no physical form are intangible – for example, goodwill (see Chapter 16) which is often paid by the purchaser when buying an existing business.

Because of the nature of non-current assets – their high cost and long-term use within the business – management will keep careful control over capital transactions. For example, the purchase of a new computer system costing £500,000 will be authorised by a meeting of senior management; by contrast the purchase of new wastepaper baskets for the office at a cost of £50 will be authorised by the office supervisor.

Before we study the procedures for authorising the purchase, control and final disposal of non-current assets, we will look at a Case Study which shows the accounting entries to record the life of a non-current asset.

Case Study

ACCOUNTING FOR NON-CURRENT ASSETS

situation

Eveshore Growers Limited is a co-operative venture which sells fruit, vegetables and flowers grown by its members in the Vale of Eveshore. The company's financial year end is 31 December.

On 4 January 20-1 the company buys a Supra XL computer for use in the administration office. The cost is £2,000 + VAT at 20% (Eveshore Growers Limited is registered for VAT); the amount is paid from the bank.

The computer is depreciated using the straight-line method at a rate of 25 per cent each year. It is company policy to charge a full year's depreciation in the year of purchase, but none in the year of sale.

By mid-20-4 the computer is beginning to show its age and it is decided to replace it by a more up-to-date model. The old computer is sold on 12 July 20-4 for £400 + VAT at 20%, a payment being received into the bank.

Show the journal and accounting entries to record:

- acquisition of the computer
- depreciation
- disposal

solution

The cost of the non-current asset is £2,000 + VAT (at 20%) of £400. This is entered in the journal (see Chapter 11) as the book of prime entry and then recorded in the double-entry accounts:

Journal

Date	Details	Reference	Dr	Cr
20-1			£	£
4 Jan	Computer	GL	2,000	
	VAT	GL	400	
	Bank	CB		2,400
			2,400	2,400
	Purchase of Supra XL computer			
	for use in the administration office;			
	capital expenditure authorisation			
	number 015/20-1			

Tutorial note: the journal is a book of prime entry which is used to list transactions before they are entered in the double-entry accounts; its use will be discussed in Chapter 11.

Dr		**Computer at cost account**		Cr
20-1		£	20-1	£
4 Jan	Bank	2,000		

Dr		**Value Added Tax account**		Cr
20-1		£	20-1	£
4 Jan	Bank	400		

Cash book (payments)

		Cash	Bank	VAT	Purchases ledger	Sundry
20-1		£	£	£	£	£
4 Jan	Computer		2,400	400		2,000

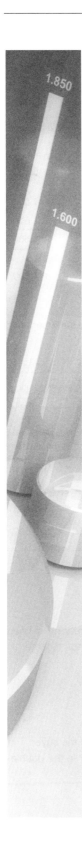

Note that, as Eveshore Growers Limited is registered for VAT, it will debit its VAT account with the tax. The amount is then included with VAT paid on inputs (purchases and expenses) and set-off against VAT charged on outputs (sales and services).

DEPRECIATION

Depreciation at 25 per cent straight-line per year is as follows:

year ended 31 December 20-1	£500 (full year's depreciation)
year ended 31 December 20-2	£500
year ended 31 December 20-3	£500

Note that, following company policy, no depreciation is charged in 20-4, being the year of disposal.

Depreciation charges are recorded in the journal (first year only shown) and in the depreciation charge account, machinery: accumulated depreciation and income statement as follows:

Journal

Date	Details	Reference	Dr	Cr
20-1			£	£
31 Dec	Income statement	GL	500	
	Depreciation charge	GL		500
	Depreciation charge for year on			
	Supra XL computer			
31 Dec	Depreciation charge	GL	500	
	Computer: accumulated depreciation	GL		500
	Transfer of depreciation charge for year			
	to accumulated depreciation			

Dr			**Depreciation charge account**		Cr
20-1		£	20-1		£
31 Dec	Computer: accumulated depreciation	500	31 Dec	Income statement	500
20-2			20-2		
31 Dec	Computer: accumulated depreciation	500	31 Dec	Income statement	500
20-3			20-3		
31 Dec	Computer: accumulated depreciation	500	31 Dec	Income statement	500

Dr			Computer: accumulated depreciation account		Cr
20-1		£	20-1		£
31 Dec	Balance c/d	500	31 Dec	Depreciation charge	500
20-2			20-2		
31 Dec	Balance c/d	1,000	1 Jan	Balance b/d	500
			31 Dec	Depreciation charge	500
		1,000			1,000
20-3			20-3		
31 Dec	Balance c/d	1,500	1 Jan	Balance b/d	1,000
			31 Dec	Depreciation charge	500
		1,500			1,500
			20-4		
			1 Jan	Balance b/d	1,500

The extended trial balance shows the following amounts for the income statement and the statement of financial position.

Year	Income statement		Statement of financial position	
	Dr	Cr	Dr	Cr
	Expense	*Income*	*Cost*	*Accumulated depreciation*
	£	£	£	£
20-1	500	–	2,000	500
20-2	500	–	2,000	1,000
20-3	500	–	2,000	1,500

DISPOSAL

The accounting entries to deal with the disposal of non-current assets have been described in Chapter 6 (pages 94-97). The asset disposal account brings together

- the original cost of the computer
- accumulated depreciation over the asset's life
- disposal proceeds

The computer is sold for £400 + VAT at 20%; payment is received from the buyer. The transaction is recorded in the journal as the book of prime entry, and in the double-entry accounts as follows:

Journal

Date	Details	Reference	Dr	Cr
20-4			£	£
12 Jul	Disposals	GL	2,000	
	Computer at cost	GL		2,000
	Computer: accumulated depreciation	GL	1,500	
	Disposals	GL		1,500
	Bank	CB	480	
	Disposals	GL		400
	VAT	GL		80
	Income statement	GL	100	
	Disposals	GL		100
			4,080	4,080
	Sale of Supra XL computer; loss on disposal of £100 transferred to income statement			

Dr				**Computer disposals account**		Cr
20-4		£		20-4		£
12 Jul	Computer at cost	2,000		12 Jul	Computer: accumulated depreciation	1,500
				12 Jul	Bank	400
				12 Jul	Income statement (loss on disposal)	100
		2,000				2,000

Dr				**Computer at cost account**		Cr
20-4		£		20-4		£
1 Jan	Balance b/d	2,000		12 Jul	Disposals	2,000

Dr				**Computer: accumulated depreciation account**		Cr
20-4		£		20-4		£
12 Jul	Disposals	1,500		1 Jan	Balance b/d	1,500

Dr				**Value Added Tax account**		Cr
20-4		£		20-4		£
				12 Jul	Bank	80

Cash book (receipts)

		Cash	Bank	VAT	Sales ledger	Sundry
20-4		£	£	£	£	£
12 Jul	Computer disposal		480	80		400

Income statement for the year ended 31 December 20-4		
	Dr *Expense* £	Cr *Income* £
Loss on disposal of computer	100	–

The loss on disposal here is because of under-depreciation; if over-depreciation had occurred, a profit on disposal would be shown as income.

CAPITAL EXPENDITURE AND REVENUE EXPENDITURE

The importance of distinguishing between capital expenditure and revenue expenditure has been highlighted in Chapter 8 (page 136). For example, the purchase of the computer seen in the Case Study is capital expenditure, which is recorded as a non-current asset of the business. Certain costs associated with the delivery and installation of the non-current asset can be capitalised (ie included in the cost of the asset) – for guidance, see the diagram on page 138.

Most non-current assets are depreciated, which means that the costs of the assets are spread over the period during which they are used by the business and charged as an expense to the income statement – an application of the *accruals concept*.

ACQUISITION AND CONTROL OF NON-CURRENT ASSETS

Because of the often large amounts of money involved, and the non-routine nature of their purchase, the acquisition of non-current assets is monitored and controlled by the business. In particular, their purchase will have to be approved by the business' managers or owners, or by a committee which appraises capital expenditure projects and decides which will be approved. The stages in the acquisition and control of non-current assets are as follows:

application and authorisation

The section of the business that wishes to purchase the non-current asset must submit an application for capital expenditure to the appropriate level of management:

- the *manager* responsible for a section of the business will be able to approve relatively low-cost items, eg the purchase of a filing cabinet

- the *capital expenditure committee* of a large business will approve significant cost items, eg the proposed installation of a new computer system

- the *owners/directors* will approve the largest applications

Much will depend on the size of the business as to who makes the decisions and how – a small business will do things very differently from a large limited company. Nevertheless, there does need to be an approval process in place for all sizes of business.

The form of the application will vary from a single sheet capital expenditure authorisation form, through to a fully documented proposal which includes an assessment of the likely costs and resources to be used over the life of the asset. Many businesses require two or three prices or quotations to be obtained, so that they can see that they are getting the best value for money.

Before giving their approval to capital projects, particularly those involving large sums of money, the managers responsible for authorising the expenditure will consider a number of wider issues:

- the expenditure must fit in with the business' plans and budgets

- the method of funding (see pages 157-158) the expenditure must be considered

  - is there sufficient money in the bank account?

  - can old assets be sold or part exchanged to provide some of the money?

  - will a bank or finance company loan need to be arranged?

  - is hire purchase or a finance lease to be used?

- staffing and training implications
  - will there be redundancies?
  - can staff be retrained? at what cost?
  - will new staff need to be employed? at what pay rates?
- productivity of the business
  - will the capital expenditure increase the output of the business?
  - will the quality of output be improved?
- profitability of the business
  - is there a market for the increased output? what will be the sales revenue?
  - by how much will our costs increase?
  - will the business be more profitable?

monitoring and control

Once authorisation has been granted for a particular project, it is important that the actual costs are monitored and controlled against the costs in the original application. For relatively small projects, it is easy to compare the original quotation against the actual price charged. For major projects, where a number of contractors are involved, it will be necessary for the buyer to monitor costs carefully – staff might be appointed specifically for this role. Cost overruns and cost savings need to be investigated to see why they have occurred, and what lessons can be learned for the future.

the use of a non-current asset register

In order to keep a record of non-current assets, many businesses make use of a *non-current asset register* – shown on the next page. This separates out each class of non-current asset – eg premises, vehicles, machinery, computers, office equipment – and records details of each asset owned, in the appropriate class, such as:

- asset description and/or serial number (a number often marked on the asset in order to give it a positive identification)
- date of acquisition
- original cost
- the method and rate of depreciation
- depreciation charge for each year of ownership
- carrying amount (net book value), ie cost less accumulated depreciation
- funding method, such as cash purchase, part exchange, or borrowing (loans, hire purchase and finance lease)
- disposal date
- disposal proceeds

NON-CURRENT ASSET REGISTER

Description/serial no	Acquisition date	Cost £	Depreciation £	Carrying amount* £	Funding method	Disposal proceeds £	Disposal date
Office equipment							
Computer, Supra XL	4/1/-1	2,000.00			Cash		
Year ended 31/12/-1			500.00	1,500.00			
Year ended 31/12/-2			500.00	1,000.00			
Year ended 31/12/-3			500.00	500.00			
Year ended 31/12/-4						400.00	12/7/-4

* carrying amount (net book value), ie cost less accumulated depreciation

The details of the computer from the Case Study are shown in the non-current asset register. Note that there is no set layout for the register – a business will use whatever method suits it best: some will show each asset over its entire life on a separate page (as shown in the example); others will list several assets on the same page for one year only, carrying forward assets owned at the end of each year to a new page.

The non-current asset register enables a business to keep control of such assets; from time-to-time the accounting staff will ensure that the capital records are being kept up-to-date – in accordance with the organisation's policies and procedures – and will check the physical items of non-current assets listed in the register. Discrepancies may occur because:

- the non-current asset register has not been kept up-to-date
  - new assets have not been recorded
  - sold or scrapped assets have not been written out of the register
  - assets which have become obsolete or inadequate for the job have not been written down in value
- assets have been stolen and their theft has not been reported or recorded
- there are errors in recording details in the register

Accounts assistants are often required to check the non-current asset register against the physical items. Any discrepancies that are identified, if they cannot be resolved, should be referred to the appropriate person – usually the accounts supervisor. It is for the management of a business, or the owners, to decide what action to take over discrepancies. If discrepancies prove to be occurring more frequently than is considered acceptable, it may be appropriate to review the way in which the capital records are maintained and to seek suggestions for improvements from the staff involved.

disposal of non-current assets

An important aspect of the control of non-current assets includes dealing with their disposal in an orderly way. In most cases old assets are replaced at the end of their useful lives with new assets, eg an old computer system is replaced with a new one. Sometimes, however, assets may become surplus to requirements part-way through their lives, eg a section of the business is closed. Whatever the circumstances, it is essential that disposal of assets is handled in such a way that the business receives the maximum amount of cash.

Old and surplus assets may be

- sold for their scrap value
- used as a part exchange value to help fund the acquisition of new assets
- sold on the secondhand market
- sold to employees

Before assets are disposed of, the approval of the appropriate person or department must be received. For example, the office manager in a small company may have authority to deal with disposals. In larger companies, a separate department may handle disposals and, for the closure of a section of the business, specialist staff may be brought in to ensure the orderly disposal of assets.

The disposal proceeds, or part exchange value, must be accounted for correctly through asset disposals account (see pages 94-98). At the same time, the non-current asset register must be updated to:

- identify the correct asset being disposed

- remove it from the register

- record the disposal proceeds and the date of disposal

FUNDING NON-CURRENT ASSETS

Funding methods for non-current assets include cash purchase, part-exchange, loans, hire purchase and finance leases. The accounts involved will be:
- non-current asset at cost account (eg machinery, vehicles)
- bank/cash account

cash purchase

This is where the business has sufficient cash in its bank account – or in an interest-bearing deposit account – to pay in full for the new asset. Alternatively, a business might buy an asset on standard commercial credit terms, eg 30 days, and then make payment for the asset from the bank account before the end of the term – legal title to the asset is usually acquired at the date of purchase, ie before the date of payment.

part exchange

This is where an old asset is 'traded in' as part of the purchase price of the new asset, the balance remaining due being paid either in cash or by borrowing (the book-keeping entries for a part exchange have been seen in Chapter 6); part exchange is especially common when a new vehicle – car or van – is being purchased.

loans

A loan agreement with a bank or a finance company is a method of funding the purchase of non-current assets, such as vehicles, machinery, computers and office equipment. The bank or finance company lends an agreed sum of money to the business, which uses the funds to purchase the asset. Ownership of the asset belongs to the business from the start – unlike hire purchase and finance leases – although the bank or finance company will often require security to back their loan. The borrower makes agreed repayments which cover the cost and the interest (which may be fixed for the term of the loan). Loans are available for periods of up to seven years (sometimes longer).

The book-keeping entries for loans and their repayment are shown on page 21.

Note that a bank overdraft is not the same as a loan – instead it is a short term facility which allows a business to overdraw its bank account and, usually, is reviewed each year. A bank overdraft is not a suitable funding method for non-current assets.

hire purchase

A hire purchase agreement from a finance company enables a business (the hirer) to have the use of a non-current asset on payment of a deposit. The finance company owns the asset and the hirer makes regular instalment payments – monthly, quarterly or half-yearly – which pay back the cost plus interest over a set period. At the end of the hire purchase period, ownership of the asset usually passes from the finance company to the business. Hire purchase is often used to finance non-current assets such as vehicles, machinery, computers and office equipment.

finance leases

Finance leases are medium term (up to seven years) arrangements used to fund non-current assets such as vehicles, machinery, computers and office equipment. With a leasing agreement, a business (the lessee) has the use of an asset owned by a finance company (the lessor). The lessee makes regular rental payments to the lessor over the period of the lease, which might be up to seven years. There is normally no provision in a finance lease for legal ownership of the leased asset to pass to the lessee at the end of the lease.

Note: in AAT Assessments you will need only an awareness of hire purchase and finance leases – no accounting entries or technical knowledge will be required.

Chapter Summary

- ■ Capital transactions concern all aspects of non-current assets – through purchasing, control and final disposal.

- ■ Tangible non-current assets – such as premises, vehicles, equipment – have a physical existence; intangible non-current assets – such as goodwill – have no physical form.

- ■ A non-current asset register is used to record details of assets.

- ■ Funding methods for non-current assets include cash purchase, part-exchange, loans, hire purchase and finance leases.

non-current assets	non-current assets are tangible items that are:
	– held for use in the production or supply of goods or services
	– are expected to be used during more than one accounting period
non-current asset register	used for control purposes; records details of purchase, depreciation, disposal of all non-current assets owned by a business
hire purchase	agreement between a finance company and a hirer which enables the hirer to have the use of a non-current asset against a deposit and regular instalment payments
finance lease	agreement between a finance company (lessor) and a business (lessee) which enables the lessee to have the use of a non-current asset against regular hire or rental payments

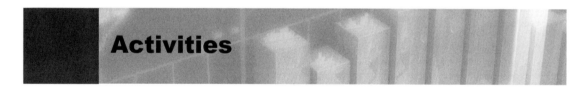

Activities

9.1   Which one of the following is a tangible non-current asset?

(a)   premises

(b)   goodwill

(c)   trade receivables

(d)   bank loan

Answer (a) or (b) or (c) or (d)

9.2   The owner of a taxi company, Mary Sampson, wishes to develop a policy for authorisation of new taxi purchases. Which one of the following is most suitable to authorise such purchases?

(a)   the owner of the business, Mary Sampson

(b)   her bank manager

(c)   her accounts assistant

(d)   the driver of the vehicle

Answer (a) or (b) or (c) or (d)

9.3 A finance lease is a:

(a) medium term agreement where a finance company funds an asset and the business makes instalment payments to buy it

(b) medium term agreement under which the lessee has the use of an asset owned by a finance company

(c) medium term agreement under which a bank or finance company lends the funds to a business for it to buy the asset

(d) type of hire purchase agreement

Answer (a) or (b) or (c) or (d)

9.4 (a) The non-current asset register of Wyvern Building Supplies is shown below. You are to complete the register with depreciation on the non-current asset for the year ended 31 December 20-3.

(b) The asset is sold on 10 February 20-4 for £500 (net of VAT); it is company policy not to charge depreciation in the year of sale. You are to complete the non-current asset register showing the asset's disposal.

NON-CURRENT ASSET REGISTER

Description/serial no	Acquisition date	Cost £	Depreciation £	Carrying amount £	Funding method	Disposal proceeds £	Disposal date
Office equipment							
Computer, Supra ML	12/3/-1	3,000.00			Cash		
Year ended 31/12/-1			1,500.00	1,500.00			
Year ended 31/12/-2			750.00	750.00			

9.5 QuickPrint Limited is a photographic processing company with a financial year end of 31 December. On 10 January 20-1 it buys an automated machine to develop and print (d & p) films; the cost is £32,000 (paid by cheque). The machine is expected to last for five years, after which its estimated value will be £2,500. Depreciation is charged at 40% each year, using the reducing balance method. It is company policy to charge a full year's depreciation in the year of purchase, but none in the year of sale.

The printing and developing machine works well but it is decided to replace it in 20-4 by a more up-to-date model. The old machine is sold on 17 August 20-4 for a part-exchange price of £5,000.

(a) You are to show the journal and accounting entries (cash book not required) to record the machine's:
- acquisition
- depreciation
- disposal

Note: VAT is to be ignored

(b) Complete the non-current asset register – below – to show the machine's acquisition, depreciation and disposal.

NON-CURRENT ASSET REGISTER							
Description/serial no	Acquisition date	Cost £	Depreciation £	Carrying amount £	Funding method	Disposal proceeds £	Disposal date
Machinery							

9.6 John Aziz runs a taxi company called Silver Link Cabs. He started in business on 24 January 20-1 when he bought two taxis, registration numbers WV01 XNP and WV01 YNP, at a cost of £15,000 each (paid from the bank).

John charges depreciation at the rate of 30 per cent each year, using the straight-line method. He charges a full year's depreciation in the year of purchase, but none in the year of sale.

On 17 February 20-3 he buys another taxi, registration number WV03 ZNP, at a cost of £17,500 (paid from the bank). On 13 October 20-3 he sells WV01 XNP for £6,500 (paid into the bank).

You are to show the accounting entries (journal and cash book not required) to record the acquisition, depreciation and disposal of his taxis for the years ended 31 December 20-1, 20-2 and 20-3.

Notes:
- VAT is to be ignored
- use one non-current asset account for all three taxis, one depreciation charge account, and one accumulated depreciation account

9.7 This Activity is about recording information for non-current assets for a business known as Diamond Trading. Diamond Trading is registered for VAT.

The following is a purchase invoice received by Diamond Trading:

To: Diamond Trading Unit 6, Elmtree Estate Wyvern WV5 2LU	Invoice 517 Norse Supplies plc Belmont Road Mereford ME5 4XS		**Date:** 28 March 20-7
Executive desk	Reference 45129X	1	635.00
Delivery		1	25.00
Desk protector mats @ £25.00 each		2	50.00
VAT @ 20%			142.00
Total			852.00
Settlement terms: strictly 30 days net			

The following information relates to the sale of a car:

Registration number	WV04 JEC
Date of sale	10 March 20-7
Selling price	£8,500.00

- Diamond Trading has a policy of capitalising expenditure over £500.
- Vehicles are depreciated at 25% on a reducing balance basis.
- Office equipment is depreciated at 30% on a straight-line basis assuming no residual value.
- Non-current assets are depreciated in the year of acquisition but not in the year of disposal.

Record the following information in the non-current asset register on the next page.

(a) Any acquisitions of non-current assets during the year ended 31 March 20-7

(b) Any disposals of non-current assets during the year ended 31 March 20-7

(c) Depreciation for the year ended 31 March 20-7

NON-CURRENT ASSET REGISTER							
Description/serial no	Acquisition date	Cost £	Depreciation £	Carrying amount £	Funding method	Disposal proceeds £	Disposal date
Office equipment							
Telephone system	30/09/-4	1,500.00			Cash		
Year end 31/03/-5			450.00	1,050.00			
Year end 31/03/-6			450.00	600.00			
Year end 31/03/07							
Year end 31/03/-7							
Vehicles							
WV04 JEC	15/04/-4	18,000.00			Cash		
Year end 31/03/-5			4,500.00	13,500.00			
Year end 31/03/-6			3,375.00	10,125.00			
Year end 31/03/-7							
WV55 DBC	30/10/-5	12,000.00			Part-exchange		
Year end 31/03/-6			3,000.00	9,000.00			
Year end 31/03/-7							

9.8 A-Z Taxis needs a new taxi to meet an increase in business. The business is profitable but the owner, Ken Molina, doesn't want to use current monies to fund the purchase. Which one of the following funding methods would you suggest he considers?

(a) cash purchase

(b) purchase on 30 days' credit terms

(c) bank overdraft

(d) hire purchase

10 Control accounts

this chapter covers...

Control accounts are 'master' accounts which record by means of totals the transactions passing through the accounts that they control.

In this chapter we will look at:

- *the double-entry system and division of the ledger*

- *the concept of control accounts*

- *the layout of sales ledger and purchases ledger control accounts*

- *the use of control accounts as an aid to the management of a business*

- *control accounts and book-keeping*

- *making reconciliations with*
    - *sales ledger control account to sales ledger*
    - *purchases ledger control account to purchases ledger*
    - *bank account to bank statement*

DIVISION OF THE LEDGER

The double-entry system of book-keeping involves making two entries in the ledger accounts for each business transaction. The traditional meaning of a ledger is a weighty leather-bound volume into which each account was entered on a separate page. With such a hand-written book-keeping system, as more and more accounts were opened, the point was reached where another ledger book was needed. Finally, in order to sort the accounts into a logical order, the accounting system was divided into four main sections, and this practice continues today:

- *sales ledger*, containing the accounts of receivables
- *purchases ledger*, containing the accounts of payables
- *cash book*, containing bank and cash records of the receipts and payments of the business
- *general ledger*, containing all the other accounts

These four divisions comprise 'the ledger', and are illustrated on the next page. Note that sales and purchases ledgers are subsidiary ledgers, with control accounts (explained in this chapter) held in the general ledger.

THE CONCEPT OF CONTROL ACCOUNTS

Control accounts are 'master' accounts which control a number of subsidiary ledger accounts.

Control accounts work in the following way:

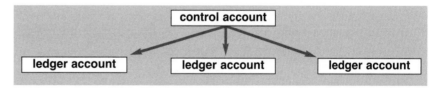

The control account (also known as a *totals account*) is used to record the totals of transactions passing through the subsidiary accounts. In this way, the balance of the control account will always be equal to the total balances of the subsidiary accounts, unless an error has occurred. Two commonly-used control accounts are:

- **sales ledger control account**, which controls the sales ledger
- **purchases ledger control account**, which controls the purchases ledger

(Later in the chapter we see how VAT control account is used to bring together totals of VAT from books of prime entry.)

DIVISION OF THE LEDGER

sales ledger

Sales ledger contains the accounts of receivables, and records:
- sales made on credit to customers of the business
- sales returns by customers
- payments received from customers
- settlement discount allowed for prompt settlement

Cash sales are not recorded in this ledger.

Sales ledger contains an account for each receivable and records the transactions with that customer. The total of the sales ledger account balances should agree with the balance of sales ledger control account in the general ledger.

purchases ledger

Purchases ledger contains the accounts of payables, and records:
- purchases made on credit from suppliers of the business
- purchases returns made by the business
- payments made to suppliers
- settlement discount received for prompt settlement

Cash purchases are not recorded in this ledger.

Purchases ledger contains an account for each payable and records the transactions with that supplier. The total of the purchases ledger account balances should agree with the balance of purchases ledger control account in the general ledger.

cash books

Cash Book

– records all transactions for bank account and cash account

– is also often used for listing the amounts of settlement (cash) discount received and allowed, and for recording amounts of Value Added Tax on cash sales and cash purchases

Note that cash book is included amongst the general ledger accounts for the purposes of a trial balance.

general ledger

The general ledger contains the other accounts of the business:
- sales account (cash and credit sales)
- purchases account (cash and credit purchases)
- sales returns, purchases returns
- expenses and income
- loan
- capital, drawings
- Value Added Tax (where the business is VAT-registered)
- non-current assets, eg premises, computers, motor vehicles
- other assets, eg cash, bank balance, inventory
- control accounts, eg sales ledger, purchases ledger

In the illustration on page 165 we have seen how a control account acts as a master account for a number of subsidiary accounts. The principle is that, if the total of the opening balances for subsidiary accounts is known, together with the total of amounts increasing these balances, and the total of amounts decreasing these balances, then the total of the closing balances for the subsidiary accounts can be calculated.

For example:

	£
Total of opening balances	50,000
Add increases	10,000
	60,000
Less decreases	12,000
Total of closing balances	48,000

The total of the closing balances can now be checked against a separate listing of the balances of the subsidiary accounts to ensure that the two figures agree. If so, it proves that the ledgers within the section are correct, subject to any errors. Let us now apply this concept to one of the divisions of the ledger – sales ledger.

The diagram on the next page shows the personal accounts which form the entire sales ledger of a particular business – in practice there would, of course, be more than four accounts involved. The sales ledger control account acts as a totals account, which records totals of the transactions passing through the subsidiary accounts that it controls. Notice how transactions appear in the control account *on the same side* as they appear in the subsidiary accounts. The sales ledger control account can be reconciled with the balances of the subsidiary accounts which it controls (see below). Thus, control accounts act as an aid to locating errors: if the control account and subsidiary accounts agree, then the error is likely to lie elsewhere. In this way the control account acts as a checking and control device – proving the arithmetical accuracy of the ledger section.

Normally the whole of a ledger section is controlled by one control account, eg sales ledger control account or purchases ledger control account. However, it is also possible to have a number of separate control accounts for sections of the subsidiary ledgers, eg sales ledger control account A-K, purchases ledger control account S-Z, etc. It is for a business – the user of the accounting system – to decide what is most suitable, taking into account the number of accounts in the subsidiary ledgers, together with the type of accounting system – manual or computerised.

From the diagram on the next page the sales ledger control account and sales ledger accounts are agreed at the beginning and end of the month, as follows:

Dr		Sales Ledger Control Account		Cr	
20-6		£	20-6		£
1 Jan	Balance b/d	500	31 Jan	Bank	443
31 Jan	Sales	700	31 Jan	Discount allowed	7
			31 Jan	Sales returns	70
			31 Jan	Balance c/d	680
		1,200			1,200
1 Feb	Balance b/d	680			

Dr		A Ackroyd		Cr	
20-6		£	20-6		£
1 Jan	Balance b/d	100	10 Jan	Bank	98
6 Jan	Sales	150	10 Jan	Discount allowed	2
			31 Jan	Balance c/d	150
		250			250
1 Feb	Balance b/d	150			

Dr		B Barnes		Cr	
20-6		£	20-6		£
1 Jan	Balance b/d	200	13 Jan	Bank	195
6 Jan	Sales	250	13 Jan	Discount allowed	5
			27 Jan	Sales returns	50
			31 Jan	Balance c/d	200
		450			450
1 Feb	Balance b/d	200			

Dr		C Cox		Cr	
20-6		£	20-6		£
1 Jan	Balance b/d	50	20 Jan	Bank	50
15 Jan	Sales	200	29 Jan	Sales returns	20
			31 Jan	Balance c/d	180
		250			250
1 Feb	Balance b/d	180			

Dr		D Douglas		Cr	
20-6		£	20-6		£
1 Jan	Balance b/d	150	30 Jan	Bank	100
20 Jan	Sales	100	31 Jan	Balance c/d	150
		250			250
1 Feb	Balance b/d	150			

Reconciliation of sales ledger control account		
	1 January 20-6	*31 January 20-6*
	£	£
A Ackroyd	100	150
B Barnes	200	200
C Cox	50	180
D Douglas	150	150
Sales ledger control account	500	680

The business will decide how often to reconcile (agree) the control account with the subsidiary accounts – weekly, monthly, quarterly or annually. Any discrepancy should be investigated immediately and the error(s) or omission(s) traced.

SALES LEDGER CONTROL ACCOUNT

The layout of sales ledger control account (also known as trade receivables control account) is shown below, with sample figures. Study the layout carefully and then read the text which explains the additional items.

Dr		Sales Ledger Control Account		Cr
	£			£
Balance b/d	2,900	Cash/bank receipts from customers		12,100
Credit sales	14,000	Settlement (cash) discount allowed		290
Returned cheques	930	Sales returns		870
		Irrecoverable debts		1,590
		Set-off entries		250
		Balance c/d		2,730
	17,830			17,830
Balance b/d	2,730			

balance b/d

The figure for balance b/d on the debit side of the control account represents the total of the balances of the individual receivables' accounts in the sales ledger. This principle is illustrated in the diagram on the previous page. Remember that, at the end of the month (or other period covered by the control account), the account must be balanced and carried down (on the credit side) on the last day of the month, and then brought down (on the debit side) on the first day of the next month.

Note that it is possible for a receivable's account to have a credit balance, instead of the usual debit balance. This may come about, for example, because the customer has paid for goods and then returned them, or has overpaid in error: the business owes the amount due, ie the receivable has a credit balance for the time being. Most accounting systems 'net off' any such credit balances against the debit balances to give an overall figure for receivables.

credit sales

Only credit sales – and not cash sales – are entered in the control account because only credit sales are recorded in the sales ledger accounts. The total sales of the business will comprise both credit and cash sales.

returned cheques

If a customer's cheque is returned unpaid by the bank, ie the cheque has 'bounced', then authorisation for the entries to be made in the double-entry system must be given by the accounts supervisor. These entries are:

– *debit* receivable's account

– *credit* cash book (bank columns)

As a transaction has been made in a receivable's account, then the amount must also be recorded in the sales ledger control account – on the debit side.

irrecoverable debts

The book-keeping entries for writing off an irrecoverable debt (see Chapter 7) are:

– *debit* irrecoverable debts account

– *credit* trade receivable's account

A credit transaction is entered in a trade receivable's account. This is because the control account 'masters' the sales ledger and so the transaction must also be recorded as a credit transaction in the control account.

Tutorial note: The allowance for doubtful debts – and any changes to the allowance – are never entered in sales ledger control account. This is because the double-entry transactions do not affect the accounts of individual receivables – see pages 112-114.

set-off entries

See page 173.

PURCHASES LEDGER CONTROL ACCOUNT

The layout of purchases ledger control account (also known as trade payables control account) is shown below, with sample figures.

Dr		**Purchases Ledger Control Account**		Cr
	£			£
Cash/bank payments to suppliers	8,200	Balance b/d		5,000
Settlement (cash) discount received	260	Credit purchases		8,500
Purchases returns	1,070			
Set-off entries	250			
Balance c/d	3,720			
	13,500			13,500
		Balance b/d		3,720

balance b/d

The figure for balance b/d on the credit side of the control account represents the total of the balances of the individual payables' accounts in the purchases ledger. This principle is illustrated in the diagram on the next page.

Note that it is possible for a payable's account to have a debit balance, instead of the usual credit balance – for example, if the supplier has been overpaid. Most accounting systems 'net off' any such debit balances against the credit balances to give an overall figure for payables.

credit purchases

Only credit purchases – and not cash purchases – are entered in the control account. However, the total purchases of the business will comprise both credit and cash purchases.

set-off entries

See page 173.

reconciliation of purchases ledger control account

The diagram on the next page shows how a purchases ledger control account acts as a totals account for the purchases ledger of a business. Reconciliation (agreement) of the balances on the purchases ledger control account and subsidiary accounts is shown on page 173.

Dr		Purchases Ledger Control Account		Cr	
20-6		£	20-6		£
31 Jan	Purchases returns	150	1 Jan Balance b/d		1,000
31 Jan	Bank	594	31 Jan Purchases		1,700
31 Jan	Discount received	6			
31 Jan	Balance c/d	1,950			
		2,700			2,700
			1 Feb Balance b/d		1,950

Dr		F Francis			Cr
20-6		£	20-6		£
17 Jan	Bank	98	1Jan Balance b/d		100
17 Jan	Discount received	2	3 Jan Purchases		200
31 Jan	Balance c/d	200			
		300			300
			1 Feb Balance b/d		200

Dr		G Gold			Cr
20-6		£	20-6		£
15 Jan	Purchases returns	50	1 Jan Balance b/d		200
28 Jan	Bank	100	9 Jan Purchases		300
31 Jan	Balance c/d	350			
		500			500
			1 Feb Balance b/d		350

Dr		H Harris			Cr
20-6		£	20-6		£
28 Jan	Purchases returns	100	1 Jan Balance b/d		300
30 Jan	Bank	200	17 Jan Purchases		500
31 Jan	Balance c/d	500			
		800			800
			1 Feb Balance b/d		500

Dr		I Ingram			Cr
20-6		£	20-6		£
22 Jan	Bank	196	1 Jan Balance b/d		400
22 Jan	Discount received	4	27 Jan Purchases		700
31 Jan	Balance c/d	900			
		1,100			1,100
			1 Feb Balance b/d		900

Reconciliation of purchases ledger control account		
	1 January 20-6	31 January 20-6
	£	£
F Francis	100	200
G Gold	200	350
H Harris	300	500
I Ingram	400	900
Purchases ledger control account	1,000	1,950

Any discrepancy should be investigated immediately and the error(s) or omission(s) traced.

SET-OFF ENTRIES

Set-off (or contra) entries occur when the same person or business has an account in both subsidiary ledgers – sales ledger and purchases ledger – ie they are both buying from, and selling to, the business whose accounts we are preparing. For example, M Patel Limited has the following accounts in the subsidiary sales and purchases ledgers:

SALES LEDGER

Dr		A Smith		Cr
	£			£
Balance b/d	200			

PURCHASES LEDGER

Dr		A Smith		Cr
	£			£
		Balance b/d		300

From these accounts we can see that:
- A Smith owes M Patel Limited £200 (sales ledger)
- M Patel Limited owes A Smith £300 (purchases ledger)

To save each having to send a payment to the other, it is possible (with A Smith's agreement) to set-off one account against the other, so that they can settle their net indebtedness with one payment. The book-keeping entries in M Patel's books will be:

– *debit* A Smith (purchases ledger) £200

– *credit* A Smith (sales ledger) £200

Note that it is always the smaller of the two amounts owing – here £200 – that is the set-off amount.

The accounts will now appear as:

SALES LEDGER

Dr		A Smith		Cr
	£			£
Balance b/d	200	Set-off: purchases ledger		200

PURCHASES LEDGER

Dr		A Smith		Cr
	£			£
Set-off: sales ledger	200	Balance b/d		300

The net result is that M Patel Limited owes A Smith £100. The important point to note is that, because transactions have been recorded in the subsidiary accounts, an entry needs to be made in the two control accounts:

– *debit* purchases ledger control account

– *credit* sales ledger control account

Set-off transactions should be appropriately documented with a journal entry (see Chapter 11) authorised by the accounts supervisor. The journal entry records the transactions in a book of prime entry and gives the authority to record the transactions in the double-entry accounts.

SOURCES OF INFORMATION FOR CONTROL ACCOUNTS

Control accounts use totals (remember that their other name is 'totals accounts') for the week, month, quarter or year – depending on what time period is decided upon by the business. The totals come from a number of sources in the accounting system:

sales ledger control account

- total credit sales (including VAT) – from the 'total' column of the sales day book
- total sales returns (including VAT) – from the 'total' column of the sales returns day book
- total cash/bank receipts from receivables – from the cash book
- returned cheques – from the cash book
- total settlement discount allowed – from the discount allowed column of the cash book, or from discount allowed account
- irrecoverable debts – from the journal, or irrecoverable debts account
- set-off entries – from the journal

purchases ledger control account

- total credit purchases (including VAT) – from the 'total' column of the purchases day book
- total purchases returns (including VAT) – from the 'total' column of the purchases returns day book
- total cash/bank payments to payables – from the cash book
- total settlement discount received – from the discount received column of the cash book, or from discount received account
- set-off entries – from the journal

CONTROL ACCOUNTS AS AN AID TO MANAGEMENT

When the manager of a business needs to know the figure for receivables or payables the balance of the appropriate control account will give the information immediately: there is no need to add up the balances of all the individual accounts. With a computer accounting system, control accounts can be printed at any time.

The use of control accounts makes fraud more difficult – particularly in a manual accounting system. If a fraudulent transaction is to be recorded on a subsidiary account, the transaction must also be entered in the control account. As the control account will be either maintained by a supervisor, or checked regularly by the manager, the control accounts add another level of security within the accounting system.

We have already seen in this chapter how control accounts can help in locating errors. Remember, though, that a control account only proves the arithmetical accuracy of the accounts which it controls – there could still be errors or omissions (see Chapter 11) within the ledger section.

A further use of control accounts is to help with the preparation of financial statements when a business has not kept double-entry accounts and a trial balance cannot be extracted – see Chapter 14, which deals with *incomplete records*.

CONTROL ACCOUNTS AND BOOK-KEEPING

A business must decide how to use control accounts in its book-keeping system. The usual way of doing this is to incorporate the control accounts into double-entry book-keeping.

The control accounts form part of the double-entry system in general ledger. The balances of the sales ledger control account and the purchases ledger control account are recorded in the trial balance or extended trial balance as the figures for receivables and payables respectively. This means that the individual accounts are not part of double-entry, but are *subsidiary memorandum accounts* which record how much each receivable owes, and how much is owed to each payable. From time-to-time, the balances of the subsidiary memorandum accounts are reconciled (agreed) with the balance of the appropriate control account.

The diagrams on the next two pages show how the sales ledger control account and the purchases ledger control account are incorporated into general ledger, with the individual receivables' and payables' accounts kept in the form of subsidiary memorandum accounts.

VALUE ADDED TAX (VAT) CONTROL ACCOUNT

VAT control account brings together amounts of VAT from books of prime entry – the day books, the journal and cash book.

It is from VAT control account that the VAT return is prepared, checked and then sent to HM Revenue and Customs – often quarterly, ie every three months. VAT return shows

- either, the money amount due to be paid by the business when VAT collected from sales is greater than the VAT paid on purchases
- or, the money amount due as a refund from HM Revenue and Customs to the business when VAT collected from sales is less than the VAT paid on purchases

The balance of VAT control account must reconcile with the amount shown on the business' VAT return – any discrepancy should be investigated immediately and the error(s) traced.

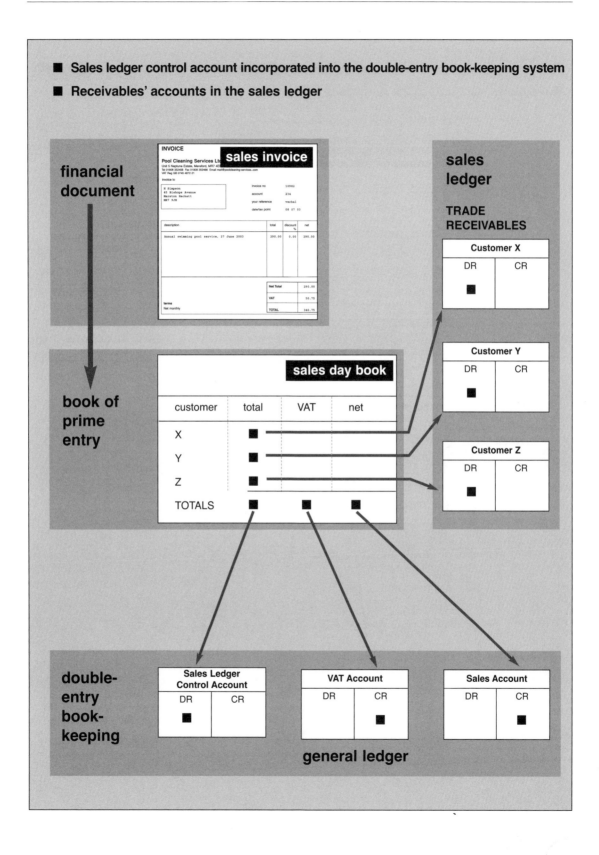

- Sales ledger control account incorporated into the double-entry book-keeping system
- Receivables' accounts in the sales ledger

■ **Purchases ledger control account incorporated into the double-entry book-keeping system**

■ **Payables' accounts in the purchases ledger**

financial document

purchases invoice

Tel 01908 352456 Fax 01908 352466 Email mail@poolclearing-services.com
VAT Reg GB 0745 4872 21

invoice to

R Simpson
45 Bishops Avenue
Marston Hackett
MR7 9JN

invoice no	10982	
account	234	
your reference	verbal	
date/tax point	08 07 03	

description	total	discount %	net
Annual swimming pool service, 27 June 2003	290.00	0.00	290.00

Net Total	290.00
VAT	50.75
TOTAL	340.75

terms
Net monthly

purchases ledger

TRADE PAYABLES

Supplier A	
DR	CR
	■

Supplier B	
DR	CR
	■

Supplier C	
DR	CR
	■

book of prime entry

purchases day book

supplier	total	VAT	net
A	■		
B	■		
C	■		
TOTALS	■	■	■

double-entry book-keeping

Purchases Ledger Control Account	
DR	CR
	■

VAT Account	
DR	CR
■	

Purchases Account	
DR	CR
■	

general ledger

The layout of a VAT control account, with sample figures, is shown below. Study the set-out carefully and then read the text which follows.

Dr		VAT Control Account		Cr
	£			£
Purchases	30,000	Sales		40,000
Sales returns	1,500	Purchases returns		1,000
Cash purchases	4,000	Cash sales		5,000
Other cash expenses	700	Other cash income		300
Balance c/d	10,100			
	46,300			46,300
		Balance b/d		10,100

purchases

This is the VAT paid by the business on its credit purchases.

sales returns

This is the VAT allowed back to customers of the business on the sales returns they make.

cash purchases and other cash expenses

This is the VAT paid on the cash purchases of the business, including other expenses – both capital and revenue – paid for as cash/bank transactions.

sales

This is the VAT charged by the business on its credit sales.

purchases returns

This is the VAT allowed back to the business by its suppliers on purchases returns.

cash sales and other cash income

This is the VAT charged on the cash/bank sales of the business, including other income – both capital and revenue – received as cash transactions.

balance

The balance on VAT control account can be either debit or credit:

- a debit balance brought down indicates that the amount is due as a refund to the business from HM Revenue and Customs

- a credit balance brought down indicates that the amount is due to be paid by the business to HM Revenue and Customs (which is the situation for the majority of businesses)

The balance of the account will be settled with a bank payment either from or to HM Revenue and Customs.

VAT control account in the accounting system

VAT control account is a general ledger account which uses amounts from the books of prime entry – day books, the journal and cash book. The account is the source information for preparation of the VAT return of the business, which is sent to HM Revenue and Customs. The balance of VAT control account must reconcile (agree) with the VAT return.

PREPARING RECONCILIATIONS

An important part of an accounting system is to carry out checks at regular intervals to ensure that balances are reconciled. If we can show that sections of the accounting system are reconciled we can be reasonably certain that no errors occur within that section – we will be looking in more detail at the correction of errors in the next chapter.

In this section we look at how to make adjustments to reconcile:

- sales ledger control account to sales ledger
- purchases ledger control account to purchases ledger
- cash book bank columns to the bank statement

Whenever an error is found it needs to be corrected by means of a journal entry – we will look at these in detail in Chapter 11.

sales ledger control account

Discrepancies between sales ledger control account and sales ledger (the individual accounts of receivables) include:

- *credit sales*
  - omitted or understated
  - entered twice or overstated

- *sales returns*
  - omitted or understated
  - entered twice or overstated
- *payments received from receivables*
  - omitted or understated
  - entered twice or overstated
- *settlement (cash) discount allowed to receivables*
  - omitted or understated
  - entered twice or overstated
- *irrecoverable debts*
  - omitted or understated
  - entered twice or overstated
- *other differences*
  - set-off entries omitted or entered twice, or understated or overstated
  - debit amounts entered on the credit side
  - credit amounts entered on the debit side

The following shows examples of the adjustments that will be necessary to reconcile sales ledger control account to sales ledger.

The sales ledger has been compared with sales ledger control account and the following differences identified:

1. The total column of sales day book has been undercast (underadded) by £100.

2. Settlement (cash) discount of £320 allowed to trade receivables and entered in their sales ledger accounts has not been entered in sales ledger control account.

3. A credit sale of £250 to J Williams has been debited to the account of J Wilson – both are sales ledger accounts.

4. The account of T Basili, £150, has been written off as irrecoverable in sales ledger, but has not been recorded in sales ledger control account.

The total of the account balances in sales ledger is £28,340 debit and the balance of sales ledger control account is £28,710 debit.

The following table shows the three adjustments that need to be made to sales ledger control account.

Adjustment number	Amount £	Debit ✓	Credit ✓
1.	100	✓	
2.	320		✓
4.	150		✓

Tutorial notes:

1. As the total column of sales day book has been undercast (underadded) this error will be carried through into sales ledger control account. It is necessary to increase the amount for sales by debiting sales ledger control account with £100.

2. Settlement (cash) discount allowed is credited to sales ledger control account – here it has been omitted, so the adjustment is a credit of £320.

3. Although there is an error – which needs to be corrected – it is an error within sales ledger, so there is no adjustment to make to sales ledger control account.

4. The irrecoverable debt of £150 must be recorded in sales ledger control account as a credit entry.

All of these adjustments will need to be corrected by means of a journal entry (see Chapter 11) which gives the book-keeper the authority to record the transactions in the double-entry accounts.

purchases ledger control account

Discrepancies between purchases ledger control account and purchases ledger (the individual accounts of payables) include:

* *credit purchases*
    - omitted or understated
    - entered twice or overstated

- *purchases returns*
  - omitted or understated
  - entered twice or overstated
- *payments made to payables*
  - omitted or understated
  - entered twice or overstated
- *settlement (cash) discount received from payables*
  - omitted or understated
  - entered twice or overstated
- *other differences*
  - set-off entries omitted or entered twice, or understated or overstated
  - debit amounts entered on the credit side
  - credit amounts entered on the debit side

The following shows examples of the adjustments that will be necessary to reconcile purchases ledger control account to purchases ledger.

The purchases ledger has been compared with purchases ledger control account and the following differences identified:

1. The total column of purchases day book has been overcast (overadded) by £100.

2. A payment of £200 made to J Smithson has been debited to the account of T Simpson – both are purchases ledger accounts.

3. Settlement (cash) discount of £450 received from trade payables has been entered on the wrong side of purchases ledger control account.

4. A set-off entry for £450 has been entered as £540 in purchases ledger control account.

The total of the account balances in purchases ledger is £44,235 credit and the balance of purchases ledger control account is £45,145 credit.

The table on the next page shows the three adjustments that need to be made to purchases ledger control account.

Adjustment number	Amount £	Debit ✓	Credit ✓
1.	100	✓	
3.	900	✓	
4.	90		✓

Tutorial notes:

1. As the total column of purchases day book has been overcast (overadded) this error will be carried through into purchases ledger control account. It is necessary to decrease the amount for purchases by debiting purchases ledger control account with £100.

2. Although there is an error – which needs to be corrected – it is an error within purchases ledger, so there is no adjustment to make to purchases ledger control account.

3. The amount of settlement (cash) discount received should be debited to purchases ledger control account – here it has been credited. To correct this error we need to double the amount of £450 to £900 (if we correct only £450 all that we do is to cancel out the error). £900 is debited to purchases ledger control account. In practice, rather than showing the difference, it is better to correct this error by taking out the wrong amount and recording the correct amount.

4. Set-off entries are debited to purchases ledger control account. Here the amount recorded has been overstated, so we must credit purchases ledger control account with the difference being £540 – £450 = £90. Again, it would be better to correct by taking out the wrong amount and recording the correct amount.

All of these adjustments will need to be corrected by means of a journal entry (see Chapter 11) which gives the book-keeper the authority to record the transactions in the double-entry accounts.

cash book bank columns

In a similar way to reconciling control accounts for sales and purchases ledgers, the bank columns of the cash book can be checked against the bank statement. Such a reconciliation demonstrates that we can be reasonably certain that no errors occur within the bank columns of the cash book. Indeed you may already be familiar, from your previous studies, with the preparation of a bank reconciliation statement.

A bank statement – which is either posted to customers at regular intervals or, increasingly, is available on-line – is the record of customer transactions from the bank's viewpoint. As such we must remember that a debit balance or entry in cash book (eg money paid into the bank) will be a credit entry on the bank statement (from the bank's view it owes the money to the customer); in the same way a credit balance or entry in cash book (eg a direct debit payment made) will be a debit entry on the bank statement (the bank has paid money out of the account on behalf of the customer).

Items appearing on bank statements include a number of different forms of receipt or payment. These include:

* *cheque* – a written instruction to a bank by a customer to pay a specified amount of money to a payee
* *BACS* – Bankers Automated Clearing Services, which is the banks' computer payment transfer system
* *standing order* – regular BACS payments, set up by the customer for the bank to make, usually for fixed amounts
* *direct debit* – regular BACS payments, set up by the organisation receiving the payments and agreed by the customer, for amounts which can be fixed or variable to be paid from the bank account

Discrepancies between the bank columns of the cash book and the bank statement include:

* unpresented cheques – cheques issued, not yet recorded on the bank statement
* outstanding lodgements – amounts paid into the bank, not yet recorded on the bank statement

These two are called timing differences – because they will correct themselves over time – as they have been recorded in the cash book but are not yet on the bank statement.

Other discrepancies which will need adjustment in the cash book include:

* *BACS credits*, such as payments from receivables
* *standing order payments*, if not already written up in the cash book
* *direct debit payments*, if not already written up in the cash book
* *unpaid cheques*, that is cheques received by the business and paid in to the bank which have 'bounced'
* *bank charges and interest*, that is service charges to operate the bank account and internet charged on borrowings

If an error is discovered that has been made by the bank, it should be queried immediately and the item and amount should not be entered into the cash book until it has been resolved.

The following shows examples of the adjustments that will be necessary to reconcile the bank columns of the cash book to the bank statement.

The bank statement has been compared with the bank columns of the cash book and the following differences identified:

1. Bank charges and interest paid of £170 have not been entered in the cash book.

2. A bank lodgement for £1,200 made yesterday is not showing on the bank statement.

3. A payment from a customer by BACS for £450 has not been entered in the cash book.

4. A standing order payment made by the bank for £280 has been incorrectly entered in the cash book as £820.

The balance showing on the bank statement is a credit of £1,900 and the balance in the cash book is a debit of £2,280.

The following table shows the three adjustments that need to be made to the cash book.

Adjustment number	Amount £	Debit ✓	Credit ✓
1.	170		✓
3.	450	✓	
4.	540	✓	

Tutorial notes:

1. As this transaction has not yet been recorded in the firm's double-entry accounts, it needs to be shown on the credit side of cash book, and debited to bank charges and interest account in general ledger.

2. This is a timing difference – the cash book is correct and the bank statement will record the lodgement in the next day or so.

3. This transaction needs to be recorded in the firm's double-entry accounts as follows:

   - debit cash book

   - credit sales ledger control account

   The amount will also be recorded in the customer's account in sales ledger.

4. Cash book is showing a payment for £540 (£820 – £280) too much. therefore to correct this a debit is shown in cash book – the other double-entry account needs to be checked to see what amount has been recorded. In practice, rather than showing the difference, it is better to correct this error by taking out the wrong amount and recording the correct amount.

    Adjustment 4 will need to be corrected by means of a journal entry. Adjustments 1 and 3 need to be recorded in the double-entry accounts – many businesses use a bank statement as a 'reminder' about standing orders, direct debits and BACS receipts that need to be entered into the accounts. No action is needed for adjustment 2, which is a timing difference.

Chapter Summary

■ The ledger is divided for convenience into four sections: sales ledger, purchases ledger, cash book and general ledger

■ Control accounts (or totals accounts) are 'master' accounts, which control a number of subsidiary accounts within the ledger.

■ Two commonly used control accounts are:
  – sales ledger control account, which controls the sales ledger
  – purchases ledger control account, which controls the purchases ledger

■ Transactions are recorded on the same side of the control account as on the subsidiary accounts.

■ Set-off (or contra) entries occur when one person has an account in both subsidiary ledgers – sales and purchases ledger – and it is agreed to set-off one balance against the other to leave a net balance. This usually results in the following control account entries:
  – debit purchases ledger control account
  – credit sales ledger control account
  Note that it is always the smaller of the two amounts owing that is set-off.

■ Control accounts are an aid to management:
  – they give up-to-date information on the total of receivables and payables
  – by making fraud more difficult
  – in helping to locate errors and omissions
  – in assisting with the preparation of financial statements from incomplete records

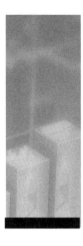

■ Control accounts are usually incorporated into the general ledger of the double-entry book-keeping system. The individual accounts of receivables and payables are set up as separate subsidiary memorandum accounts.

■ A further control account is VAT control account which brings together amounts of VAT from books of prime entry.

■ At regular intervals it is good practice to carry out reconciliations to check sections of the accounting system. Such reconciliations include:

 – sales ledger control account to sales ledger

 – purchases ledger control account to purchases ledger

 – cash book bank columns to the bank statement

Key Terms		
control account	a 'master' account which controls a number of subsidiary accounts
sales ledger control account	a 'master' account which controls the sales ledger
purchases ledger control account	'master' account which controls the purchases ledger
set-off entries	where balances in sales ledger and purchases ledger are to be set-off against one another
subsidiary account	an account which is not part of the double-entry system
VAT control account	account which brings together amounts of VAT from books of prime entry

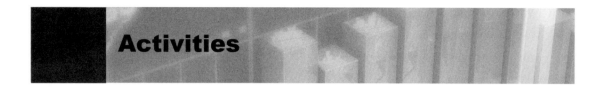

Activities

10.1 Which one of the following is the reason why a sales ledger control account is used?

(a)   to show how much each individual customer owes

(b)   to show the total sales of the business

(c)   to enable the manager to know the total of trade receivables

(d)   to enable the production of individual customer statements

Answer (a) or (b) or (c) or (d)

10.2 Which one of the following is the reason why subsidiary purchases ledgers are used?

(a)   to enable the manager to know the total of trade payables

(b)   to show how much each individual supplier is owed

(c)   to show potential irrecoverable debts

(d)   to show the total purchases of the business

Answer (a) or (b) or (c) or (d)

10.3 You have the following information:

• opening payables balances at start of month	£18,600
• cash/cheques paid to trade payables during month	£9,400
• credit purchases for month	£9,100
• purchases returns for month	£800

What is the figure for closing payables balances at the end of the month?

(a)   £18,100

(b)   £19,100

(c)   £36,300

(d)   £17,500

Answer (a) or (b) or (c) or (d)

10.4   Which one of the following does not appear in sales ledger control account?

(a)   irrecoverable debts

(b)   settlement (cash) discount received

(c)   sales returns

(d)   cash/cheques received from receivables

Answer (a) or (b) or (c) or (d)

10.5   Prepare a sales ledger control account for the month of June 20-8 from the following information:

20-8		£
1 Jun	Sales ledger balances	17,491
30 Jun	Credit sales for month	42,591
	Sales returns	1,045
	Payments received from trade receivables	39,024
	Settlement (cash) discount allowed	593
	Irrecoverable debts	296

The trade receivables figure at 30 June is to be entered as the balancing figure.

10.6   Prepare a purchases ledger control account for the month of April 20-9 from the following information:

20-9		£
1 Apr	Purchases ledger balances	14,275
30 Apr	Credit purchases for month	36,592
	Purchases returns	653
	Payments made to trade payables	31,074
	Settlement (cash) discount received	1,048
	Set-off of credit balances to sales ledger	597

The trade payables figure at 30 April is to be entered as the balancing figure.

10.7   The sales ledger of Rowcester Traders contains the following accounts on 1 February 20-4:

Arrow Valley Retailers, balance £826.40 debit

B Brick (Builders) Limited, balance £59.28 debit

Mereford Manufacturing Company, balance £293.49 debit

Redgrove Restorations, balance £724.86 debit

Wyvern Warehouse Limited, balance £108.40 debit

The following transactions took place during February:

3 Feb	Sold goods on credit to Arrow Valley Retailers £338.59, and to Mereford Manufacturing Company £127.48
7 Feb	Redgrove Restorations returned goods £165.38
15 Feb	Received a bank payment from Wyvern Warehouse Limited for the balance of the account after deduction of 2.5% settlement (cash) discount
17 Feb	Sold goods on credit to Redgrove Restorations £394.78, and to Wyvern Warehouse Limited £427.91
20 Feb	Arrow Valley Retailers settled an invoice for £826.40 by bank payment after deducting 2.5% settlement (cash) discount
24 Feb	Mereford Manufacturing Company returned goods £56.29
29 Feb	Set-off the balance of Mereford Manufacturing Company's account to the company's account in the purchases ledger
29 Feb	Wrote off the account of B Brick (Builders) Limited as an irrecoverable debt

You are to:

(a) write up the accounts in the sales ledger of Rowcester Traders for February 20-4, balancing them at the end of the month

(b) prepare a sales ledger control account for February 20-4, balancing it at the end of the month

(c) reconcile the control account balance with the subsidiary accounts at 1 February and 29 February 20-4.

Note: VAT is to be ignored on all transactions and day books are not required.

10.8 Which one of the following is the reason why a VAT control account is used?

(a) to bring together amounts of VAT from books of prime entry

(b) to calculate the amount of VAT on sales invoices

(c) to remind the business when it is time to submit VAT returns

(d) to ensure that the VAT calculated on purchases invoices allows for settlement discount

Answer (a) or (b) or (c) or (d)

10.9 This Activity is about preparing reconciliations.

The sales ledger has been compared with sales ledger control account and the following differences identified:

1. The total column of sales returns day book has been overcast (overadded) by £200.

2. A set-off entry for £150 has been omitted from sales ledger control account.

3.   The account of D Clarke, £125, has been written off as irrecoverable in sales ledger, but has not been recorded in sales ledger control account.

4.   Settlement (cash) discount of £20 has been credited to the sales ledger account of K Fairbank instead of the sales ledger account of S Fairweather.

The total of the account balances in sales ledger is £32,705 debit and the balance of sales ledger control account is £33,180 debit.

Use the following table to show the three adjustments you need to make to sales ledger control account.

Adjustment number	Amount £	Debit ✓	Credit ✓

10.10 This Activity is about preparing reconciliations.

The purchases ledger has been compared with purchases ledger control account and the following differences identified:

1.   The total of settlement (cash) discount received from trade payables of £240 has been recorded in purchases ledger control account as £420.

2.   A payment of £195 has been debited to the purchases ledger account of M Touoson instead of the purchases ledger account of B Toulson.

3.   The total column of purchases returns day book has been undercast (underadded) by £400.

4.   A set-off entry for £220 has been entered on the wrong side of purchases ledger control account.

The total of the account balances in purchases ledger is £29,640 credit and the balance of purchases ledger control account is £30,300 credit.

Use the following table to show the three adjustments you need to make to purchases ledger control account.

Adjustment number	Amount £	Debit ✓	Credit ✓

10.11 This Activity is about preparing reconciliations.

The bank statement has been compared with the bank columns of the cash book and the following differences identified:

1.   Cheques totalling £2,540 paid into the bank yesterday are not showing on the bank statement.

2.   A direct debit payment made by the bank for £550 has not been entered in the cash book.

3.   A payment cheque to a supplier for £680 has been incorrectly entered in the cash book as £860.

4.   Bank charges and interest of £210 have not been entered in the cash book.

The balance showing on the bank statement is a credit of £1,090 and the balance in the cash book is a debit of £4,210.

Use the following table to show the three adjustments you need to make to the cash book.

Adjustment number	Amount £	Debit ✓	Credit ✓

11 The journal and correction of errors

this chapter covers...

The journal is the book of prime entry for non-regular transactions, eg purchase and disposal of non-current assets, correction of errors, end-of-year transfers (such as depreciation and allowance for doubtful debts), and other transfers.

As a book of prime entry, the journal is not part of double-entry book-keeping; instead the journal is used to list transactions before they are entered into the accounts. In this way, journal entries record amounts in a book of prime entry and give the book-keeper the authority to record the transactions in the double-entry accounts.

USES OF THE JOURNAL

The journal provides the book of prime entry for non-regular transactions, which are not recorded in any other book of prime entry. Such non-regular transactions include:

* year end transfers, including accruals and prepayments, depreciation, irrecoverable debts and allowance for doubtful debts

* purchase and sale of non-current assets on credit, and gain/loss on disposal

* correction of errors found in the double-entry system

The reasons for using a journal are:

* to provide a book of prime entry for non-regular transactions

* to eliminate the need for remembering why non-regular transactions were put through the accounts – the journal acts as a notebook

* to give the book-keeper the authority to record transactions in the double-entry accounts

* to reduce the risk of fraud, by making it difficult for unauthorised transactions to be entered in the double-entry system

* to reduce the risk of errors, by listing the transactions that are to be put into the double-entry accounts

* to ensure that entries can be traced back to an authorised financial document (note that documentation is stored securely for possible future reference)

THE JOURNAL – A BOOK OF PRIME ENTRY

The journal is a book of prime (or original) entry; it is not, therefore, part of the double-entry book-keeping system. The journal is used to list the transactions that are then to be put through the accounts. The accounting system for non-regular transactions is as follows:

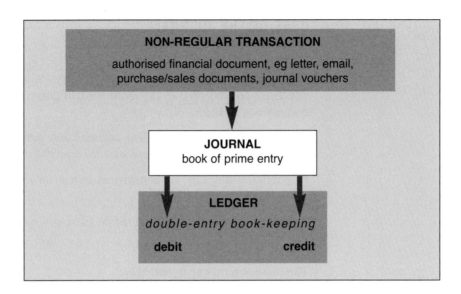

The journal is set out in the following way, with a sample transaction.

Date	Details	Reference	Dr	Cr
20-4			£	£
1 Jul	Vehicle at cost	GL	5,000	
	Bank	CB		5,000

Notes:

- journal entries are prepared from authorised financial documents (which are stored securely for possible future reference)
- the names of the accounts to be debited and credited in the double-entry system are written in the details column; it is customary to show the debit transaction first
- the money amount of each debit and credit is stated in the appropriate columns
- the reference column shows where each account is found, eg GL = general ledger, CB = cash book, SL = sales ledger, PL = purchases ledger; the reference may include an account number
- a journal entry always balances, ie debit and credit entries are for the same amount or total
- it is usual to include a brief narrative (ie a few words) explaining why the transaction is being carried out, and making reference to the financial document whenever possible (you should always include a narrative unless told otherwise)

- each journal entry is complete in itself and is ruled off to separate it from the next entry

Note that any journal entries involving sales ledger control account and purchases ledger control account must also be recorded in the subsidiary memorandum accounts in sales ledger and purchases ledger.

YEAR END TRANSFERS

Many non-regular transactions take place at the end of a business' financial year and need to be recorded in the journal. In this section, we will look at journal entries to account for:

- transfers to income statement
- closing inventory
- accruals and prepayments of expenses and income
- depreciation charge on non-current assets
- irrecoverable debts
- allowance for doubtful debts

As we have seen earlier (Chapter 4), the income statement forms part of the double-entry system. Therefore, each amount recorded in the income statement must have an opposite entry in another account: such transfers are recorded in the journal as the book of prime entry, as shown by the entries which follow.

transfers to income statement

The three journal entries which follow are examples of year end transfers which close off income and expense accounts by transfer to the income statement. With these examples, the full balance of the account is transferred – we will see how to deal with accruals and prepayments on page 199.

31 Dec 20-4   *Balance of sales account at the year end, £155,000, transferred to income statement (debit sales account; credit income statement)*

Date	Details	Reference	Dr	Cr
20-4			£	£
31 Dec	Sales	GL	155,000	
	Income statement	GL		155,000
	Transfer to income statement of			
	sales for the year			

31 Dec 20-4   *Balance of purchases account at the year end, £105,000, transferred to income statement (debit income statement; credit purchases account)*

Date	Details	Reference	Dr	Cr
20-4			£	£
31 Dec	Income statement	GL	105,000	
	Purchases	GL		105,000
	Transfer to income statement of purchases for the year			

31 Dec 20-4   *Balance of wages account, £23,500, transferred to income statement (debit income statement; credit wages account)*

Date	Details	Reference	Dr	Cr
20-4			£	£
31 Dec	Income statement	GL	23,500	
	Wages	GL		23,500
	Transfer to income statement of expenditure for the year			

closing inventory

31 Dec 20-4   *Closing inventory has been valued at £12,500 and is to be entered into the financial statements*

Date	Details	Reference	Dr	Cr
20-4			£	£
31 Dec	Closing inventory – statement of financial position	GL	12,500	
	Closing inventory – income statement	GL		12,500
	Inventory valuation at 31 December 20-4 transferred to the financial statements			

The journal entry shows that the closing inventory valuation for the year is recorded in the statement of financial position as an asset.

accruals and prepayments

The amounts of accruals and prepayments of expenses and income (see Chapter 5) are recorded in the accounts: such transfers are recorded in the journal as the book of prime entry.

accrual of expense

31 Dec 20-4   *The balance of telephone account at the year end is £500. A telephone bill for £100 is received on 4 January 20-5 and relates to costs incurred in 20-4.*

Date	Details	Reference	Dr	Cr
20-4			£	£
31 Dec	Income statement	GL	600	
	Telephone	GL		500
	Accruals	GL		100
			600	600
	Transfer to income statement			
	of expenditure for the year			

This transaction shows the:

* transfer to income statement of expenditure for the year
* amount of the accrual which is shown as a liability on the statement of financial position

prepayment of expense

31 Dec 20-4   *The balance of rent paid account at the year end is £750. Of this, £675 relates to 20-4, while £75 is a prepayment for 20-5*

Date	Details	Reference	Dr	Cr
20-4			£	£
31 Dec	Income statement	GL	675	
	Prepayments	GL	75	
	Rent paid	GL		750
			750	750
	Transfer to income statement			
	of expenditure for the year			

This transaction shows the:

* transfer to income statement of expenditure for the year
* amount of the prepayment which is shown as an asset on the statement of financial position

accrual of income

31 Dec 20-4   *The balance of commission received account at the year end is £1,250. A further £250 was received on 10 January 20-5 and relates to work done in 20-4.*

Date	Details	Reference	Dr	Cr
20-4			£	£
31 Dec	Commission received	GL	1,250	
	Accrual of income	GL	250	
	Income statement	GL		1,500
			1,500	1,500
	Transfer to income statement of income for the year			

This transaction shows the:

- transfer to income statement of income for the year
- amount of the accrual of income which is shown as an asset on the statement of financial position

prepayment of income

31 Dec 20-4   *The balance of rent received account at the year end is £2,850. Of this, £2,450 relates to 20-4, while £400 is a prepayment of income for 20-5*

Date	Details	Reference	Dr	Cr
20-4			£	£
31 Dec	Rent received	GL	2,850	
	Prepayment of income	GL		400
	Income statement	GL		2,450
			2,850	2,850
	Transfer to income statement of income for the year			

This transaction shows the:

- transfer to income statement of income for the year
- amount of the prepayment of income which is shown as a liability on the statement of financial position

depreciation charge on non-current assets

As we have seen in Chapter 6, the amount of depreciation on non-current assets is recorded in the income statement:

- – debit income statement
- – credit depreciation charge account

31 Dec 20-4   *Depreciation charge on a machine is calculated at £400 for the year*

The journal entry is:

Date	Details	Reference	Dr	Cr
20-4			£	£
31 Dec	Income statement	GL	400	
	Depreciation charge	GL		400
	Transfer to income statement of			
	depreciation charge for year			
	on machine			

As already seen in Chapter 6, the amount credited to depreciation charge account (the annual charge for depreciation) is then transferred to accumulated depreciation account (which records the total of depreciation for each class of asset):

– *debit* depreciation charge account

– *credit* accumulated depreciation account

The journal entry for the transfer to accumulated depreciation account is:

Date	Details	Reference	Dr	Cr
20-4			£	£
31 Dec	Depreciation charge	GL	400	
	Machinery: accumulated depreciation	GL		400
	Transfer of depreciation charge			
	for year to accumulated			
	depreciation account			

irrecoverable debts

We have already seen, in Chapter 7, the double-entry transaction to write off a receivable's account as irrecoverable:

– *debit* irrecoverable debts account

– *credit* sales ledger control account

15 Dec 20-4   *Write off the sales ledger account of T Hughes, which has a balance of £25, as irrecoverable*

The journal entry is:

Date	Details	Reference	Dr	Cr
20-4			£	£
15 Dec	Irrecoverable debts	GL	25	
	Sales ledger control	GL		25
	Account of T Hughes written off			
	as irrecoverable:			
	in the sales ledger			
	– credit T Hughes £25			

At the end of the financial year, the balance of irrecoverable debts account is transferred to the income statement as follows:

– *debit* income statement

– *credit* irrecoverable debts account

The journal entry for the transfer to income statement is:

Date	Details	Reference	Dr	Cr
20-4			£	£
31 Dec	Income statement	GL	25	
	Irrecoverable debts	GL		25
	Transfer to income statement of			
	irrecoverable debts for year			

allowance for doubtful debts

In Chapter 7 we saw that the creation of an allowance for doubtful debts is recorded in the income statement:

– *debit* income statement

– *credit* allowance for doubtful debts: adjustment account

31 Dec 20-4   An allowance for doubtful debts of £500 is to be created

The journal entry is:

Date	Details	Reference	Dr	Cr
20-4			£	£
31 Dec	Income statement	GL	500	
	Allowance for doubtful debts:			
	adjustment	GL		500
	Creation of an allowance for			
	doubtful debts			

As already seen in Chapter 7, the amount credited to allowance for doubtful debts: adjustment account (the annual change in the allowance) is then transferred to allowance for doubtful debts account (which records the accumulated allowance):

– *debit* allowance for doubtful debts: adjustment account

– *credit* allowance for doubtful debts account

The journal entry for the transfer to allowance for doubtful debts is:

Date	Details	Reference	Dr	Cr
20-4			£	£
31 Dec	Allowance for doubtful debts:			
	adjustment	GL	500	
	Allowance for doubtful debts	GL		500
	Transfer of amount for year to			
	allowance for doubtful debts			
	account			

An existing allowance for doubtful debts will usually be increased or decreased as the level of receivables changes. The book-keeping entries (see Chapter 7) are:

increasing the allowance

– *debit* income statement

– *credit* allowance for doubtful debts: adjustment account

decreasing the allowance

– *debit* allowance for doubtful debts: adjustment account

– *credit* income statement

31 Dec 20-5   The existing allowance for doubtful debts is to be increased by £250

The journal entry is:

Date	Details	Reference	Dr	Cr
20-5			£	£
31 Dec	Income statement	GL	250	
	Allowance for doubtful debts:			
	adjustment	GL		250
	Transfer to income statement of			
	increase in allowance for doubtful			
	debts			

The journal entry for the transfer to allowance for doubtful debts account is:

Date	Details	Reference	Dr	Cr
20-5			£	£
31 Dec	Allowance for doubtful debts:			
	adjustment	GL	250	
	Allowance for doubtful debts	GL		250
	Transfer of increase for year to			
	allowance for doubtful debts account			

Note that a decrease in the allowance will have the opposite journal entries to these.

PURCHASE AND SALE OF NON-CURRENT ASSETS ON CREDIT

The purchase and sale of non-current assets are non-regular business transactions which are recorded in the journal as the book of prime entry. Only *credit* transactions are entered in the journal (because cash/bank transactions are recorded in the cash book as the book of prime entry). However, a business (or an Activity or an Assessment) may choose to journalise cash book entries: strictly, though, this is incorrect as two books of prime entry are being used.

purchase of non-current asset

15 Apr 20-4   Bought a machine for £1,000 plus VAT (at 20%) on credit from Machinery Supplies Limited, purchase order no 2341.

Date	Details	Reference	Dr	Cr
20-4			£	£
15 Apr	Machinery at cost	GL	1,000	
	VAT	GL	200	
	Purchases ledger control*	GL		1,200
			1,200	1,200
	Purchase of machine on credit from Machinery Supplies Limited: purchase order 2341			

* Instead of entering this transaction in the purchases ledger, an alternative treatment would be to open a general ledger account for Machinery Supplies Limited. This would avoid confusion with trade payables – in the purchases ledger.

sale of non-current asset

20 May 2004   Car sold for £2,500 on credit to Wyvern Motors Limited (no VAT chargeable).

Date	Details	Reference	Dr	Cr
20-4			£	£
20 May	Sales ledger control**	GL	2,500	
	Disposals	GL		2,500
	Sale of car, registration no QV01 HAB			
	to Wyvern Motors Limited			

** As with the purchase transaction, in order to avoid confusion with trade receivables, a general ledger account could be opened for Wyvern Motors Limited for this sale transaction.

disposal of non-current assets

When a non-current asset is sold or disposed, the double-entry transactions (see page 108) bring together:

- the original cost of the asset
- accumulated depreciation over the life of the asset
- disposal proceeds

31 Dec 20-6   *A machine had been bought on 1 January 20-4 (ie three years ago) for £2,000 (net of VAT). Accumulated depreciation (including the current year) totals £1,200. On 31 December 20-6 the machine is sold for £600 (net of VAT) received into the bank.*

The journal entry is:

Date	Details	Reference	Dr	Cr
20-6			£	£
31 Dec	Disposals	GL	2,000	
	Machinery at cost	GL		2,000
	Machinery: accumulated			
	depreciation	GL	1,200	
	Disposals	GL		1,200
	Bank	CB	720	
	Disposals	GL		600
	VAT	GL		120
	Income statement	GL	200	
	Disposals	GL		200
			4,120	4,120
	Sale of machine no. xxxx; loss on			
	disposal £200 debited to income			
	statement			

(If you wish to check the double-entry transactions for this disposal, they are set out in full on pages 95-97.)

CORRECTION OF ERRORS

In any accounting system there is always the possibility of errors. These can to some extent be reduced through the use of sound accounting techniques. But some errors may still occur. In this section, we will look at:

- correction of errors **not** revealed by a trial balance
- correction of errors revealed by a trial balance, using a suspense account

errors not revealed by a trial balance

In Chapter 3 (see page 45) we have explained errors that are **not** revealed by a trial balance. These are: error of principle, mispost/error of commission, error of original entry, error of omission, reversal of entries and compensating error.

Although these errors are not revealed by a trial balance, they are likely to come to light through checking procedures and customer response. For example, a customer will soon let you know if her account has been debited with goods she did not buy. When an error is found, it needs to be corrected by means of a journal entry showing the double-entry transactions made.

We will now look at an example of each of the errors not revealed by a trial balance, and will see how it is corrected by means of a journal entry. Note that, for all journal entries shown below which involve sales ledger or purchases ledger, we have assumed that control accounts are used, which are incorporated into the double-entry system in general ledger.

ERROR OF PRINCIPLE

The cost of diesel fuel, £50 (excluding VAT) on receipt no 1234 has been debited to vehicles account; the error is corrected on 20 May 20-4

Date	Details	Reference	Dr	Cr
20-4			£	£
20 May	Vehicle expenses	GL	50	
	Vehicles at cost	GL		50
	Correction of error: receipt 1234			

With this type of error it is the wrong class of account being used. In this example, the vehicle expenses must be kept separate from the cost of the asset (the vehicle), otherwise the expense and asset accounts will be incorrect, leading to profit for the year being overstated and the non-current asset being shown in the statement of financial position at too high a figure.

MISPOST/ERROR OF COMMISSION

Credit sales of £60, including VAT (at 20%), on invoice no 321 have been debited to the account of J Adams, instead of the account of J Adams Limited; the error is corrected on 15 May 20-4

Date	Details	Folio	Dr	Cr
20-4			£	£
15 May	Sales ledger control	GL	60	
	Sales ledger control	GL		60
	Correction of mispost in the sales			
	ledger:			
	– debit J Adams Limited £60			
	– credit J Adams £60			

This type of error can be avoided, to some extent, by the use of account numbers, and by persuading the customer to quote the account number or reference on each transaction.

ERROR OF ORIGINAL ENTRY

Postages of £45 paid from the bank entered in the accounts as £54; the error is corrected on 27 May 20-4

Date	Details	Reference	Dr	Cr
20-4			£	£
27 May	Bank	CB	54	
	Postages	GL		54
	Postages	GL	45	
	Bank	CB		45
			99	99
	Correction of error: postages of £45			
	entered into the accounts as £54			

This error could have been corrected by debiting bank and crediting postages with £9, being the difference between the two amounts. However, there was no original transaction for this amount, and it is better to reverse the wrong transaction and put through the correct one. Where figures are reversed there is always a difference of nine (as above), or an amount divisible by nine. An error of original entry can also be a 'bad' figure written on a financial document, eg an invoice, which is entered wrongly into both accounts.

ERROR OF OMISSION

Credit sale of goods, £200 plus VAT (at 20%) on invoice 4967 to H Jarvis completely omitted from the accounting system; the error is corrected on 12 May 20-4

Date	Details	Reference	Dr	Cr
20-4			£	£
12 May	Sales ledger control	GL	240	
	Sales	GL		200
	VAT	GL		40
			240	240
	Invoice 4967 omitted from accounts:			
	in the sales ledger –			
	debit H Jarvis £240			

This type of error can happen in a very small business – often where the double-entry accounts are kept by one person. For example, a completed sales invoice is 'lost' down the back of a filing cabinet. In a large business, particularly one using a computer accounting system, it should be impossible for this error to occur. Also, if documents are numbered serially, then none should be mislaid.

REVERSAL OF ENTRIES

A payment, on 5 May 20-4 from the bank of £50 to a supplier, S Wright has been debited in the cash book and credited to purchases ledger control and Wright's account in purchases ledger; the error is corrected on 14 May 20-4

Date	Details	Reference	Dr	Cr
20-4			£	£
14 May	Purchases ledger control	GL	50	
	Bank	CB		50
	Purchases ledger control	GL	50	
	Bank	CB		50
			100	100
	Correction of reversal of entries:			
	in the purchases ledger			
	– debit S Wright £50			
	– debit S Wright £50			

To correct this type of error it is best to reverse the entries that have been made incorrectly (the first two journal entries), and then to put through the correct entries. This is preferable to debiting £100 to purchases ledger control account and crediting £100 to bank account: there was never a transaction for this amount – the original transaction was for £50.

As noted earlier, it is often an idea to write out the 'T' accounts, complete with the error, and then to write in the correcting entries. As an example, the two accounts involved in this last error are shown with the error made on 5 May, and the corrections made on 14 May indicated by the shading:

Dr	Purchases Ledger Control Account			Cr
20-4		£	20-4	£
14 May Bank		50	5 May Bank	50
14 May Bank		50		

Dr	Bank Account			Cr
20-4		£	20-4	£
5 May Purchases ledger control	50		14 May Purchases ledger control	50
			14 May Purchases ledger control	50

The accounts now show a net debit transaction of £50 on purchases ledger control account, and a net credit transaction of £50 on bank account.

COMPENSATING ERROR

Rates account is added up by £100 more than it should be (ie it is overadded, or overcast); sales account is also overcast by the same amount; the error is corrected on 29 May 20-4

Date	Details	Folio	Dr	Cr
20-4			£	£
29 May	Sales	GL	100	
	Rates	GL		100
	Correction of overcast on rates account and sales account			

Here an account with a debit balance (rates) has been overcast and compensated by an overcast on an account with a credit balance (sales). There are several variations on this: eg two debit balances, one overcast, one undercast; or a debit balance undercast and a credit balance undercast.

ERRORS SHOWN BY THE TRIAL BALANCE: JOURNAL ENTRIES

There are several types of errors revealed by a trial balance; these include:

- one-sided entry (ie only one of the two parts of a double-entry transaction has been recorded)
- entry duplicated on one side, nothing on the other (ie two debits or two credits have been recorded for a transaction)
- unequal entries (ie different amounts have been recorded for the debit and credit entries)
- account balance incorrectly transferred to the trial balance

When errors are shown, the trial balance is 'balanced' by recording the difference in a suspense account, as shown in the following Case Study.

Case Study

TEMESIDE TRADERS: SUSPENSE ACCOUNT

The book-keeper of Temeside Traders is unable to balance the trial balance on 30 June 20-4. As the error or errors cannot be found quickly the trial balance is balanced by recording the difference in a suspense account, as follows:

	Dr	Cr
	£	£
Trial balance totals	99,950	100,000
Suspense account	50	
	100,000	100,000

A suspense account is opened in the general ledger with, in this case, a debit balance of £50.

Dr			Suspense Account		Cr
20-4		£	20-4		£
30 Jun	Trial balance difference	50			

A detailed examination of the book-keeping system is now made in order to find the errors. As errors are found, they are corrected by means of a journal entry. The journal entries will balance, with one part of the entry being either a debit or credit to suspense account. In this way, the balance on suspense account is eliminated by double-entry transactions. Using the above suspense account, the following errors are found and corrected on 15 July 20-4:

- telephone expenses of £55 were not recorded in the expenses account
- stationery expenses £48 have been debited to both stationery account and bank account
- a payment to a supplier, A Wilson, for £65, has been recorded in the bank as £56
- the balance of rent paid account is £3,100 but it has been recorded in the trial balance as £3,000

These errors are corrected by the journal entries shown on the next few pages.

one-sided entry

Telephone expenses of £55 were not recorded in the expenses account.

As only the bank entry has been recorded, the correcting entry must complete double-entry by debiting telephone expenses account with £55. The correcting journal entry is:

Date	Details	Reference	Dr	Cr
20-4			£	£
15 Jul	Telephone expenses	GL	55	
	Suspense	GL		55
	Omission of entry in expenses account.			

entry duplicated on one side, nothing on the other

Stationery expenses £48 have been debited to both stationery account and bank account.

As bank account has been debited in error with £48, the correcting journal entry must be in two parts to remove the incorrect entry and record the correct entry

Date	Details	Reference	Dr	Cr
20-4			£	£
15 Jul	Suspense	GL	48	
	Bank	CB		48
	Suspense	GL	48	
	Bank	CB		48
			96	96
	Correction of error: payment from bank debited in error to bank account			

unequal entries

A £65 payment to a supplier, A Wilson, has been recorded in the bank as £56.
As the credit entry in bank account has been entered incorrectly, the correcting journal entry must be in two parts to remove the incorrect entry and record the correct entry

Date	Details	Reference	Dr	Cr
20-4			£	£
15 Jul	Bank	CB	56	
	Suspense	GL		56
	Suspense	GL	65	
	Bank	CB		65
			121	121
	Payment to a supplier entered in bank account as £56 instead of £65			

account balance incorrectly transferred

The balance of rent paid account has been recorded in the trial balance as £3,000; further checking shows that the correct balance is £3,100.

To correct this type of error needs a journal entry to take the wrong amount from suspense account and then to record the correct amount, ie a two-part journal entry. As rent paid account has a debit balance the journal entry is firstly to take out the wrong balance (debit suspense account and credit rent paid account in the trial balance) and then to record the correct balance (debit rent paid account in the trial balance and credit suspense account).

Date	Details	Reference	Dr	Cr
20-4			£	£
15 Jul	Suspense	GL	3,000	
	Rent paid	GL		3,000
	Rent paid	GL	3,100	
	Suspense	GL		3,100
			6,100	6,100
	Incorrect balance of rent paid account transferred to the trial balance			

The entries in suspense account are shown below

suspense account

After the journal entries have been recorded in the double-entry accounts, suspense account appears:

Dr				Suspense Account		Cr
20-4			£	20-4		£
30 Jun	Trial balance difference		50	15 Jul	Telephone expenses	55
15 Jul	Bank		48	15 Jul	Bank	56
15 Jul	Bank		48	15 Jul	Rent paid	3,100
15 Jul	Bank		65			
15 Jul	Rent paid		3,000			
			3,211			3,211

Thus all the errors have now been found, and suspense account has a nil balance.

EFFECT ON PROFIT AND STATEMENT OF FINANCIAL POSITION

The correction of errors, whether shown by a trial balance or not, often has an effect on the profit figure calculated before the errors were found. For example, an undercast of sales account, when corrected, will increase profit and, of course, the profit figure taken to the statement of financial position. Some errors, however, only affect the statement of financial position, eg errors involving receivables' and payables' accounts. The diagram below shows the effect of errors, when corrected, on the profit figure and the statement of financial position.

	correction of error	profit	statement of financial position
income statement	sales undercast/understated	increase	profit increase
	sales overcast/overstated	decrease	profit decrease
	purchases undercast/understated	decrease	profit decrease
	purchases overcast/overstated	increase	profit increase
	opening inventory undervalued	decrease	profit decrease
	opening inventory overvalued	increase	profit increase
	closing inventory undervalued	increase	profit increase/inventory increase
	closing inventory overvalued	decrease	profit decrease/inventory decrease
	expense undercast/understated	decrease	decrease in profit
	expense overcast/overstated	increase	increase in profit
	income undercast/understated	increase	increase in profit
	income overcast/overstated	decrease	decrease in profit
statement of financial position	asset undercast/understated	–	increase asset
	asset overcast/overstated	–	decrease asset
	liability undercast/understated	–	increase liability
	liability overcast/overstated	–	decrease liability

MAKING JOURNAL ENTRIES

As we have seen in this chapter, the journal is the book of prime entry for non-regular transactions. Because of the irregular nature of journal transactions, it is important that they are correctly authorised by the appropriate person – such as the accounts supervisor, the manager of the organisation, the owner of the business. The authorisation will, ideally, be written – eg letter, memo, email or other document – but may well be verbal – eg "make the year end transfers to income statement", or "find the errors and put them right".

A great deal of tact and courtesy is needed when investigating business transactions. For example, when investigating errors, it is likely that the person who made the errors will be the one who can be of most assistance to you in correcting them – that person invariably knows the double-entry system better than you do, and his or her co-operation is needed, firstly, to put the errors right and, secondly, to see that they do not happen again.

It might well be that not all errors can be corrected without the assistance of other people, eg the accounts supervisor. Under such circumstances you, as an accounts assistant, should make the corrections that you are able to do – which may go some way to reducing the imbalance shown by suspense account – and then seek assistance from the appropriate person for help in resolving any outstanding items.

At another level, the investigation of errors may reveal that fraudulent transactions have been entered into the accounts. Tact and courtesy are needed to ensure that such transactions are investigated thoroughly, and the appropriate person in the organisation advised of the findings so that further action can be taken.

With journal entries for year end transfers it is essential to ensure that the organisation's policies, regulations, procedures and timescales are observed in relation to the preparation of financial statements. Thus journal entries are needed for income statement transfers, accruals and prepayments, depreciation, irrecoverable debts and allowance for doubtful debts – all of these must be made at the correct time for the organisation and for the correct amounts.

It is good practice in an organisation to ensure that journal entries are checked by an appropriate person before they are entered into the double-entry system. It is all too easy to get a journal entry the wrong way round resulting in an error becoming twice as much as it was in the first place!

Chapter Summary

■ The journal is used to list non-regular transactions.

■ The journal is a book of prime entry – it is not a double-entry account.

■ The journal is used for:
– year end transfers
– purchase and sale of non-current assets on credit
– correction of errors found in the double-entry system

■ Correction of errors is always a difficult topic to put into practice: it tests knowledge of double-entry procedures and it is all too easy to make the error worse than it was in the first place! The secret of dealing with this topic well is to write down – in account format – what has gone wrong. It should then be relatively easy to see what has to be done to put the error right.

■ Errors not revealed by a trial balance: error of principle, mispost/error of commission, error of original entry, error of omission, reversal of entries and compensating error.

■ Errors revealed by a trial balance include: one-sided entry, entry duplicated on one side, nothing on the other, unequal entries, account balance incorrectly transferred to the trial balance.

■ All errors are non-regular transactions and need to be corrected by means of a journal entry: the journal entry gives the book-keeper the authority to record the transactions in the double-entry accounts.

■ When error(s) are shown by a trial balance, the amount of the error is placed in a suspense account. As the errors are found, journal entries are made which 'clear out' the suspense account.

■ Correction of errors may have an effect on profit calculated before the errors were found, and on the statement of financial position.

Key Terms

journal — the book of prime entry for non-regular transactions

suspense account — account in which to place an error in the trial balance, pending further investigation

Activities

11.1 Which one of the following will *not* be recorded in the journal?

(a)   credit purchase of a non-current asset

(b)   cash sale of goods to a customer

(c)   write-off of an irrecoverable debt

(d)   correction of an error not shown by the trial balance

Answer (a) or (b) or (c) or (d)

11.2 A trial balance fails to agree by £75 and the difference is placed to a suspense account. Later it is found that a credit sale for this amount has not been entered in the sales account. Which one of the following journal entries is correct?

(a)   debit suspense account £75; credit sales account £75

(b)   debit suspense account £150; credit sales account £150

(c)   debit sales account £75; credit suspense account £75

(d)   credit sales account £75

Answer (a) or (b) or (c) or (d)

11.3 The trial balance of Thomas Wilson balanced. However, a number of errors have been found in the book-keeping system:

(a)   Credit sale of £150 to J Rigby has not been entered in the accounts.

(b)   The cost of a new delivery van, £10,000, has been entered to vehicle expenses account.

(c)   Postages of £55, paid by cheque, have been entered on the wrong sides of both accounts.

(d)   A bank payment for £89 from L Johnson, a trade receivable, has been entered in the accounts as £98.

(e)   The totals of the purchases day book and the purchases returns day book have been undercast by £100.

(f)   A bank payment for £125 to H Price Ltd, a trade payable, has been recorded in the account of H Prince.

You are to take each error in turn and:
- state the type of error
- show the correcting journal entry

Notes:
- *VAT is to be ignored*
- *a blank journal entry is given in the Appendix*

11.4 Jeremy Johnson extracts a trial balance on 30 September 20-7. Unfortunately the trial balance fails to balance and the difference, £19 debit, is placed to a suspense account in the general ledger pending further investigation.

The following errors are later found:

(a) A bank payment of £85 for office expenses has been entered in the cash book but no entry has been made in the office expenses account.

(b) A bank payment for photocopying of £87 by cheque has been correctly entered in the cash book, but is shown as £78 in the photocopying account.

(c) The balance of sales returns account has been recorded in the trial balance as £2,500; further checking shows that the current balance is £2,400.

(d) Commission received of £25 has been entered twice in the account.

You are to:

• show the correcting journal entries

• show the suspense account after the errors have been corrected

Note: a blank journal entry is given in the Appendix

11.5 Show the journal entries for the following transfers which relate to Trish Hall's business for the year ended 31 December 20-8:

(a) Closing inventory is to be recorded in the financial statements at a valuation of £22,600.

(b) Telephone expenses for the year, amounting to £890, are to be transferred to the income statement.

(c) Salaries account shows a balance of £22,950, but £980 is owing; the expenditure for the year is to be transferred to the income statement.

(d) Photocopying expenses account shows a balance of £1,240, but this includes copier rental of £80 in respect of January and February 20-9; the expenditure for the year is to be transferred to the income statement.

(e) Rent received account shows a balance of £4,800, but £400 of this relates to a payment for January 20-9; the income for the year is to be transferred to the income statement.

(f) Depreciation charge on fixtures and fittings for the year is calculated at £500, but no entries have been made in the accounts.

(g) A machine had been bought on 1 January 20-6 for £5,000 (net of VAT). Accumulated depreciation (including the current year) totals £3,750. On 31 December 20-8 the machine is sold for £2,000 (net of VAT) received into the bank.

(h) The following accounts in the sales ledger are to be written off as irrecoverable: Nick Marshall, £55; Crabbe & Company, £30; A Hunt, £40.

These are the only irrecoverable debts during the year; the total is to be transferred to the income statement.

(i) The allowance for doubtful debts is £550; the amount is to be reduced to £450.

Note: a blank journal entry is given in the Appendix

11.6 This Activity is about recording journal entries.

You are working on the financial statements of a business with a year end of 31 March. A trial balance has been drawn up and a suspense account opened with a debit balance of £9,700. You now need to make some corrections and adjustments for the year ended 31 March 20-1.

Record the journal entries needed in the general ledger to deal with the items below. You should:

• remove any incorrect entries, where appropriate

• post the correct entries

You do not need to give narratives.

Do NOT enter zeros into unused column cells.

Ignore VAT.

(a) **Entries need to be made for an irrecoverable debt of £220.**

Journal

	Dr £	Cr £

(b) **A purchase of a delivery vehicle for £12,500 has been made from the bank. The correct entry was made to the bank account, but no other entries were made.**

Journal

	Dr £	Cr £

(c) No entries have been made for closing inventory for the year end 31 March 20-1. Closing inventory has been valued at cost at £25,400. Included in this figure are some items costing £1,850 that will be sold for £1,200.

Journal

	Dr £	Cr £

(d) The figures from the columns of the sales day book for 31 March have been totalled correctly as follows:

Sales column	£7,000
VAT column	£1,400
Total column	£8,400

The amounts have been posted as follows:

Cr Sales	£7,000
Dr VAT	£1,400
Dr Sales ledger control	£8,400

Journal

	Dr £	Cr £

11.7   This Activity is about recording adjustments in the extended trial balance and closing off accounts.

You are working on the financial statements of a business with a year end of 31 March. A trial balance has been drawn up and a suspense account opened with a credit balance of £2,150. You now need to make some corrections and adjustments for the year ended 31 March 20-1.

(a)   **Record the adjustments needed on the extract from the extended trial balance to deal with the items below.**

You will not need to enter adjustments on every line. Do NOT enter zeros into unused cells.

(i)   Entries need to be made for an irrecoverable debt of £78.

(ii)   A payment of £2,500 for rent has been made from the bank account. The correct entry was made in rent paid account, but no other entries were made.

(iii)   No entries have been made for closing inventory for the year end 31 March 20-1. Closing inventory has been valued at cost at £42,000. Included in this figure are some items costing £2,300 that will be sold for £1,500.

(iv)   The figures from the columns of the sales day book for 31 March have been totalled correctly as follows:

Sales column	£2,000
VAT column	£400
Total column	£2,400

The amounts have been posted as follows:

Cr Sales	£2,000
Cr VAT	£400
Dr Sales ledger control	£2,000

Extract from extended trial balance

	Ledger balances		Adjustments	
	Dr £	**Cr** £	**Dr** £	**Cr** £
Allowance for doubtful debts		720		
Bank	9,500			
Closing inventory – statement of financial position				
Closing inventory – income statement				
Depreciation charge	2,000			
Irrecoverable debts				
Office expenses	5,300			
Rent paid	14,200			
Sales		245,000		
Sales ledger control	47,400			
Suspense		2,150		
VAT		7,300		
Vehicles – accumulated depreciation		6,000		

(b) The ledgers are ready to be closed off for the year ended 31 March 20-1. Fill in the account names and tick to show the entries to close off the office expenses account. Give an appropriate narrative.

Account	Dr ✓	Cr ✓
Narrative:		

11.8 This Activity is about completing an extended balance.

You have the following extended trial balance. The adjustments have already been correctly entered.

Extend the figures into the income statement and statement of financial position.

Do NOT enter zeros into unused column cells.

Make the columns balance by entering figures in the correct places.

Extended trial balance

Ledger account	Ledger balances		Adjustments		Income statement		Statement of financial position	
	£ Dr	£ Cr	£ Dr	£ Cr	£ Dr	£ Cr	£ Dr	£ Cr
Allowance for doubtful debts		1,700		200				
Allowance for doubtful debts adjustment			200					
Bank		16,200		300				
Capital		20,500						
Closing inventory			18,500	18,500				
Depreciation charge			3,500					
Office expenses	18,600		400					
Opening inventory	12,500							
Payroll expenses	40,800		200					
Purchases	260,000		1,000					
Purchases ledger control		32,500						
Sales revenue		375,000						
Sales ledger control	60,100							
Selling expenses	21,000							
Suspense	1,300		300	1,600				
VAT		2,900						
Vehicles at cost	45,000							
Vehicles accumulated depreciation		10,500		3,500				
Profit/loss for the year								
	459,300	459,300	24,100	24,100				

Section 2

Accounts Preparation 2

This section focuses on the preparation of conventional year end financial statements for sole traders and partnerships. These use the trial balance, or extended trial balance, as their starting point. Accounting adjustments – accruals and prepayments, depreciation of non-current assets, irrecoverable debts and allowance for doubtful debts – are applied to the financial statements.

Incomplete records shows how techniques such as control accounts, margins and mark-ups, bank statements and journal entries are used to calculate missing figures for the financial statements when double-entry accounts are not in use, or where no trial balance is available.

The financial statements of partnerships include the sharing of profits or losses, and the use of partners' capital and current accounts. The accounting treatments for admission of a partner, retirement of a partner, and changes in profit-sharing ratios are also studied.

12 Sole trader financial statements

this chapter covers...

In this chapter we look at preparing the year end financial statements of a sole trader (that is, one person running their own business) using the conventional format. In Accounts Preparation 1 we have made extensive use of the extended trial balance format to show the income statement (profit and loss account) and the statement of financial position (balance sheet).

The extended trial balance format gives an understanding of the principles of financial statements and it is often used by accountancy firms as a first step towards preparing year end accounts for their clients. We will now take the extended trial balance and develop it into the conventional format of financial statements as used by accountancy firms.

We see the structure of the conventional format income statement and statement of financial position and also revise the accounting equation (which we saw in Chapter 1) and see its effect on the financial statements.

At the end of the financial year, double-entry transfers are made so that items such as sales, purchases, expenses and closing inventory are transferred to the income statement.

SOLE TRADERS

Sole traders are people who run their own business: they run shops, factories, farms, garages, local franchises, etc. The businesses are generally small because the owner usually has a limited amount of capital. Profits are often small and, after the owner has taken out drawings, are usually ploughed back into the business.

advantages and disadvantages

Sole trader businesses are cheap and easy to set up; the **advantages** are:

- the owner has independence and can run the business, often without the need to consult others
- in a small business with few, if any, employees, personal service and supervision by the owner are available at all times
- the business is easy to establish legally – either using the owner's name, or a trading name such as 'The Fashion Shop' or 'Wyvern Plumbers'

The **disadvantages** are:

- the owner has unlimited liability for the debts of the business – this means that if the sole trader should become insolvent, the owner's personal assets may be used to pay business debts
- expansion is limited because it can only be achieved by the owner ploughing back profits, or by borrowing from a lender such as a bank
- the owner usually has to work long hours and it may be difficult to find time to take holidays; if the owner should become ill the work of the business will either slow down or stop altogether

FINANCIAL STATEMENTS AND THE TRIAL BALANCE

financial statements

The financial statements of a sole trader comprise:

- income statement (profit and loss account)
- statement of financial position (balance sheet)

These financial statements can be produced more often than once a year in order to give information to the sole trader on how the business is progressing. However, it is customary to produce annual accounts for the benefit of HM Revenue and Customs, the bank manager and other interested parties. In this way the income statement covers an accounting period of a financial year (which can end at any date – it doesn't have to be the calendar year), and the statement of financial position shows the state of the business at the end of the accounting period.

trial balance

The trial balance provides an initial check of the accuracy of the double-entry book-keeping. As we have seen in Chapter 11, the trial balance will reveal errors in the book-keeping such as:

- one-sided entries

- entry duplicated on one side, nothing on the other

- unequal entries

- account balances incorrectly transferred to the trial balance

We have seen how these errors occur and how to correct them by means of journal entries in Chapter 11.

Once any errors have been corrected, the trial balance then provides the starting point for the preparation of year end financial statements. However, note the limitations of a trial balance:

- there may be errors in the double-entry book-keeping that are not revealed by the trial balance – errors of principle, original error, omission, and reversal of entries (see Chapter 11)

- amounts recorded in the trial balance do not distinguish between those that relate to the income statement and those that relate to the statement of financial position

- the two-column trial balance does not give a profit figure – only when figures from the trial balance are used in the income statement can profit be calculated

- closing inventory needs to be recognised in both the income statement and the statement of financial position as an adjustment to the trial balance

The book-keeper's two-column trial balance is often developed into an extended trial balance – as we saw in Chapter 4. The extended trial balance gives an understanding of the principles of financial statements and is often used by accountancy firms as a first step towards preparing year end accounts for their clients. The way in which accountants present financial statements is often described as being in the conventional format.

Shortly we will use the extended trial balance of Tara Smith (seen in Chapter 4) to prepare her sole trader financial statements, using the conventional format.

INCOME STATEMENT

income   minus   **expenses**   equals   **profit (or loss) for the year**

The income statement (profit and loss account) shows the income a business has received over a given period for goods sold or services provided (together with any small amounts of other income, eg rent received). It also sets out the expenses incurred – the cost of the product, and the expenses (eg wages, administration expenses, rent, and so on). The difference between income and expenses is the profit for the year (net profit) of the business. If expenses are greater than income, then a loss has been made. The profit (or loss) belongs to the owner of the business. For a business that trades in goods, a figure for gross profit shows the profit made before expenses are deducted, and a profit for the year after expenses are deducted.

The format of an income statement is as follows:

	Sales revenue
less	Cost of sales* (cost of purchases of goods, adjustment for change in inventories)
equals	**Gross profit**
less	Expenses (wages, administration expenses, rent, etc)
equals	**Profit for the year (net profit)**

* often referred to as 'cost of goods sold'

Note that where an extended trial balance is being used, profit for the year can be checked against the figure shown in the ETB's income statement columns.

Remember that, by transferring the balances of revenue and expense accounts to the income statement, we are clearing those accounts ready for the start of the next financial year.

STATEMENT OF FINANCIAL POSITION

assets   minus   **liabilities**   equals   **capital**

The statement of financial position (balance sheet) uses the accounting equation (see page 10) to give a 'snapshot' of the business at a particular date – the end of the financial year. A typical business statement of financial position will show:

assets

What the business owns:

- non-current (fixed) assets comprise the long-term items owned by a business:

    - intangible non-current assets which do not have material substance, eg goodwill (the amount paid for the reputation and connections of a business that has been bought – see page 311)

    - tangible non-current assets which have material substance, eg premises, vehicles, machinery, office equipment

- current assets comprise short-term assets which change regularly, eg inventory (stock) held for resale, receivables (debtors), VAT repayable*, bank and cash balances

liabilities

What the business owes:

- current liabilities, where payment is due within twelve months of the date of the statement of financial position, eg payables (creditors), bank overdraft, VAT payable*

- non-current liabilities, where payment is due in more than one year from the date of the statement of financial position, eg loans, mortgages, long-term bank loans

net assets

The total of non-current and current assets, less current and non-current liabilities. The net assets are financed by the owner of the business, in the form of capital. Net assets therefore equals the total of the 'financed by' section – the statement of financial position 'balances'.

capital

Where the resources (eg money) to finance the business have come from – the owner's investment and business profits.

* Note that the balance of VAT control account can be either a current asset or a current liability in the statement of financial position:

- it is a current asset when a business is due on repayment of VAT from HM Revenue and Customs, eg where VAT paid on purchases and expenses exceeds VAT collected on sales, or where a business sells goods that are zero-rated for VAT (eg food, children's clothing) or exempt from VAT (eg postal services, loans of money)

- it is a current liability when a business owes the VAT it has collected on sales, less the VAT paid on purchases and expenses, to HM Revenue and Customs; this is the situation for most businesses

significance of the statement of financial position

The conventional format statement of financial position uses the accounting equation of assets minus liabilities equals capital to show the assets used by the business and how they have been financed. The format is as follows:

	Non-current assets
plus	Net current assets (current assets – current liabilities)
minus	Non-current liabilities
equals	Net assets
equals	Capital

Remember we have seen in Chapter 1, page 10, how every business transaction will change the statement of financial position and the equation – but the equation always balances.

For example, the purchase of a new machine on credit for use in the business has the following effect:

- debit non-current assets (assets)
- credit payables (liabilities)

When the machine is paid for from the bank the effect is:

- debit payables (liabilities)
- credit bank (asset, assuming that there is money in the bank)

If the business had a bank overdraft, the effect of paying for the machine would affect only the liabilities section of the statement of financial position:

- debit payables (liabilities)
- credit bank (liabilities)

In Activities and AAT Assessments you may well be asked to demonstrate your knowledge of the effect of business transactions on the accounting equation.

TARA SMITH: FROM ETB TO FINANCIAL STATEMENTS IN CONVENTIONAL FORMAT

situation

Please refer to the extended trial balance of Tara Smith's business on the next page. (We have seen this before, in Chapter 4.) We will use this ETB to prepare Tara Smith's sole trader financial statements, using the conventional format.

Note that the adjustments for closing inventory are already included in the ledger balance columns.

solution

The ETB does not present the financial statements in the conventional format, as used by accountants. While accountancy firms often use the ETB as a first step, the figures have to be taken from the income statement columns of the ETB and presented in vertical format – running down the page.

Tara Smith's income statement is shown in conventional format on page 233. Study it carefully and see how the figures can be identified on the ETB on the next page. Note that the income statement includes a figure for gross profit (because Tara's business trades in goods) which is the profit made before expenses are deducted, and a profit for the year after expenses are deducted.

Tara Smith's statement of financial position is shown in the conventional format on page 235. Study it carefully and see how the figures can be identified on the ETB shown on the next page.

Tutorial note:

In the income statement (profit and loss account) on page 233 and in the statement of financial position (balance sheet) on page 235 we have used IAS (international accounting standards) terms, and have also shown UK terms in brackets, for example: 'non-current (fixed) assets'.

With the increasing use of IAS terms in the UK, future financial statements in this book will use only IAS terms. A glossary of terms is given on the introduction page for your reference.

AAT Assessments may make use of either IAS or UK terminology.

EXTENDED TRIAL BALANCE   TARA SMITH TRADING AS "THE FASHION SHOP"   31 DECEMBER 20-4

Account name	Ledger balances Dr £	Ledger balances Cr £	Adjustments Dr £	Adjustments Cr £	Income statement Dr £	Income statement Cr £	Statement of financial position Dr £	Statement of financial position Cr £
Opening inventory	12,500				12,500			
Purchases	105,000				105,000			
Sales revenue		155,000				155,000		
Administration expenses	6,200				6,200			
Wages	23,500				23,500			
Rent paid	750				750			
Telephone	500				500			
Interest paid	4,500				4,500			
Travel expenses	550				550			
Premises at cost	100,000						100,000	
Shop fittings at cost	20,000						20,000	
Sales ledger control	10,500						10,500	
Bank	5,450						5,450	
Cash	50						50	
Capital		75,000						75,000
Drawings	7,000						7,000	
Loan from bank		50,000						50,000
Purchases ledger control		14,500						14,500
Value Added Tax		2,000						2,000
Closing inventory: income statement		10,500				10,500		
Closing inventory: statement of financial position	10,500						10,500	
Profit/loss for the year					12,000			12,000
	307,000	307,000			165,500	165,500	153,500	153,500

Income statement includes a figure for gross profit because Tara Smith's business trades in goods. Income statement finishes with profit for the year (net profit) for the accounting period, ie profit after expenses.

The amounts for **sales revenue** and **purchases** include only items in which the business trades – eg a clothes shop buying clothes from the manufacturer and selling to the public. Note that items bought for use in the business, such as a new till for the shop, are not included with purchases but are *capital expenditure* shown as assets on the statement of financial position.

Cost of sales, or cost of goods sold, represents the cost to the business of the goods which have been sold in this financial year. Cost of sales is:

	opening inventory	(inventory bought previously)
plus	purchases	(purchased during the year)
minus	closing inventory	(inventory left unsold at the end of the year)
equals	cost of sales	(cost of what has actually been sold)

Gross profit is calculated as:

sales revenue – cost of sales = gross profit

Expenses, or overheads, are the running costs of the business – known as *revenue expenditure*. The categories of expenses or overheads used vary according to the needs of each business.

Profit for the year (net profit) is calculated as:

gross profit – expenses = profit for the year

If expenses are more than gross profit, the business has made a loss.

The profit for the year is the amount the business earned for the owner, and is subject to taxation. The owner can draw some or all of the profit for personal use in the form of drawings. Part of the profit might well be left in the business in order to help build up the business for the future.

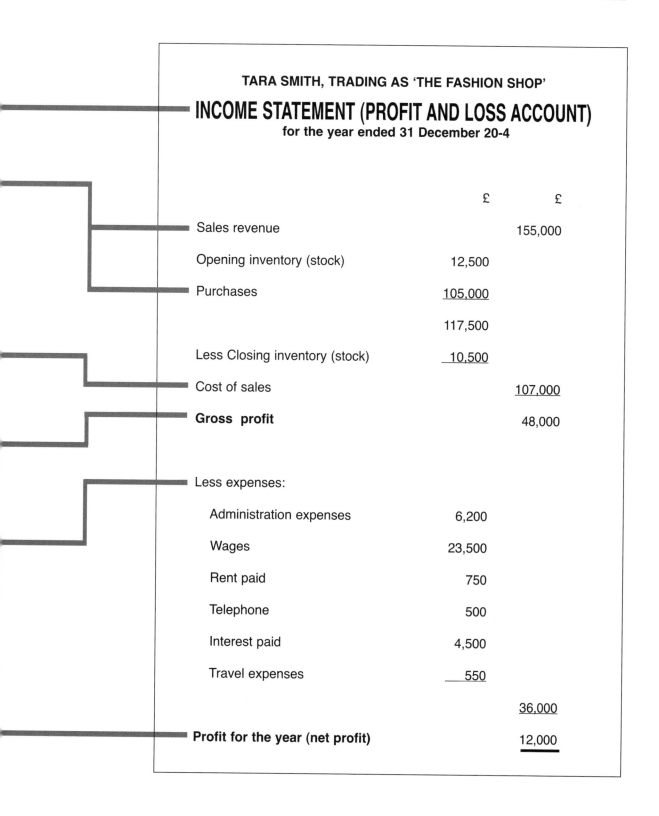

TARA SMITH, TRADING AS 'THE FASHION SHOP'

INCOME STATEMENT (PROFIT AND LOSS ACCOUNT)
for the year ended 31 December 20-4

	£	£
Sales revenue		155,000
Opening inventory (stock)	12,500	
Purchases	105,000	
	117,500	
Less Closing inventory (stock)	10,500	
Cost of sales		107,000
Gross profit		48,000
Less expenses:		
Administration expenses	6,200	
Wages	23,500	
Rent paid	750	
Telephone	500	
Interest paid	4,500	
Travel expenses	550	
		36,000
Profit for the year (net profit)		12,000

Non-current assets comprise the long-term items owned by a business:
- intangible non-current assets, which do not have material substance, eg goodwill (the amount paid for the reputation and connections of a business that has been bought)
- tangible non-current assets, which have material substance, eg premises, vehicles, machinery, office equipment

Current assets comprise short-term assets which change regularly, eg inventory held for resale, receivables, bank balances and cash. These items will alter as the business trades, eg inventory will be sold, or more will be bought; receivables will make payment to the business, or sales on credit will be made; the cash and bank balances will alter with the flow of money paid into the bank account, or as withdrawals are made.

Current liabilities are where payment is due within twelve months of the date of the statement of financial position, eg payables, and bank overdraft (which is usually repayable on demand, unlike a bank loan which is negotiated for a particular time period).

Net current assets is the excess of current assets over current liabilities, ie current assets – current liabilities = net current assets. Without adequate net current assets, a business will find it difficult to continue to operate. Net current assets is also often referred to as *working capital* .

Non-current liabilities are where payment is due in more than one year from the date of the statement of financial position; they are often described by terms such as loans, mortgages, long-term bank loans.

Net assets is the total of non-current and current assets, less current and non-current liabilities. The net assets are financed by the owner of the business, in the form of capital. Net assets therefore equals the total of the 'financed by' section – ie the statement of financial position 'balances'.

Capital is the owner's investment, and is a liability of a business, ie it is what the business owes the owner. Opening capital + profit for the year – drawings = closing capital (the owner's investment at the end of the year, ie the date of the statement of financial position)

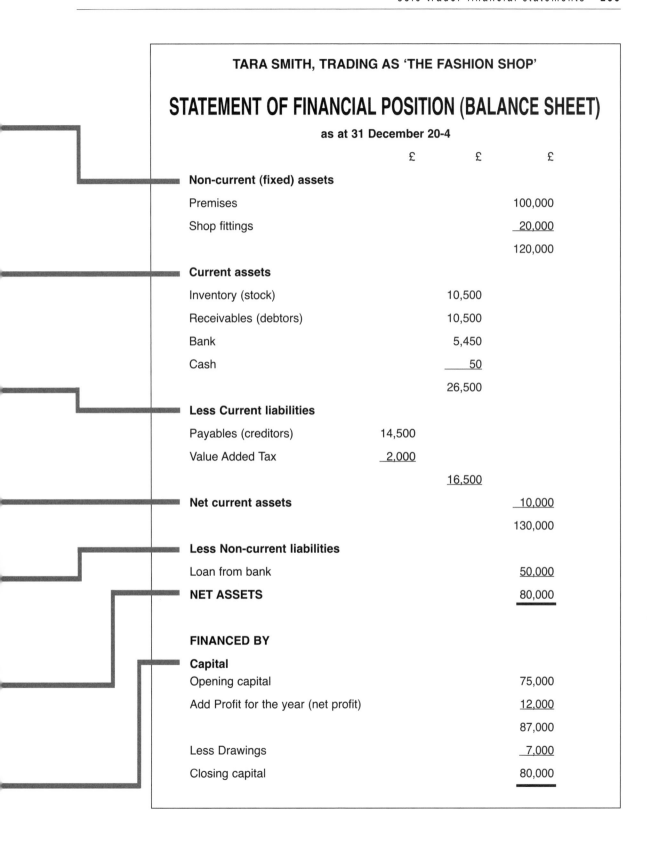

TARA SMITH, TRADING AS 'THE FASHION SHOP'

STATEMENT OF FINANCIAL POSITION (BALANCE SHEET)

as at 31 December 20-4

	£	£	£
Non-current (fixed) assets			
Premises			100,000
Shop fittings			20,000
			120,000
Current assets			
Inventory (stock)		10,500	
Receivables (debtors)		10,500	
Bank		5,450	
Cash		50	
		26,500	
Less Current liabilities			
Payables (creditors)	14,500		
Value Added Tax	2,000		
	16,500		
Net current assets			10,000
			130,000
Less Non-current liabilities			
Loan from bank			50,000
NET ASSETS			80,000
FINANCED BY			
Capital			
Opening capital			75,000
Add Profit for the year (net profit)			12,000
			87,000
Less Drawings			7,000
Closing capital			80,000

PREPARATION OF FINANCIAL STATEMENTS FROM A TRIAL BALANCE

The trial balance contains the basic figures necessary to prepare the year end financial statements but, as we have seen in earlier chapters, the figures are transferred from the double-entry accounts of the business. The information needed for the preparation of the financial statements is picked out from the trial balance in the following way:

- go through the trial balance and write against the items the financial statement in which each appears

- 'tick' each figure as it is used – each item from the trial balance appears in the financial statements once only

- here the closing inventory figure is listed in the trial balance, but may sometimes be shown as a note; you will remember that it appears twice in the financial statements – in the income statement, and in the statement of financial position (as a current asset)

If this routine is followed with the trial balance of Tara Smith, it appears as follows . . .

Trial balance of Tara Smith as at 31 December 20-4				
	Dr £	Cr £		
Opening inventory	12,500		IS (cost of sales)	✔
Purchases	105,000		IS (cost of sales)	✔
Sales revenue		155,000	IS (cost of sales)	✔
Administration expenses	6,200		IS (expense)	✔
Wages	23,500		IS (expense)	✔
Rent paid	750		IS (expense)	✔
Telephone	500		IS (expense)	✔
Interest paid	4,500		IS (expense)	✔
Travel expenses	550		IS (expense)	✔
Premises at cost	100,000		SFP (non-current asset)	✔
Shop fittings at cost	20,000		SFP (non-current asset)	✔
Sales ledger control	10,500		SFP (current asset)	✔
Bank	5,450		SFP (current asset)	✔
Cash	50		SFP (current asset)	✔
Capital		75,000	SFP (capital)	✔
Drawings	7,000		SFP (capital)	✔
Loan from bank		50,000	SFP (non-current liabs)	✔
Purchases ledger control		14,500	SFP (current liability)	✔
Value Added Tax		2,000	SFP (current liability)	✔
Closing inventory: income statement		10,500	IS (cost of sales)	✔
Closing inventory: statement of financial position	10,500		SFP (current asset)	✔
	307,000	307,000		

Note: IS = income statement; SFP - statement of financial position

In the trial balance illustrated here, items are grouped together – for example, all the income statement expenses are listed together. This has been done to help you at these early stages in the preparation of conventional financial statements.

However, this grouping into categories will not always be the case. In particular, in Activities and Assessments, you will often find that the items listed in the trial balance appear in alphabetical order. This does have the effect of, for example, putting administration expenses (an income statement expense) next to bank (which appears in the statement of financial position). It is time well spent to go through the trial balance carefully and to indicate where each item appears in the financial statements.

double-entry transfers for income and expenses

All of the items in the trial balance marked 'IS' must be transferred to the income statement by means of a double-entry transfer. Such items are for sales, purchases, expenses and closing inventory – the accounts are closed off at the end of the year by transfer to the income statement. These accounts will then be ready to record business transactions in the next financial year.

Examples of double-entry transfers, using amounts from Tara Smith's trial balance are as follows:

income account

Dr		Sales revenue account			Cr
20-4		£	20-4		£
31 Dec	Income statement	155,000	31 Dec	Balance b/d	155,000

amount transferred to income statement

amount shown in the trial balance

cost of sales and expenses accounts

Dr		Purchases account			Cr
20-4		£	20-4		£
31 Dec	Balance b/d	105,000	31 Dec	Income statement	105,000

amount shown in the trial balance

amount transferred to income statement

Dr		Administration expenses account			Cr
20-4		£	20-4		£
31 Dec	Balance b/d	6,200	31 Dec	Income statement	6,200

All other expenses accounts – in Tara Smith's trial balance for wages, rent paid, telephone, interest paid and travel expenses – are closed off by transfer to the income statement in the same way.

inventory account

Dr			Inventory account			Cr
20-4		£	20-4			£
31 Dec	Balance b/d	12,500	31 Dec	Income statement		12,500
31 Dec	Income statement	10,500				

closing inventory of £10,500 transferred from income statement; the amount is an asset which is shown on the statement of financial position

opening inventory of £12,500 transferred to income statement

Note that there are other ways of accounting for closing inventory: a cost of sales account can be used (see page 258), or separate accounts can be used for opening and closing inventory.

profit and drawings

Profit for the year and the amount of drawings relate to the owner of the business. The amounts are transferred to capital account as follows:

Dr			Capital account			Cr
20-4		£	20-4			£
31 Dec	Drawings	7,000	31 Dec	Balance b/d		75,000
31 Dec	Balance c/d	80,000	31 Dec	Profit for the year		12,000
		87,000				87,000
20-5			20-5			
			1 Jan	Balance b/d		80,000

£80,000 is the amount of closing capital on the statement of financial position (see page 235)

assets and liabilities

All of the remaining items from the trial balance form the assets and liabilities of the statement of financial position. The account balances are carried forward into next year's financial statements.

The balance of capital account is shown in the 'financed by' section where it is usual to show the following:

	Opening capital
add	Profit for the year
less	Drawings
equals	Closing capital

FINANCIAL STATEMENTS: POINTS TO NOTE

assets and the order of liquidity

In the statement of financial position it is customary to list the assets – non-current assets and current assets – in an 'increasing order of liquidity'. In accounting, liquidity means nearness to cash, so the most permanent assets – ie those that are furthest away from cash – are listed first. Thus premises, which would take time to turn into cash, heads the list, with other non-current assets – such as shop fittings, machinery and vehicles – following. For current assets, the usual order is to start with inventory, then receivables, bank (if not overdrawn), and cash. In this way, the assets are listed from the most permanent (usually premises) to the most liquid (cash itself).

The reason for this order is historical – nineteenth-century business owners wanted to impress upon readers of their financial statements the solid assets that they owned. The top line of the balance sheet (as it was known in the nineteenth century) was the first to be read and that showed the value of their premises. The following lines listed their other assets. This traditional approach lives on into twenty-first century financial statements.

adjustments to financial statements

Whilst the starting point for the preparation of financial statements is the book-keeper's two-column trial balance, if we used only the trial balance figures (which record the financial transactions that have taken place) the resultant financial statements would show an inaccurate picture of the state of the business. Adjustments are made with the aim of improving the accuracy of the financial statements in showing the profit, and the assets and liabilities of the business.

The main adjustments to financial statements are for:

- closing inventory
- accruals and prepayments of expenses and income
- depreciation of non-current assets
- irrecoverable debts written off
- allowance for doubtful debts

In Chapters 4, 5, 6 and 7 we have already seen how these adjustments affect the extended trial balance, and we also looked at the double-entry accounting involved. In the next chapter we see how these adjustments affect the conventional format financial statements.

SOLE TRADER FINANCIAL STATEMENTS: LAYOUT

A layout or pro-forma for the financial statements of a sole trader is included in the Appendix. This may be photocopied (it is advisable to enlarge it up to A4 size); alternatively, the layout can be downloaded from the website www.osbornebooks.co.uk. It shows:

– an income statement
– a statement of financial position

Note that when used for partnership financial statements (see Chapter 15), the layout will need to be adjusted to take note of the appropriation of profits and of the partners' capital and current accounts.

FURTHER ITEMS IN FINANCIAL STATEMENTS

There are a number of further double-entry items that may have to be incorporated into the income statement. These items include:

• carriage in
• carriage out
• sales returns
• purchases returns
• discount received
• discount allowed

carriage in

This is the expense to a buyer of the carriage (transport) costs. For example, if an item is purchased on the internet, the buyer usually has to pay the additional cost of delivery.

In an income statement, the cost of carriage in is added to the cost of purchases. The reason for doing this is so that all purchases are at a 'delivered to the door' price.

carriage out

This is where the seller pays the expense of the carriage charge. For example, an item is sold to the customer and described as 'post free' or 'carriage free'.

In the income statement, the cost of carriage out on sales is shown as an expense of the business.

sales returns

Sales returns (or *returns in*) is where a credit customer returns goods to the business.

In conventional format financial statements, the amount of sales returns is deducted from the figure for sales revenue in the income statement.

purchases returns

Purchases returns (or *returns out*) is where a business returns goods to a supplier.

In conventional format financial statements, the amount of purchases returns is deducted from the figure for purchases in the income statement.

discount received

Discount received is an allowance offered by suppliers on purchases invoice amounts for quick settlement, eg 2% cash discount for settlement within seven days.

In financial statements, the amount of discount received is shown in the income statement as income received.

discount allowed

This is an allowance offered to customers on sales invoice amounts for quick settlement.

In financial statements, the amount of discount allowed is shown in the income statement as an expense.

NATASHA MORGAN:
INCOME STATEMENT – FURTHER ITEMS

situation

An extract from the trial balance of Natasha Morgan is as follows:

Trial balance (extract) as at 30 June 20-8

	Dr £	Cr £
Opening inventory	12,350	
Sales revenue		250,000
Purchases	156,000	
Sales returns	5,400	
Purchases returns		7,200
Carriage in	1,450	
Carriage out	3,250	
Discount received		2,500
Discount allowed	3,700	
Other expenses	78,550	
Closing inventory: income statement		16,300

Natasha asks for your help in the preparation of her income statement, using the conventional format.

solution

There are a number of further items to be incorporated into the layout of the income statement. In particular, the calculation of cost of sales is made in the following way:

	opening inventory
+	purchases
+	carriage in
–	purchases returns
–	closing inventory
=	cost of sales

The income statement for Natasha Morgan's business is shown on the next page. Note the use of three money columns.

NATASHA MORGAN
INCOME STATEMENT
for the year ended 30 June 20-8

	£	£	£
Sales revenue			250,000
Less Sales returns			5,400
Net sales revenue			244,600
Opening inventory		12,350	
Purchases	156,000		
Add Carriage in	1,450		
	157,450		
Less Purchases returns	7,200		
Net purchases		150,250	
		162,600	
Less Closing inventory		16,300	
Cost of sales			146,300
Gross profit			98,300
Add income: Discount received			2,500
			100,800
Less expenses:			
Discount allowed		3,700	
Carriage out		3,250	
Other expenses		78,550	
			85,500
Profit for the year			15,300

SERVICE SECTOR BUSINESSES

The financial statements of a service sector business – such as a secretarial agency, solicitor, estate agent, doctor – do not normally include a calculation of gross profit. This is because the business, instead of trading in goods, supplies services.

The income statement commences with the income from the business activity – such as 'fees', 'income from clients', 'charges', 'work done'. Other items of income – such as discount received – are added, and the expenses are then listed and deducted to give the profit or (loss) for the year. An example of a service sector income statement is shown on the next page:

JEMMA SMITH, TRADING AS 'WYVERN SECRETARIAL AGENCY'
INCOME STATEMENT
for the year ended 31 December 20-8

	£	£
Income from clients		110,000
Less expenses:		
Salaries	64,000	
Heating and lighting	2,000	
Telephone	2,000	
Rent and rates	6,000	
Sundry expenses	3,000	
		77,000
Profit for the year		**33,000**

The layout of the statement of financial position for a service sector business is identical to that seen earlier (page 235); the only difference is that there is unlikely to be much, if any, inventory in the current assets section.

Chapter Summary

■ Sole traders are people who run their own business; generally their businesses are small because the owner usually has a limited amount of capital.

■ The extended trial balance (ETB) format is a first step towards preparing year end financial statements. From the ETB can be developed financial statements in the conventional format used by accountants.

■ The trial balance provides
  – an initial check of the accuracy of the double-entry book-keeping
  – the starting point for the preparation of year end financial statements

■ In the conventional format, the financial statements of a sole trader comprise
  – income statement (which may include a figure for gross profit)
  – statement of financial position

■ Further book-keeping items incorporated into financial statements include
  – carriage in
  – carriage out
  – sales returns
  – purchases returns
  – discount received
  – discount allowed

■ The next chapter shows how adjustments for accruals and prepayments, depreciation of non-current assets, irrecoverable debts and allowance for doubtful debts are dealt with in conventional format financial statements.

Key Terms

conventional format	the form of financial statements used by accountants
sole trader	one person running their own business
service sector business	a business which supplies services, eg secretarial agency, solicitor, estate agent
gross profit	sales revenue minus cost of sales, ie the profit made before expenses are deducted
profit for the year	gross profit minus expenses, ie the profit which belongs to the owner of the business
assets	items owned by the business, split between non-current assets and current assets
liabilities	items owed by the business, split between current liabilities and non-current liabilities
capital	the owner's investment in the business

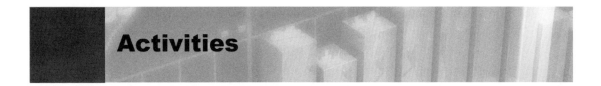

Activities

Blank photocopiable layouts of the income statement and the statement of financial position are included in the Appendix – it is advisable to enlarge them up to A4 size.

12.1   This Activity is about calculating missing balances and the accounting equation.

You are given the following information about a sole trader as at 1 April 20-6:

The value of assets and liabilities was:

- Non-current assets at carrying amount   £21,500
- Trade receivables   £8,750
- Bank (overdrawn)   £1,290
- Trade payables   £5,480

There were no other assets or liabilities.

(a)   Calculate the capital account balance as at 1 April 20-6.

£

(b)   On 30 April 20-6, a new vehicle is purchased on credit for use in the business. Tick the boxes to show what effect this transaction will have on the balances. You must choose ONE answer for EACH line.

	Debit ✓	Credit ✓	No change ✓
Non-current assets			
Trade receivables			
Trade payables			
Bank			
Capital			

(c)   Which of the following is best described as a current liability? Tick ONE answer.

	✓
A bank loan repayable in two years' time	
A bank overdraft	
Drawings by the owner of the business	
Inventory sold and awaiting collection by the customer	

12.2 The following trial balance has been extracted by Nick Johnson on 31 December 20-3:

	Dr £	Cr £
Opening inventory	25,000	
Purchases	210,000	
Sales revenue		310,000
Administration expenses	12,400	
Wages	41,000	
Rent paid	7,500	
Telephone	1,000	
Interest paid	9,000	
Travel expenses	1,100	
Premises at cost	200,000	
Machinery at cost	40,000	
Sales ledger control	31,000	
Bank	900	
Cash	100	
Capital		150,000
Drawings	14,000	
Loan from bank		100,000
Purchases ledger control		29,000
Value Added Tax		4,000
Closing inventory: income statement		21,000
Closing inventory: statement of financial position	21,000	
	614,000	614,000

You are to prepare the financial statements of Nick Johnson for the year ended 31 December 20-3, using the conventional format.

12.3   The following trial balance has been extracted by the book-keeper of Alan Harris at 30 June 20-4:

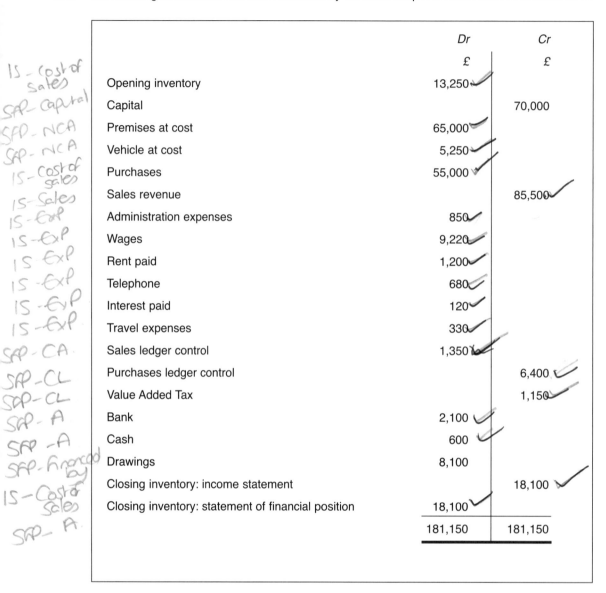

	Dr	Cr
	£	£
Opening inventory	13,250	
Capital		70,000
Premises at cost	65,000	
Vehicle at cost	5,250	
Purchases	55,000	
Sales revenue		85,500
Administration expenses	850	
Wages	9,220	
Rent paid	1,200	
Telephone	680	
Interest paid	120	
Travel expenses	330	
Sales ledger control	1,350	
Purchases ledger control		6,400
Value Added Tax		1,150
Bank	2,100	
Cash	600	
Drawings	8,100	
Closing inventory: income statement		18,100
Closing inventory: statement of financial position	18,100	
	181,150	181,150

You are to prepare the financial statements of Alan Harris for the year ended 30 June 20-4, using the conventional format.

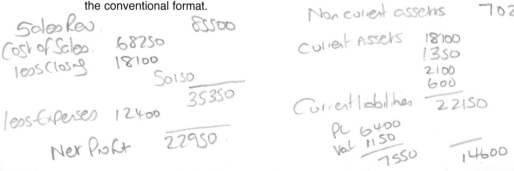

12.4 An extract from the trial balance of Christine Lorraine is as follows:

Trial balance (extract) as at 30 June 20-1

	Dr	Cr
	£	£
Opening inventory	15,140	
Sales revenue		175,000
Purchases	102,000	
Sales returns	4,100	
Purchases returns		8,300
Carriage in	1,210	
Carriage out	5,680	
Discount received		790
Discount allowed	1,460	
Other expenses	58,230	
Closing inventory: income statement		18,350

You are to prepare the income statement of Christine Lorraine for the year ended 30 June 20-1, using the conventional format.

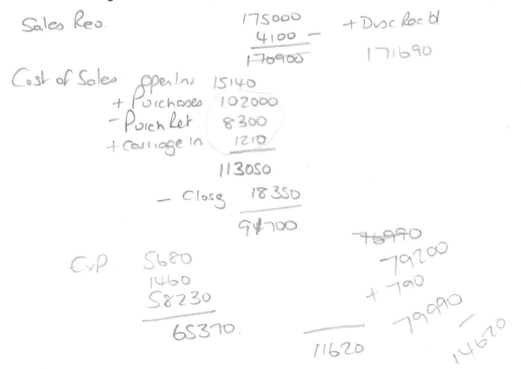

13 Adjustments to sole trader financial statements

this chapter covers...

This chapter shows how conventional format financial statements are adjusted to

- *present a more relevant and reliable view of profit, and assets and liabilities*
- *enable comparisons to be made with financial statements from previous years*
- *enable users of financial statements to understand the information given*

We begin by considering how the accounting policies of a business fit in with the objectives of relevance, reliability, comparability and ease of understanding. All of these help to make financial information useful to users of financial statements.

The chapter continues with conventional format financial statements by bringing together into a trial balance the adjustments for:

- *closing inventory*
- *accruals and prepayments*
- *depreciation of non-current assets*
- *irrecoverable debts*
- *allowance for doubtful debts*

We have already seen in Chapters 4, 5, 6 and 7 how these adjustments affect the extended trial balance – together with the double-entry accounting involved. In this chapter we see how these adjustments are incorporated into the conventional format financial statements.

ACCOUNTING POLICIES

Accounting policies are the methods used by a business to show the effect of business transactions, and to record assets and liabilities in the statement of financial position. For example, a business may choose as its accounting policy to depreciate its office equipment, using the straight-line method, at 25 per cent per year.

In order for financial information to be useful, it is important for a business to select its accounting policies to fit in with the objectives of:

- *relevance* – financial information that is useful to users of the financial statements

- *reliability* – financial information that can be depended upon by users

- *comparability* – financial statements that can be compared with those from previous years

- *ease of understanding* – users of the financial statements can understand the information given

These four objectives that make financial information useful are shown in the following diagram.

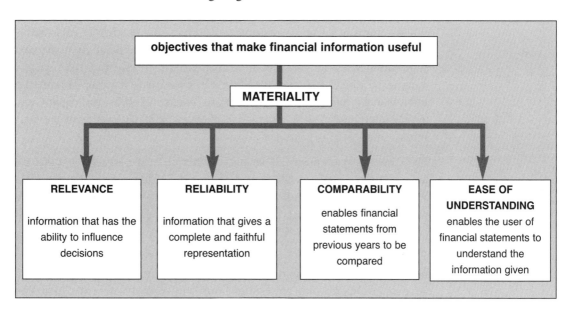

For financial information to be relevant, it must also be *material*. The accounting concept of materiality has been discussed earlier (page 128). What it means is that information is material when its omission or misstatement could have an influence on decisions made by users of financial statements – eg to invest, or not to invest, in a business.

In practical terms, materiality means that items above a certain money amount are recorded separately in the accounts – eg the purchase cost of non-current assets such as a new vehicle – while items below the money amount are recorded together as expenses – eg the purchase cost of waste paper baskets for the office. If information is not material, then it cannot be relevant in the preparation of financial statements or to the users of the information.

Of course, materility depends very much on the size of the busines. For example, a large company may consider that the cost of items of less than £1,000 are not material; by contrast, a small business may use a much lower amount, perhaps £100. It is for a business to set a policy as to what amount is material and what is not. As an accounts assistant, the business policy manual will give guidance; for further clarification, you should consult the accounts supervisor.

FINANCIAL STATEMENTS: THE ADJUSTMENTS

Many Activities and Assessments focus on aspects of the preparation of financial statements in the conventional format used by accountants. For example, you may be asked to prepare some, or all, of an income statement and statement of financial position. There may be a number of adjustments incorporated into the year end financial statements. The diagram on the next page summarises the year end adjustments and their effect on the financial statements. Remember that the adjustments are made in order to present a more relevant and reliable view of profit, assets, liabilities and capital, and to enable comparisons to be made with financial statements from previous years.

The Case Study on page 254 brings together all of the adjustments that we have seen previously in Chapters 4, 5, 6 and 7. Although in total the Case Study is more complex than would be required in an Assessment, it does provide a useful reference point which shows the adjustments incorporated into the financial statements of a sole trader.

The Activities at the end of this chapter are based on the preparation of financial statements from a trial balance and provide practice to help with your studies in preparing conventional format financial statements. Note that in AAT Assessments you will always be given a balancing trial balance, which incorporates the adjustments; you will also be given an outline 'pro-forma' of the financial statements.

SUMMARY OF YEAR END ADJUSTMENTS FOR FINANCIAL STATEMENTS		
ADJUSTMENT	**INCOME STATEMENT**	**STATEMENT OF FINANCIAL POSITION**
closing inventory	• deduct from purchases	• current asset
accrual of expenses	• add to expense	• current liability
prepayment of expenses	• deduct from expense	• current asset
accrual of income	• add to income	• current asset
prepayment of income	• deduct from income	• current liability
depreciation charge/ accumulated depreciation of non-current assets	• depreciation charge: expense	• non-current assets reduced by accumulated depreciation to give carrying amount
irrecoverable debts	• expense	• deduct from trade receivables
disposal of non-current asset	• debit balance: expense • credit balance: income	• non-current assets reduced by disposal
creation of, or increase in, allowance for doubtful debts	• expense	• trade receivables figure reduced by total amount of allowance
decrease in allowance for doubtful debts	• income	• trade receivables figure reduced by total amount of allowance
goods taken by the owner for own use	• deduct from purchases	• add to drawings

Note that, in AAT Assessments, you may be required to combine account balances before transferring the net amount or total amount to the income statement or statement of financial position. Examples include sales minus sales returns equals net sales, purchases minus purchases returns equals net purchases, trade receivables less allowance for doubtful debts equals net trade receivables. An Assessment will always tell you when such combining is to be done – usually in the form of a statement of the business' policy.

Case Study

1.850

1.600

SOLE TRADER FINANCIAL STATEMENTS

situation

You are the accountant to Olivia Boulton, a sole trader, who runs a kitchen and cookware shop. Her book-keeper extracted the year end trial balance and you have incorporated into it the adjustments advised to you by Olivia Boulton. The adjusted trial balance is as follows:

Trial balance of Olivia Boulton as at 31 December 20-2

	Dr £	Cr £
Opening inventory	50,000	
Purchases	420,000	
Sales revenue		557,500
Closing inventory	42,000	42,000
Shop expenses	6,200	
Shop wages	33,300	
Prepayment of shop wages	200	
Telephone expenses	600	
Accrual of telephone expenses		100
Interest paid	8,000	
Travel expenses	550	
Discounts allowed	450	
Discounts received		900
Disposal of non-current asset		250
Premises at cost	250,000	
Shop fittings at cost	40,000	
Premises: depreciation charge	5,000	
Shop fittings: depreciation charge	6,400	
Premises: accumulated depreciation		15,000
Shop fittings: accumulated depreciation		14,400
Sales ledger control	10,000	
Irrecoverable debts	500	
Allowance for doubtful debts		250
Allowance for doubtful debts: adjustment	50	
Purchases ledger control		11,250
Bank	2,650	
Capital		125,000
Drawings	24,000	
Loan from bank (repayable in 20-9)		130,000
Value Added Tax		3,250
	899,900	899,900

You are to prepare the financial statements of Olivia Boulton for the year ended 31 December 20-2, using the conventional format.

solution

The financial statements incorporating these adjustments are shown on the next two pages. A summary of the effect of each adjustment is given below.

closing inventory

- deduct £42,000 from purchases in the income statement
- show inventory at £42,000 as a current asset in the statement of financial position

prepayment of expenses

- show £200 prepayment of shop wages as a current asset in the statement of financial position

accrual of expenses

- show £100 accrual of telephone expenses as a current liability in the statement of financial position

depreciation of non-current assets

- in the income statement show as expenses the depreciation charges for premises £5,000 and shop fittings £6,400
- in the statement of financial position show accumulated depreciation amounts deducted from non-current assets to give carrying amounts (net book values) as follows:

	£	£	£
	Cost	Accumulated depreciation	Carrying amount
Premises	250,000	15,000	235,000
Shop fittings	40,000	14,400	25,600
	290,000	29,400	260,600

disposal of non-current asset

During the year a non-current asset has been sold. The book-keeping entries for disposals have been made and all that remains is a credit balance of £250 on disposals account. This amount is shown as income, being a profit on disposal, in the income statement. (A debit balance on disposals account would mean a loss on disposal – this would be shown as an expense in the income statement.)

irrecoverable debts

- record irrecoverable debts of £500 as an expense in the income statement

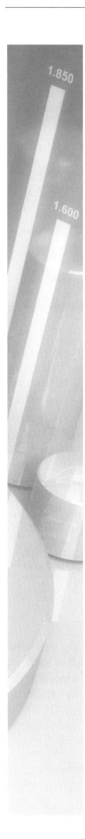

allowance for doubtful debts: adjustment

- in the income statement record the £50 amount of the increase (debit side of trial balance) in allowance for doubtful debts as an expense

- in the statement of financial position deduct £250 from the trade receivables figure of £10,000 to give net receivables of £9,750 – it is this amount that is listed in current assets

Note that, where there is a reduction in the allowance for doubtful debts, show the amount of the reduction as income in the income statement.

financial statements

The financial statements of Olivia Boulton that you prepare are shown below.

<table>
<tr><td colspan="3" align="center">**OLIVIA BOULTON**
INCOME STATEMENT
for the year ended 31 December 20-2</td></tr>
<tr><td></td><td align="center">£</td><td align="center">£</td></tr>
<tr><td>Sales revenue</td><td></td><td>557,500</td></tr>
<tr><td>Opening inventory</td><td>50,000</td><td></td></tr>
<tr><td>Purchases</td><td>420,000</td><td></td></tr>
<tr><td></td><td>470,000</td><td></td></tr>
<tr><td>Less Closing inventory</td><td>42,000</td><td></td></tr>
<tr><td>Cost of sales</td><td></td><td>428,000</td></tr>
<tr><td>**Gross profit**</td><td></td><td>129,500</td></tr>
<tr><td>Add other income:</td><td></td><td></td></tr>
<tr><td>Discounts received</td><td></td><td>900</td></tr>
<tr><td>Profit on disposal of non-current asset</td><td></td><td>250</td></tr>
<tr><td></td><td></td><td>130,650</td></tr>
<tr><td>Less expenses:</td><td></td><td></td></tr>
<tr><td>Shop expenses</td><td>6,200</td><td></td></tr>
<tr><td>Shop wages</td><td>33,300</td><td></td></tr>
<tr><td>Telephone</td><td>600</td><td></td></tr>
<tr><td>Interest paid</td><td>8,000</td><td></td></tr>
<tr><td>Travel expenses</td><td>550</td><td></td></tr>
<tr><td>Discounts allowed</td><td>450</td><td></td></tr>
<tr><td>Depreciation charges: premises</td><td>5,000</td><td></td></tr>
<tr><td>shop fittings</td><td>6,400</td><td></td></tr>
<tr><td>Irrecoverable debts</td><td>500</td><td></td></tr>
<tr><td>Allowance for doubtful debts: adjustment</td><td>50</td><td></td></tr>
<tr><td></td><td></td><td>61,050</td></tr>
<tr><td>**Profit for the year**</td><td></td><td>69,600</td></tr>
</table>

Note that the balances of accounts such as discounts received, interest received, commission received, profit on disposal of non-current asset etc are listed in the income statement under the heading of **other income**.

STATEMENT OF FINANCIAL POSITION
as at 31 December 20-2

	£	£	£
Non-current assets	Cost	Accumulated depreciation	Carrying amount
Premises	250,000	15,000	235,000
Shop fittings	40,000	14,400	25,600
	290,000	29,400	260,600
Current assets			
Inventory		42,000	
Trade receivables	10,000		
Less allowance for doubtful debts	250		
		9,750	
Prepayment of expenses		200	
Bank		2,650	
		54,600	
Less Current liabilities			
Trade payables	11,250		
Accrual of expenses	100		
Value Added Tax	3,250		
		14,600	
Net current assets			40,000
			300,600
Less Non-current liabilities			
Loan from bank			130,000
NET ASSETS			170,600
FINANCED BY			
Capital			
Opening capital			125,000
Add Profit for the year			69,600
			194,600
Less Drawings			24,000
Closing capital			170,600

THE USE OF COST OF SALES ACCOUNT

In some trial balances there is a debit column balance given for cost of sales (also referred to as cost of goods sold). This happens because the cost of sales calculation has been done already, and no amounts are shown in the trial balance for:

- in the debit column
  - opening inventory
  - purchases
- in the credit column
  - purchases returns (if any)
  - closing inventory (but the debit column balance for closing inventory is still shown, as this is the amount which is an asset for the statement of financial position)

The calculation for cost of sales (cost of goods sold) is:

	Opening inventory
plus	Purchases
less	Purchases returns (if any)
less	Closing inventory
equals	Cost of sales

It is the final figure for cost of sales that is shown in the debit column of the trial balance – the other amounts are not shown – when the business is using a cost of sales account.

cost of sales account

This account brings together the amounts that make up cost of sales, as follows (using the figures from Olivia Boulton's trial balance on page 254):

Dr		Cost of sales account		Cr
20-2		£	20-2	£
31 Dec	Opening inventory	50,000	31 Dec Purchases returns*	–
31 Dec	Purchases	420,000	31 Dec Closing inventory	42,000
			31 Dec Balance c/d	428,000
		470,000		470,000
31 Dec	Balance b/d	428,000	31 Dec Income statement	428,000

* Note: there were no purchases returns in Olivia Boulton's trial balance

The balance of cost of sales account, £428,000, is transferred to the income statement where it is deducted from sales to give gross profit:

OLIVIA BOULTON
INCOME STATEMENT (extract)
for the year ended 31 December 20-2

	£	£
Sales revenue (less sales returns, if any)		557,500
Less Cost of sales		428,000
Gross profit		129,500

As you see, this is the same gross profit as we have seen already on page 256, but here gross profit has been calculated in just three lines (although there may be sales returns to deduct from sales revenue). The rest of the income statement continues as we have seen previously.

summary

In Activities and Assessments you should be ready for a trial balance to present you with two different circumstances:

either

- full cost of sales amounts
    - opening inventory, in debit column
    - purchases, in debit column
    - purchases returns (if any), in credit column
    - closing inventory, in both debit and credit columns (remember that the debit amount is an asset on the statement of financial position, while the credit amount is used in cost of sales)

or

- cost of sales account
    - cost of sales, in debit column
    - closing inventory, in debit column (an asset on the statement of financial position)

In the first circumstance you will need to calculate the figure for cost of sales on the face of the income statement. In the second circumstance it is only necessary to deduct cost of sales from the figure for sales (allowing for sales returns, if any) in order to calculate the gross profit figure – after gross profit,

Chapter Summary

the income statement continues as we have seen previously.

- ■ Accounting policies are selected to fit in with the objectives of
  - relevance
  - reliability
  - comparability
  - ease of understanding

- ■ For financial information to be relevant, it must also be material.

- ■ Adjustments are made to financial statements in order to improve their relevance and reliability.

- ■ A fully adjusted trial balance incorporates the adjustments for
  - closing inventory
  - accruals and prepayments
  - depreciation of non-current assets
  - irrecoverable debts
  - allowance for doubtful debts

- ■ A cost of sales account enables the income statement to show gross profit in three lines:

  sales revenue, less sales returns (if any)
  - cost of sales
  = gross profit

Key Terms

accounting policies
methods used by a business to show the effect of business transactions, and to record assets and liabilities in the statement of financial position

adjusted trial balance
trial balance which incorporates the accounting adjustments and from which financial statements can be prepared

cost of sales account
account which brings together amounts that make up cost of sales:

opening inventory
+ purchases
- purchases returns (if any)
- closing inventory
= cost of sales

Activities

Blank photocopiable layouts of the income statement and the statement of financial position are included in the Appendix – it is advisable to enlarge them up to A4 size.

13.1 An income statement shows a profit for the year of £10,500. It is discovered that no allowance has been made for wages prepaid of £250 and administration expenses accrued of £100 at the year end. What is the adjusted profit for the year?

(a)   £10,150
(b)   £10,350
(c)   £10,650
(d)   £10,850

Answer (a) or (b) or (c) or (d)

13.2 A year end trial balance includes the following amounts:

opening inventory	£5,500
closing inventory	£6,500
purchases	£25,000
sales revenue	£48,000
purchases returns	£1,000
sales returns	£2,000

What is the cost of sales figure for the year?

(a)   £23,000
(b)   £25,000
(c)   £26,000
(d)   £47,000

Answer (a) or (b) or (c) or (d)

13.3 An income statement shows a profit for the year of £15,750. The owner of the business wishes to reduce the allowance for doubtful debts by £500 and to write off irrecoverable debts of £300. What is the adjusted profit for the year?

(a)   £14,950
(b)   £15,550
(c)   £15,950
(d)   £16,550

Answer (a) or (b) or (c) or (d)

13.4 You have the following trial balance for a sole trader known as Zelah Trading. All the necessary year end adjustments have been made.

(a) **Prepare an income statement (on the next page) for the business for the year ended 31 March 20-4.**

Zelah Trading Trial balance as at 31 March 20-4	Dr £	Cr £
Accruals		950
Bank	3,220	
Capital		22,000
Closing inventory	6,500	6,500
Depreciation charge	3,400	
Discounts allowed	750	
Drawings	6,500	
General expenses	21,240	
Machinery at cost	24,200	
Machinery: accumulated depreciation		8,400
Opening inventory	4,850	
Prepayments	650	
Purchases	85,260	
Purchases ledger control		11,360
Rent	8,900	
Sales revenue		155,210
Sales ledger control	15,350	
Selling expenses	27,890	
Value Added Tax		4,290
	208,710	208,710

Zelah Trading Income statement for the year ended 31 March 20-4		
	£	£
Sales revenue		155210
less Opening Inventory	*4850*	
Purchases	*85260*	
Closg Inverby	*6500*	
Cost of sales	*83610*	
Gross profit		*71600*
Less expenses:		
Dep Chage	*3400*	
Disc Allowed	*750*	
General Exp	*21240*	
Rent	*8900*	
Selg Exp	*27890*	
Total expenses	*62180*	
Profit for the year		*9420*

(b) Indicate where closing inventory should be shown in the statement of financial position. Tick ONE from:

	✓
As a non-current asset	
As a current asset	✓
As a current liability	
As a deduction from capital	

(c) State the meaning of a credit balance for Value Added Tax in a trial balance. Tick ONE from:

	✓
HM Revenue and Customs owes the business	
HM Revenue and Customs is a receivable of the business	
There is an error – VAT is always a debit balance	
The business owes HM Revenue and Customs	✓

13.5 The following adjusted trial balance has been taken from the books of Helena Ostrowska, who sells soft furnishings, as at 31 March 20-5:

	Dr £	Cr £
Sales ledger control	46,280	
Purchases ledger control		24,930
Value Added Tax		3,860
Bank	10,180	
Capital		62,000
Sales revenue		243,820
Purchases	140,950	
Opening inventory	30,030	
Shop wages	40,270	
Accrual of shop wages		940
Heat and light	3,470	
Prepayment of heat and light	220	
Rent and rates	12,045	
Shop fittings at cost	30,000	
Shop fittings: depreciation charge	5,000	
Shop fittings: accumulated depreciation		15,000
Disposal of non-current asset	850	
Irrecoverable debts	200	
Drawings	31,055	
Closing inventory	34,080	34,080
	384,630	384,630

You are to prepare the financial statements of Helena Ostrowska for the year ended 31 March 20-5, using the conventional format.

13.6 The following adjusted trial balance has been taken from the books of Mark Pelisi, a landscape gardener, as at 31 March 20-7:

	Dr £	Cr £
Sales revenue		100,330
Sales returns	120	
Cost of sales	35,710	
Discounts allowed and received	170	240
Drawings	30,090	
Vehicles at cost	24,000	
Vehicles: depreciation charge	6,000	
Vehicles: accumulated depreciation		12,500
Equipment at cost	18,500	
Equipment: depreciation charge	3,500	
Equipment: accumulated depreciation		8,000
Disposal of non-current asset		160
Wages	24,110	
Accrual of wages		400
Advertising	770	
Administration expenses	14,830	
Bank	3,800	
Sales ledger control	3,480	
Irrecoverable debts	350	
Allowance for doubtful debts		620
Allowance for doubtful debts: adjustment		180
Purchases ledger control		2,760
Value Added Tax		1,840
Capital		35,040
Bank loan (repayable in 20-9)		9,000
Closing inventory	5,640	
	171,070	171,070

You are to prepare the financial statements of Mark Pelisi for the year ended 31 March 20-7, using the conventional format.

14 Incomplete records

Our studies of Accounts Preparation have so far concentrated on the double-entry system and, from this, we have extracted a trial balance and year end financial statements. However, there are a number of circumstances when full double-entry accounts are not available – the business may not keep adequate records, or information may have been lost as a result of a disaster such as a fire or a flood, or there may be discrepancies between the accounts. Whatever the circumstances, some financial information – incomplete records – will be available and, at the end of the year, it is the task of the accountant to construct the financial statements from these.

This chapter looks at

- *the information available when constructing financial statements from incomplete records*

- *how information that is required can be calculated*

- *preparing year-end financial statements from incomplete records*

- *the use of gross profit mark-up and margin in incomplete records accounting*

WHAT ARE INCOMPLETE RECORDS?

Incomplete records is the term used where some aspect of the accounting system is missing.

Incomplete records occurs when:

- information has been lost as a result of a disaster – such as a fire, a flood or the theft/loss of accounting records, including records held on a computer
- there are inadequate or missing accounting records
- there are discrepancies between
  - the inventory records and the physical inventory held by the business
  - the ledger accounts, non-current asset register and the physical non-current assets held by the business
  - the business cash book and the bank statement received from the bank
  - the purchases ledger accounts and statements received from suppliers

The task of the accountant faced with incomplete records is to construct the financial statements by

- using the information that is available (see below)
- seeing what information is not available, and how 'missing' figures can be calculated

information available to the accountant

The basic financial record kept by most businesses is a cash book which records the business cash and bank transactions. Often the cash book is operated on the *single-entry* system, ie there is no double-entry. In practice, even if a cash book has not been kept, it is usually possible to reconstruct it from banking records, although this task can prove to be time-consuming. Other financial information will be available so that, in all, the accountant has the following to work from:

- cash book – the basic record for any single entry system
- banking details – statements, paying-in books, cheque stubs and other bank transfers
- invoices – both invoices received (for purchases) and copies of invoices sent (for sales) during the year
- expenses – during the year
- lists of amounts owing to suppliers (payables), and due from customers (receivables), at the beginning and end of the year
- assets and liabilities – non-current and current assets, long-term and current liabilities, at the beginning and end of the year
- non-current assets – bought or sold during the year

Information which may not be available, and will need to be calculated includes:

- capital at the beginning of the year
- purchases and sales for the year
- cash book summary for the year
- profit for the year

the tools of accounting

From the two Case Studies which follow (below, and on page 275) we shall see how to take the financial information that is available and, using the tools of accounting, to construct the accounts that are required. The tools of accounting that may be needed are:

- the use of an opening trial balance, or statement of assets and liabilities
- the construction of a cash account and/or bank account
- the use of control accounts – sales ledger control account, purchases ledger control account and VAT control account
- the preparation of financial statements – income statement and statement of financial position

In addition, the following may be of use:

- the accounting equation (assets – liabilities = capital)
- gross profit mark-up and margin (see page 281)

The two Case Studies make use of these tools of accounting, although it should be emphasised that no two incomplete records situations are the same; however practice will help to develop your skills in this aspect of accounts preparation.

Case Study

JAYNE PERRY – STATIONERY SUPPLIES

The following information has been taken from the incomplete records of Jayne Perry, who runs a small stationery supplies business.

LIST OF ASSETS AND LIABILITIES

	1 Jan 20-4	31 Dec 20-4
	£	£
Shop fittings	8,000	8,000
Inventory	25,600	29,800
Trade receivables	29,200	20,400
Bank (money at the bank)	5,000	not known
Trade payables	20,800	16,000
Administration expenses owing	200	300

BANK SUMMARY FOR 20-4

	£
Receipts from trade receivables	127,800
Payments to trade payables	82,600
Drawings	12,500
Administration expenses	30,600

In the text which follows we shall see how Jayne Perry's accountant will construct the financial statements for 20-4 from incomplete records. The information to be calculated is:

• opening capital, at the beginning of the financial year

• cash book summary for the year

• purchases and sales for the year

• profit for the year, and a year end statement of financial position

Note: for the sake of simplicity we will ignore VAT on all transactions in this Case Study.

OPENING CAPITAL

Opening capital is needed because a year end statement of financial position is to be prepared. In other situations with incomplete records, opening capital may be known, being the difference between assets and liabilities. To calculate the capital at the beginning of the financial year, we use the accounting equation: *assets – liabilities = capital*.

This is presented as a *statement of assets and liabilities* as follows:

> **JAYNE PERRY**
> **STATEMENT OF ASSETS AND LIABILITIES**
> **as at 1 January 20-4**
>
> | | £ | £ |
> |---|---|---|
> | **Assets** | | |
> | Shop fittings | | 8,000 |
> | Inventory | | 25,600 |
> | Trade receivables | | 29,200 |
> | Bank | | 5,000 |
> | | | 67,800 |
> | **Less Liabilities** | | |
> | Trade payables | 20,800 | |
> | Administration expenses owing | 200 | |
> | | | 21,000 |
> | **Capital at 1 January 20-4** | | 46,800 |

Notes:

- Here, the bank balance is an asset, ie money in the bank; if it was marked as an overdraft, it would be included amongst the liabilities.

- Look out for the opening bank balance or overdraft being stated elsewhere in the information; for example, a bank summary may be given which starts with the bank figure at the beginning of the year – this figure must be included in the statement of assets and liabilities, which is used to calculate opening capital.

CASH BOOK SUMMARY

A cash book/bank summary enables us to find out the cash and bank balances at the year end. (Sometimes this is not necessary, as a cash book may have been prepared already by the owner of the business.) In practice, the entries on the bank statement can be used to produce a summary of bank receipts and payments for the year. In the case of Jayne Perry's business, the cash book (bank columns) are:

Dr			Cash Book (bank columns)			Cr
20-4			£	20-4		£
1 Jan	Balance b/d		5,000		Payments to trade	
	Receipts from trade				payables	82,600
	receivables		127,800		Drawings	12,500
					Administration expenses	30,600
				31 Dec	Balance c/d	7,100
			132,800			132,800
20-5				20-5		
1 Jan	Balance b/d		7,100			

missing figure

The bank balance of £7,100 on 31 December 20-4 is calculated by filling in the missing figure.

Notes:

• When preparing a cash book summary, look out for an opening bank balance that is *overdrawn*; this is entered on the credit side.

• At the end of the cash book summary, a credit balance brought down is an overdraft.

• If working from a bank statement, take care with the balances. Remember that a credit balance at the bank (money in the bank) is a debit balance in the business accounts, which represents an asset of the business. By contrast a debit balance at the bank (an overdraft) is a credit balance in the business accounts, which represents a liability of the business.

PURCHASES AND SALES

In calculating purchases and sales, we need to take note of the payables and receivables at both the beginning and the end of the year. The important point to note is that payments are *not* the same as purchases for the year (because of the change in the level of payables). Likewise, receipts are not the same as sales (because of the change in receivables). Only in a business which trades solely on cash terms and has no receivables and payables would the receipts and payments be the figures for sales and purchases.

calculating purchases and sales

The method of calculating the purchases and sales figures is:

• **purchases for year** = payments in year, *less* payables at the beginning of the year, *plus* payables at the end of the year

• **sales for year** = receipts in year, *less* receivables at the beginning of the year, *plus* receivables at the end of the year

When calculating purchases and sales, also take note of any purchases and sales returns, any cash (settlement) discounts received and allowed, and – for sales – irrecoverable debts (but ignore an allowance for doubtful debts).

The figures from Jayne Perry's business are:

purchases	= £82,600 – £20,800 + £16,000	= £77,800
sales	= £127,800 – £29,200 + £20,400	= £119,000

use of control accounts

The use of control accounts is recommended for calculating purchases and sales in incomplete records. We can use the information for purchases given in the Case Study as follows:

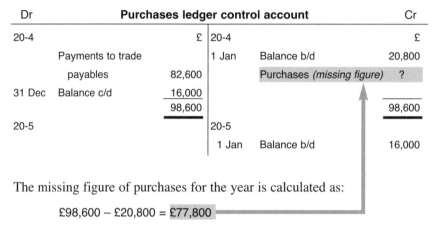

Dr		Purchases ledger control account			Cr
20-4		£	20-4		£
	Payments to trade		1 Jan	Balance b/d	20,800
	payables	82,600		Purchases *(missing figure)*	?
31 Dec	Balance c/d	16,000			
		98,600			98,600
20-5			20-5		
			1 Jan	Balance b/d	16,000

The missing figure of purchases for the year is calculated as:

£98,600 – £20,800 = £77,800

In a similar way, the sales figure can be calculated:

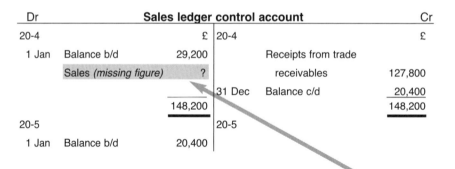

Dr		Sales ledger control account			Cr
20-4		£	20-4		£
1 Jan	Balance b/d	29,200		Receipts from trade	
	Sales *(missing figure)*	?		receivables	127,800
			31 Dec	Balance c/d	20,400
		148,200			148,200
20-5			20-5		
1 Jan	Balance b/d	20,400			

The missing figure of sales for the year is £148,200 – £29,200 = £119,000

The control account method, although its use is not essential in incomplete records, does bring a discipline to calculating the two important figures of purchases and sales. Do not forget that the control accounts give the figures for *credit* purchases and sales: cash purchases and sales need to be added, where applicable, to obtain total purchases and sales for the year.

purchases and sales – summary

Whichever method of calculating purchases or sales is used – calculation, or a control account – four pieces of information are usually required:

- opening balance
- closing balance
- bank and cash payments or receipts for the year
- purchases or sales for the year

Provided that any three are known, the fourth can be calculated – the figure for purchases and sales was missing from the examples above. However if, for example, we know the opening and closing receivables totals, together with sales for the year, then it is a simple matter to calculate the missing figure for receipts from receivables.

Remember that, if they are applicable, purchases and sales returns, cash (settlement) discounts received and allowed, and – for sales – irrecoverable debts, should also be incorporated into the control accounts.

VAT control account

Note that a VAT control account may be needed for VAT-registered businesses – see page 278 of the next Case Study. Also, with incomplete records, be ready to make VAT calculations to extract net or VAT from a gross figure which includes VAT. These calculations were covered in earlier studies at Level 2.

PREPARATION OF THE FINANCIAL STATEMENTS

income statement

Having calculated the figures for purchases and sales, we can now prepare the income statement. The section as far as gross profit is:

JAYNE PERRY		
INCOME STATEMENT		
for the year ended 31 December 20-4		
	£	£
Sales revenue		119,000
Opening inventory	25,600	
Purchases	77,800	
	103,400	
Less Closing inventory	29,800	
Cost of sales		73,600
Gross profit		45,400

The expenses section of the income statement follows but, before we are able to complete this, we need to know the figure for administration expenses for the year. The relevant information from the Case Study is:

- bank payments for administration expenses during year, £30,600
- administration expenses owing at 1 January 20-4, £200
- administration expenses owing at 31 December 20-4, £300

Like the calculation of purchases and sales, we cannot simply use the bank payments figure for expenses; we must take note of cash payments, together with accruals (and prepayments). The calculation is:

> **expenses for year** = bank and cash payments, *less* accruals at the beginning of the year (or *plus* prepayments), *plus* accruals at the end of the year (or *less* prepayments)

Thus the figure for Jayne Perry's administration expenses is:

£30,600 − £200 + £300 = £30,700.

Alternatively, the figure can be calculated by means of a control account:

Dr	**Administration expenses control account**			Cr
20-4		£	20-4	£
	Cash/bank	30,600	1 Jan Balance b/d	200
31 Dec Balance c/d		300	31 Dec Income statement *(missing figure)*	?
		30,900		30,900
20-5			20-5	
			1 Jan Balance b/d	300

The missing figure is £30,900 − £200 = £30,700

Jayne Perry's income statement concludes as follows:

	£
Gross profit	45,400
Less expenses:	
Administration expenses	30,700
Profit for the year	14,700

statement of financial position

The statement of financial position can now be prepared using the assets and liabilities from the Case Study.

JAYNE PERRY
STATEMENT OF FINANCIAL POSITION
as at 31 December 20-4

	£	£	£
Non-current assets			
Shop fittings			8,000
Current assets			
Inventory		29,800	
Trade receivables		20,400	
Bank		7,100	
		57,300	
Less Current liabilities			
Trade payables	16,000		
Accrual of administration expenses	300		
		16,300	
Net current assets			41,000
NET ASSETS			49,000
FINANCED BY			
Capital			
Opening capital			46,800
Add Profit for the year			14,700
			61,500
Less Drawings			12,500
Closing capital			49,000

Case Study

ELECTROPARTS

We will now look at a more comprehensive example of incomplete records accounting. This incorporates sales returns, VAT (including the use of VAT control account), depreciation and the sale of a non-current asset, and concludes with the preparation of financial statements. You may like to work through the Case Study before comparing your solution with the one shown.

situation

John Anstey owns a small business, Electroparts, which supplies spare parts for a wide range of electrical goods – cookers, fridges, freezers, kettles, dishwashers, etc.

His customers are self-employed repairers who buy parts for specific jobs from his trade counter – John allows them credit terms. There are no cash sales. All purchases made by John from suppliers are on credit terms.

All sales, disposals of assets and purchases are standard-rated for VAT at 20%.

John does not keep a full set of accounting records; however, the following information has been produced for the year ended 31 March 20-8:

Assets and Liabilities of Electroparts at 1 April 20-7

		£	£
ASSETS	Fixtures and fittings at cost		15,000
	Less accumulated depreciation		7,500
			7,500
	Inventory	24,400	
	Trade receivables	21,650	
	Prepayment of administration expenses	140	
			46,190
	TOTAL ASSETS		53,690
LIABILITIES	Trade payables	15,950	
	Value Added Tax	2,310	
	Bank	12,850	
	TOTAL LIABILITIES		31,110
CAPITAL			22,580

Bank account summary for the year ended 31 March 20-8

	£		£
Trade receivables	207,410	Balance b/d	12,850
Disposal of fixtures		Trade payables	139,620
and fittings (inc VAT)	1,950	Administration expenses	17,760
		Wages	18,280
		HMRC for VAT	4,360
		Drawings	15,390
		Balance c/d	1,100
	209,360		209,360

Day book summaries for the year	Net £	VAT £	Total £
Sales	196,400	39,280	235,680
Sales returns	1,560	312	1,872
Purchases	135,600	27,120	162,720
Administration expenses	14,800	2,960	17,760
Note: there were no purchases returns during the year			

further information:

– On 31 March 20-8, inventory was valued at £28,400

– Cash (settlement) discounts received during the year totalled £760; there was no cash discount allowed during the year

– Depreciation is charged at the rate of 10% on the cost of fixtures and fittings held at the end of the financial year. No depreciation is charged in the year of disposal

– Fixtures and fittings purchased on 1 April 20-5 for £2,500 (net of VAT) were sold on 30 September 20-7 for £1,950 (including VAT)

– On 31 March 20-8, £210 was owing for administration expenses

John Anstey asks you to:

1 Calculate the amount of trade receivables at 31 March 20-8

2 Calculate the amount of trade payables at 31 March 20-8

3 Calculate the profit or loss on the disposal of fixtures and fittings

4 Calculate the amount of VAT due to HM Revenue and Customs at 31 March 20-8

5 Calculate the amount of administration expenses to be shown in the income statement for the year ended 31 March 20-8

6 Prepare the income statement for the year ended 31 March 20-8

7 Prepare the statement of financial position at 31 March 20-8

solution

1

Dr		Sales ledger control account			Cr
20-7/-8		£	**20-7/-8**		£
1 Apr	Balance b/d	21,650		Sales returns day book	1,872
	Sales day book	235,680		Bank	207,410
			31 Mar	Balance c/d *(missing figure)*	48,048
		257,330			257,330

2

Dr		Purchases ledger control account			Cr
20-7/-8		£	**20-7/-8**		£
	Bank	139,620	1 Apr	Balance b/d	15,950
	Discounts received	760		Purchases day book	162,720
31 Mar	Balance c/d *(missing figure)*	38,290			
		178,670			178,670

3 **Profit or loss on disposal of fixtures and fittings**

Depreciation charge per year	£250
Number of years' depreciation	2 (20-5/-6,20-6/-7; no depreciation in year of sale)
Accumulated depreciation	£500
Disposals	£1,625 + £325 VAT = £1,950

Dr			**Disposals account**		Cr
20-7/-8		£	20-7/-8		£
30 Sep	Fixtures and fittings	2,500	30 Sep	Accumulated depreciation	500
30 Sep	VAT on disposals	325	30 Sep	Bank (disposal proceeds)	1,950
			31 Mar	Income statement (loss on disposal)	375
		2,825			2,825

4

Dr			**VAT control account**		Cr
20-7/-8		£	20-7/-8		£
	Sales returns day book	312	1 Apr	Balance b/d	2,310
	Purchases day book	27,120		Sales day book	39,280
	Administration expenses day book	2,960		Disposals	325
	Bank	4,360			
31 Mar	Balance c/d (missing figure)	7,163			
		41,915			41,915

5

Dr			**Administration expenses control account**		Cr
20-7/-8		£	20-7/-8		£
1 Apr	Balance b/d	140	31 Mar	Income statement (missing figure)	15,150
	Administration expenses day book	*14,800			
31 Mar	Balance c/d	210			
		15,150			15,150
	* net of VAT				

6

JOHN ANSTEY, TRADING AS 'ELECTROPARTS'
INCOME STATEMENT
for the year ended 31 March 20-8

	£	£
Sales revenue		196,400
Less Sales returns		1,560
Net sales		194,840
Opening inventory	24,400	
Purchases	135,600	
	160,000	
Less Closing inventory	28,400	
Cost of sales		131,600
Gross profit		63,240
Add income: Discounts received		760
		64,000
Less expenses:		
Administration expenses	15,150	
Loss on disposal of fixtures and fittings	375	
Depreciation charge: fixtures and fittings	*1,250	
Wages	18,280	
		35,055
Profit for the year		28,945

*Note

Fixtures and fittings at cost on 1 April 20-7	£15,000
Less cost price of fixtures and fittings sold 30 September 20-7	£2,500
Fixtures and fittings at cost on 31 March 20-8	£12,500
Depreciation charge at 10%	£1,250

7

JOHN ANSTEY, TRADING AS 'ELECTROPARTS'
STATEMENT OF FINANCIAL POSITION
as at 31 March 20-8

	£ Cost	£ Accumulated depreciation	£ Carrying amount
Non-current assets			
Fixtures and fittings	12,500	*8,250	4,250
Current assets			
Inventory		28,400	
Trade receivables		48,048	
Bank		1,100	
		77,548	
Less Current liabilities			
Trade payables	38,290		
Value Added Tax	7,163		
Accrual of administration expenses	210		
		45,663	
Net current assets			31,885
NET ASSETS			36,135
FINANCED BY			
Capital			
Opening capital (from assets and liabilities at 1 April 20-7)			22,580
Add Profit for the year			28,945
			51,525
Less Drawings			15,390
Closing capital			36,135

*Note

Accumulated depreciation of fixtures and fittings at 1 April 20-7	7,500
Less accumulated depreciation on asset sold	500
	7,000
Depreciation charge for year (see income statement)	1,250
Accumulated depreciation of fixtures and fittings at 31 March 20-8	8,250

THE USE OF GROSS PROFIT MARK-UP AND MARGIN

It is often necessary to use accounting ratios and percentages in the preparation of financial statements from incomplete records.

The two main percentages used for incomplete records accounting are:

* gross profit mark-up
* gross profit margin (or gross sales margin)

It is quite common for a business to establish its selling price by reference to either a mark-up or a margin. The difference between the two is that:

* mark-up is a profit percentage added to *buying* or *cost* price
* margin is a percentage profit based on the *selling* price

For example, a product is bought by a retailer at a cost of £100; the retailer sells it for £125, ie

$$\text{cost price} \quad + \quad \text{gross profit} \quad = \quad \text{selling price}$$
$$£100 \quad + \quad £25 \quad = \quad £125$$

The *mark-up* is:

$$\frac{\text{gross profit}}{\text{cost price}} \times \frac{100}{1} \quad = \quad \frac{£25}{£100} \times \frac{100}{1} \quad = \quad \mathbf{25\%}$$

The *margin* (**or gross sales margin**) is:

$$\frac{\text{gross profit}}{\text{selling price}} \times \frac{100}{1} \quad = \quad \frac{£25}{£125} \times \frac{100}{1} \quad = \quad \mathbf{20\%}$$

In incomplete records accounting, mark-up or the margin percentages can be used in a range of circumstances, as shown by the examples which follow.

WORKED EXAMPLES

example 1 – calculation of sales

* Cost of sales is £150,000
* Mark-up is 40%
* What is sales revenue?

Gross profit $= £150,000 \times \dfrac{40}{100} = £60,000$

Sales = cost of sales + gross profit, ie £150,000 + £60,000 = **£210,000**

example 2 – calculation of purchases

- Sales are £450,000
- Margin is 20%
- Opening inventory is £40,000; closing inventory is £50,000
- What are purchases?

Gross profit = £450,000 x $\frac{20}{100}$ = £90,000

Cost of sales = sales – gross profit, ie £450,000 – £90,000 = £360,000

The purchases calculation is:

	Opening inventory	£40,000
+	Purchases (missing figure)	?
–	Closing inventory	£50,000
=	Cost of sales	£360,000
Therefore purchases =		**£370,000**

example 3 – converting from a mark-up to a margin

- Mark-up is 50%
- What is the margin?

Margin = $\frac{\text{mark-up \%}}{100 + \text{mark-up \%}}$ x $\frac{100}{1}$

= $\frac{50}{100 + 50}$ x $\frac{100}{1}$ = **33.33% margin**

example 4 – converting from a margin to a mark-up

- Margin is 33.33%
- What is the mark-up?

Mark-up = $\frac{\text{margin \%}}{100 - \text{margin \%}}$ x $\frac{100}{1}$

= $\frac{33.33}{100 - 33.33}$ x $\frac{100}{1}$ = **50% mark-up**

INVENTORY LOSSES

A loss of inventory may occur as a result of an event such as a fire, a flood or a theft. When such a loss occurs, an estimate of the value of the inventory lost needs to be made in order for the business to make an insurance claim (always assuming that the inventory was adequately insured). The value is calculated by preparing an accounting summary to the date of the event, and often making use of margins and mark-ups. The calculations are best carried out in three steps:

1		Opening inventory
	+	Purchases
	=	Cost of inventory available for sale
2		Sales
	−	Gross profit (using normal gross profit margin)
	=	Cost of sales
3		Cost of inventory available for sale (from 1, above)
	−	Cost of sales (2, above)
	=	Estimated closing inventory
	−	Value of inventory remaining or salvaged
	=	Value of inventory lost through fire, flood or theft

Case Study

CLOTHING SUPPLIES: THEFT OF INVENTORY

situation

Peter Kamara runs Clothing Supplies, a small clothing wholesalers. Peter is convinced that various items of clothing have been stolen during the year and he asks you to calculate, from the accounting details, the value of inventory stolen. The following information is available:

• sales for the year, £500,000

• opening inventory at the beginning of the year, £15,000

• purchases for the year, £310,000

• closing inventory at the end of the year, £22,000

• the gross profit margin achieved on all sales is 40 per cent

solution

CALCULATION OF INVENTORY LOSS FOR THE YEAR

	£	£
Opening inventory		15,000
Purchases		310,000
Cost of inventory available for sale		325,000
Sales	500,000	
Less Normal gross profit margin (40%)	200,000	
Cost of sales		300,000
Estimated closing inventory		25,000
Less Actual closing inventory		22,000
Value of inventory loss		3,000

Chapter Summary

- Incomplete records is the term used where some aspect of the accounting system is missing.

- In order to prepare financial statements, the accountant may well have to calculate:
  - capital at the beginning of the year
  - purchases and sales for the year
  - cash book summary for the year
  - profit for the year

- On the basis of these calculations, the accountant can then construct the financial statements without recourse to a trial balance.

- Two ratios and percentages used in incomplete records accounting are:
  - gross profit mark-up
  - gross profit margin

- The value of inventory losses caused by fire, flood or theft is calculated using margins and mark-ups.

Key Terms

incomplete records	financial records where some aspect of the accounting system is missing
gross profit mark-up	profit percentage added to the buying price
gross profit margin	profit percentage based on the selling price
inventory loss	loss of inventory caused by fire, flood or theft

Activities

14.1 • Cost of sales for the year is £200,000.
 • Mark-up is 30%.
 What are sales for the year?

 (a)   £140,000

 (b)   £200,000

 (c)   £260,000

 (d)   £300,000

 Answer (a) or (b) or (c) or (d)

14.2 • Sales for the year are £100,000.
 • Gross profit margin is 25%.
 • Opening inventory is £10,000; closing inventory is £12,000.
 What are purchases for the year?

 (a)   £25,000

 (b)   £77,000

 (c)   £102,000

 (d)   £125,000

 Answer (a) or (b) or (c) or (d)

14.3 You are preparing accounts from incomplete records. Trade receivables at the start of the year were £2,500, and at the end were £3,250. Bank receipts from receivables total £17,850; cash sales total £2,500. What is the sales revenue figure for the year?

 (a)   £17,850

 (b)   £17,100

 (c)   £18,600

 (d)   £21,100

 Answer (a) or (b) or (c) or (d)

14.4   Jane Price owns a fashion shop called 'Trendsetters'. She has been in business for one year and, although she does not keep a full set of accounting records, the following information has been produced for the first year of trading, which ended on 31 December 20-4:

Summary of the business bank account for the year ended 31 December 20-4:

	£
Capital introduced	60,000
Receipts from sales	153,500
Payments to suppliers	95,000
Advertising	4,830
Wages	15,000
Rent and rates	8,750
Administration expenses	5,000
Shop fittings	50,000
Drawings	15,020

Summary of assets and liabilities as at 31 December 20-4:

	£
Shop fittings at cost	50,000
Inventory	73,900
Trade receivables	2,500
Trade payables	65,000

Other information:

* Jane wishes to depreciate the shop fittings at 20% per year using the straight-line method
* At 31 December 20-4, rent is prepaid by £250, and wages of £550 are owing

You are to:

(a)   Calculate the amount of sales during the year.

(b)   Calculate the amount of purchases during the year.

(c)   Calculate the amounts of

   • rent and rates

   • wages

   to be shown in the income statement for the year ended 31 December 20-4.

(d)   Prepare Jane Price's income statement for the year ended 31 December 20-4.

(e)   Prepare Jane Price's statement of financial position at 31 December 20-4.

Note: VAT is to be ignored on all transactions

14.5 James Harvey runs a stationery supplies shop. He is convinced that one of his employees is stealing stationery. He asks you to calculate from the accounting records the value of inventory stolen. The following information is available:

* sales for the year, £180,000
* opening inventory at the beginning of the year, £21,500
* purchases for the year, £132,000
* closing inventory at the end of the year, £26,000
* the gross profit margin achieved on all sales is 30 per cent

You are to calculate the value of inventory stolen (if any) during the year.

14.6 Colin Smith owns a business which sells specialist central heating parts to trade customers. He has been in business for a number of years. Although he does not keep a full set of accounting records, the following information is available in respect of the year ended 30 June 20-5:

Summary of assets and liabilities:

	1 July 20-4	30 June 20-5
	£	£
Assets		
Inventory	25,000	27,500
Fixtures and fittings (cost £50,000)	40,000	35,000
Trade receivables	36,000	35,000
Bank	1,500	1,210
Liabilities		
Trade payables	32,500	30,000
Accrual: administration expenses	500	700

Summary of the business bank account for the year ended 30 June 20-5:

	£
Administration expenses	30,000
Drawings	28,790
Receipts from trade receivables	121,000
Payments to trade payables	62,500

Other information:

* Fixtures and fittings are being depreciated at 10% per year using the straight line method
* Irrecoverable debts of £550 have been written off during the year

You are to:

(a) Calculate the amount of sales during the year ended 30 June 20-5

(b) Calculate the amount of purchases during the year ended 30 June 20-5

(c) Calculate the amount of administration expenses to be shown in the income statement for the year ended 30 June 20-5

(d) Prepare Colin Smith's income statement for the year ended 30 June 20-5

(e) Prepare Colin Smith's statement of financial position at 30 June 20-5

Note: VAT is to be ignored on all transactions

14.7   This Activity is about finding missing figures in ledger accounts where the records are incomplete.

You are working on the financial statements of a business for the year ended 31 March 20-9. You have the following information.

Day book summaries for the year	Net £	VAT £	Total £
Sales	168,000	33,600	201,600
Purchases	96,000	19,200	115,200

All sales and purchases are on credit terms

Balances as at:	31 March 20-8 £	31 March 20-9 £
Trade receivables	20,400	27,100
Trade payables	12,600	11,800

Further information:	Net £	VAT £	Total £
Selling expenses	12,400	2,480	14,880

Selling expenses are not included in the purchases figure in purchases day book

Bank summary	Dr £		Cr £
Balance b/d	12,460	Travel expenses	2,300
Trade receivables	192,650	Selling expenses	14,880
Interest received	55	Trade payables	112,150
		HMRC for VAT	10,425
		Drawings	21,000
		Wages	33,280
		Balance c/d	11,130
	205,165		205,165

(a) Using the figures given on the previous page, prepare the sales ledger control account for the year ended 31 March 20-9. Show clearly discounts as the balancing figure.

Sales ledger control account

(b) Find the closing balance for VAT by preparing the VAT control account for the year ended 31 March 20-9. Use the figures given on the previous page.

Note: The business is not charged VAT on its travel expenses.

VAT control account

		Balance b/d	3,050

15 Partnership financial statements

So far, when discussing financial statements, we have considered the accounts of a sole trader, ie one person in business. However, a partnership is a common form of business unit, and can be found in the form of:

- sole traders who have joined together with others in order to raise finance and expand the business

- family businesses, such as builders, car repairers, gardeners

- professional firms such as solicitors, accountants, doctors, dentists

In this chapter we look at

- the definition of a partnership

- the accounting requirements of the Partnership Act 1890

- the accounting requirements which may be incorporated into a partnership agreement

- the use of capital accounts and current accounts

- the appropriation of profits

- the layout of the capital section of the statement of financial position

- partnership financial statements, using the extended trial balance method and the conventional format

WHAT DOES A PARTNERSHIP INVOLVE?

The Partnership Act of 1890 defines a partnership as:

the relation which subsists between persons carrying on a business in common with a view of profit

Normally, partnerships consist of between two and twenty partners (exceptions being large professional firms, eg solicitors and accountants). Partnerships are often larger businesses than sole traders because, as there is more than one owner, there is likely to be more capital. A partnership may be formed to set up a new business or it may be the logical growth of a sole trader taking in partners to increase the capital.

advantages and disadvantages

Partnerships are cheap and easy to set up; the **advantages** are:

* there is the possibility of increased capital
* individual partners may be able to specialise in particular areas of the business
* with more people running the business, there is cover for illness and holidays

The **disadvantages** are:

* as there is more than one owner, decisions may take longer because other partners may need to be consulted
* there may be disagreements amongst the partners
* each partner is liable in law for the dealings and business debts of the *whole* firm (unless it is a 'limited liability partnership' set up under the Limited Liability Partnerships Act, 2000)
* the retirement or death of one partner may adversely affect the running of the business

accounting requirements of a partnership

The accounting requirements of a partnership are:

* either to follow the rules set out in the Partnership Act 1890
* or – and more likely – for the partners to agree amongst themselves, by means of a partnership agreement (see next page), to follow different accounting rules

Unless the partners agree otherwise, the Partnership Act 1890 states the following accounting rules:

* profits and losses are to be shared equally between the partners
* no partner is entitled to a salary

- partners are not entitled to receive interest on their capital
- interest is not to be charged on partners' drawings
- when a partner contributes more capital than agreed, he or she is entitled to receive interest at five per cent per annum on the excess

Note: for AAT Assessments you should be aware of these rules and the circumstances in which the provisions of the Partnership Act would be relevant.

As mentioned above, the partners may well decide to follow different accounting rules – these will be set out in a partnership agreement.

FINANCIAL STATEMENTS OF A PARTNERSHIP

A partnership prepares the same type of year end financial statements as a sole trader business:

- income statement
- statement of financial position

The main difference is that, immediately after the income statement, follows an **appropriation section** (often described as an appropriation account). This shows how the profit from the income statement is shared amongst the partners. Note that, in AAT Assessments, a pro-forma appropriation account will be given when required.

example of sharing profits

Jan, Kay and Lil are partners sharing profits and losses equally; their income statement for 20-1 shows a profit of £60,000. The appropriation of profits appears as:

JAN, KAY AND LIL PARTNERSHIP APPROPRIATION ACCOUNT for the year ended 31 December 20-1	
	£
Profit for the year	60,000
Profit share:	
Jan	20,000
Kay	20,000
Lil	20,000
	60,000

The above is a simple appropriation of profits. A more complex appropriation account (see Case Study on page 295) deals with other accounting points from the partnership agreement.

PARTNERSHIP AGREEMENT

The accounting rules from the Partnership Act are often varied with the agreement of all partners, by means of a partnership agreement. In particular, a partnership agreement will usually cover the following main points:

- division of profits and losses between partners (which may be expressed as a ratio, fraction or percentage)
- partners' salaries
- whether interest is to be allowed on partners' capital, and at what rate
- whether interest is to be charged on partners' drawings, and at what rate

The money amounts involved for each of these points (where allowed by the partnership agreement) are shown in the partnership appropriation account (see Case Study on page 295).

division of profits and losses between partners

The Partnership Act states that, in the absence of an agreement to the contrary, profits and losses are to be shared equally. A partner's share of the profits is normally taken out of the business in the form of drawings. Clearly, if one partner has contributed much more capital than the other partner(s), it would be unfair to apply this clause from the Act. Consequently, many partnerships agree to share profits and losses on a different basis – often in the same proportions as they have contributed capital. Note that, in Activities and Assessments, you will normally be told the agreed division of profits; however, if there is no mention of this, you should assume that the partners receive an equal share.

partners' salaries

Although the Act says that no partner is entitled to a salary, it is quite usual in the partnership agreement for one or more partners to be paid a salary. The reason for doing this is that often in a partnership, one of the partners spends more time working in the partnership than the other(s). The agreement to pay a salary is in recognition of the work done. Note that partners' salaries are not shown as an expense in the income statement; instead they appear in the partnership appropriation account.

Many professional partnerships, such as solicitors and accountants, have junior partners who receive a partnership salary because they work full-time in the business, but have not yet contributed any capital. In a partnership, there may not be a requirement to contribute capital, unless the partnership agreement states otherwise; however, most partners will eventually do so.

interest allowed on capital

Many partnerships include a clause in their partnership agreement which allows interest to be paid on capital; the rate of interest will be stated also. This clause is used to compensate partners for the loss of use of their capital, ie it is not available to invest elsewhere. Often, interest is allowed on capital in partnerships where profits and losses are shared equally – it is one way of partly adjusting for different capital balances. As noted earlier, the Partnership Act does not permit interest to be paid on capital, so reference to it must be made in the partnership agreement.

When calculating interest on capital, it may be necessary to allow for part years. For example:

1 January 20-1 capital balance	£20,000
1 July 20-1 additional capital contributed	£4,000
the rate of interest allowed on capital	10% per annum
the partnership's financial year end	31 December 20-1

Interest allowed on capital is calculated as:

1 January – 30 June £20,000 x 10% (for 6 months)	£1,000
1 July – 31 December £24,000 x 10% (for 6 months)	£1,200
Interest allowed on capital for year	£2,200

interest charged on partners' drawings

In order to discourage partners from drawing out too much money from the business early in the financial year, the partnership agreement may stipulate that interest is to be charged on partners' drawings, and at what rate. This acts as a penalty against early withdrawal in the year when the business may be short of cash.

The amount of interest charged on drawings for the year is shown in the partnership appropriation account, where it increases the profit to be shared amongst the partners.

Note that Activities and AAT Assessments will state the amount of interest charged – you will not need to calculate it.

CAPITAL ACCOUNTS AND CURRENT ACCOUNTS

The important book-keeping difference between a sole trader and a partnership is that each partner usually has a capital account *and* a current account. The capital account is normally *fixed,* and only alters if a permanent increase or decrease in capital contributed by the partner takes place. The current account is *fluctuating* and it is to this account that:

- share of profit is credited
- share of loss is debited
- salary is credited
- interest allowed on partners' capital is credited
- interest charged on partners' drawings is debited
- drawings and goods for own use are debited

Thus, the current account is treated as a *working* account, while capital account remains fixed, except for capital introduced or withdrawn – usually done by payments into the bank account for capital introduced, or payments out of the bank account for capital withdrawn.

A partner's current account has the following layout:

Dr	**Partner Aye: Current Account**	Cr
	£	£
Drawings/goods for own use	Balance b/d	
Interest charged on drawings*	Salary*	
Loss share	Interest on capital*	
Balance c/d	Profit share	

* if these items are allowed by the partnership agreement

Note that whilst the normal balance on a partner's current account is credit, when the partner has drawn out more than his or her share of the profits, then the balance will be debit.

Case Study

ALI AND BOB:
APPROPRIATION OF PARTNERSHIP PROFITS

As we have seen earlier in this chapter, the appropriation section (often described as the appropriation account) follows the income statement and shows how profit for the year has been divided amongst the partners. This Case Study shows a partnership salary (which is not shown as an expense in the income statement), interest allowed on partners' capital, and interest charged on partners' drawings.

situation

Ali and Bob are in partnership sharing profits and losses 60 per cent and 40 per cent respectively. Profit for the year ended 31 March 20-4 is £42,000.

At 1 April 20-3 (the start of the year), the partners have the following balances:

	Capital account	Current account
	£	£
Ali	40,000	2,000 Cr
Bob	30,000	400 Cr

- There have been no changes to the capital accounts during the year; interest is allowed on partners' capitals at the rate of eight per cent per year.
- Bob is entitled to a salary of £16,000 per year.
- During the year partners' drawings were: Ali £18,000, Bob £24,000.
- Interest charged on partners' drawings for the year was: Ali £900, Bob £1,200.

solution

The appropriation of profits will be made as follows:

ALI AND BOB **PARTNERSHIP APPROPRIATION ACCOUNT** **for the year ended 31 March 20-4**		
	£	£
Profit for the year		42,000
Add interest charged on partners' drawings:		
Ali	900	
Bob	1,200	2,100
		44,100
Less appropriation of profit:		
Salary: Bob		16,000
Interest allowed on partners' capitals:		
Ali £40,000 x 8%	3,200	
Bob £30,000 x 8%	2,400	5,600
Profit available for distribution		22,500
Profit share:		
Ali (60%)	13,500	
Bob (40%)	9,000	
Total profit distributed		22,500

Note that all of the available profit – after allowing for interest charged on drawings, salary, and interest allowed on capital – is shared amongst the partners, in the ratio in which they share profits and losses.

The partners' current accounts for the year are shown on the next page. Note that the layout for the partners' current accounts uses a normal 'T' account but in a side-by-side format with a column for each partner on both the debit and credit sides. As an alternative, separate current accounts can be produced for each partner.

Dr		Ali	Bob		**Partners' Current Accounts**	Ali	Bob	Cr
20-3/4		£	£	20-3/4		£	£	
31 Mar	Drawings	18,000	24,000	1 Apr	Balances b/d	2,000	400	
31 Mar	Interest on drawings	900	1,200		Salary	–	16,000	
31 Mar	Balance c/d	–	2,600	31 Mar	Interest on capital	3,200	2,400	
				31 Mar	Profit share	13,500	9,000	
				31 Mar	Balance c/d	200	–	
		18,900	27,800			18,900	27,800	
20-4/5				20-4/5				
1 Apr	Balance b/d	200	–	1 Apr	Balance b/d	–	2,600	

From the current accounts we can see that Ali has drawn more out than the balance of the account; accordingly, at the end of the year, Ali has a debit balance of £200 on current account. By contrast, Bob has a credit balance of £2,600 on current account.

STATEMENT OF FINANCIAL POSITION

The statement of financial position of a partnership must show the year end balances on each partner's capital and current account. However, the transactions that have taken place on each account can be shown in summary form – in the same way that, in a sole trader's statement of financial position, profit for the year is added and drawings for the year are deducted.

The other sections of the statement of financial position – non-current assets, current assets, current and long-term liabilities – are presented in the same way as for a sole trader.

The following is an example statement of financial position layout for the 'financed by' section (the other sections of the statement of financial position are not shown). It details the capital and current accounts of the partnership of Ali and Bob (see Case Study above).

ALI AND BOB, IN PARTNERSHIP			
STATEMENT OF FINANCIAL POSITION (EXTRACT) as at 31 March 20-4			
FINANCED BY	Ali	Bob	Total
	£	£	£
Capital accounts	40,000	30,000	70,000
Current accounts	(200)	2,600	2,400
	39,800	32,600	72,400

PARTNERSHIP FINANCIAL STATEMENTS FROM THE TRIAL BALANCE

Financial statements for a partnership can be prepared using the extended trial balance method and can then be set out in the conventional format. The procedures are exactly the same as for sole traders. The only differences to note are that partners' capital and current accounts are shown in the statement of financial position. Transactions affecting the partners' current accounts – share of profits, partners' salaries, interest allowed on capital, interest charged on drawings, drawings, etc – can be shown either in the form of a double-entry 'T' account (see previous page for an example), or directly on the face of the statement of financial position (see the following Case Study). Whichever is done, it is the closing balances of the capital and current accounts that are added in to the 'financed by' section of the statement of financial position.

Case Study

RAMJIT SINGH AND VETA BIX: PARTNERSHIP FINANCIAL STATEMENTS

situation

The extended trial balance for the partnership of Ramjit Singh and Veta Bix, trading as 'RaVe Music', at 31 December 20-5 is shown on the next page. All columns of the ETB have been completed ready for preparation of financial statements in the conventional format.

Note that the ETB includes the following points:

- there are both accruals and prepayments
- non-current assets have been depreciated
- during the year the partners have taken goods for their own use – purchases has been reduced and the goods charged to each partner (note that the amounts of goods for own use have been shown separately on the ETB to show clearly the accounting treatment; they can be incorporated into the figure for drawings)
- one partner, Veta Bix, receives a salary* – this is shown in the income statement columns and the statement of financial position columns
- interest has been allowed on partners' capital accounts* at a rate of 10 per cent per year – the amounts are shown in the income statement and the statement of financial position columns
- the partners share remaining profits* equally – shown in the income statement columns and the statement of financial position columns
- * in conventional format financial statements these items are shown in the partnership appropriation account, ie *after* profit for the year has been calculated – see page 300

solution

The financial statements of the partnership of Ramjit Singh and Veta Bix, trading as 'RaVe Music', are shown in ETB format on the next page and in the conventional format on pages 300 and 301.

EXTENDED TRIAL BALANCE   RAMJIT SINGH AND VETA BIX, IN PARTNERSHIP, TRADING AS 'RAVE MUSIC'   31 DECEMBER 20-5

Account name	Ledger balances		Adjustments		Income statement		Statement of financial position	
	Dr £	Cr £	Dr £	Cr £	Dr £	Cr £	Dr £	Cr £
Opening inventory	20,000				20,000			
Sales revenue		250,000				250,000		
Purchases	120,000			900	119,100			
Premises at cost	200,000						200,000	
Premises: accumulated depreciation		9,000		3,000				12,000
Fixtures and fittings at cost	20,000						20,000	
Fixtures and fittings: accumulated depreciation		8,000		2,000				10,000
Wages and salaries	35,000		1,700		36,700			
Shop expenses	20,000			800	19,200			
Sales ledger control	3,000						3,000	
Purchases ledger control		7,000						7,000
Value Added Tax		4,000						4,000
Bank		2,000						2,000
Bank loan		80,000						80,000
Capital account: Ramjit Singh		50,000						50,000
Capital account: Veta Bix		45,000						45,000
Current account: Ramjit Singh		4,000						4,000
Current account: Veta Bix		1,000						1,000
Drawings: Ramjit Singh	24,000						24,000	
Drawings: Veta Bix	18,000						18,000	
Goods for own use: Ramjit Singh			500				500	
Goods for own use: Veta Bix			400				400	
Closing inventory: income statement				30,000		30,000		
Closing inventory: statement of financial position			30,000				30,000	
Accruals				1,700				1,700
Prepayments			800				800	
Depreciation charge			5,000		5,000			
Partnership salary: Veta Bix					10,000			10,000
Interest on capital: Ramjit Singh					5,000			5,000
Interest on capital: Veta Bix					4,500			4,500
Profit/loss: Ramjit Singh					30,250			30,250
Profit/loss: Veta Bix					30,250			30,250
	460,000	460,000	38,400	38,400	280,000	280,000	296,700	296,700

**RAMJIT SINGH AND VETA BIX IN PARTNERSHIP,
TRADING AS 'RAVE MUSIC'**

INCOME STATEMENT
for the year ended 31 December 20-5

	£	£	£
Sales revenue			250,000
Opening inventory		20,000	
Purchases	120,000		
Less Goods for own use	900		
		119,100	
		139,100	
Less Closing inventory		30,000	
Cost of sales			109,100
Gross profit			140,900
Less expenses:			
Wages and salaries		36,700	
Shop expenses		19,200	
Depreciation charge:			
freehold buildings		3,000	
fixtures and fittings		2,000	
			60,900
Profit for the year			80,000
Less appropriation of profit:			
Salary: Veta Bix			10,000
Interest allowed on partners' capitals:			
Ramjit Singh	£50,000 x 10%	5,000	
Veta Bix	£45,000 x 10%	4,500	
			9,500
Profit available for distribution			60,500
Profit share:			
Ramjit Singh (50%)			30,250
Veta Bix (50%)			30,250
Total profit distributed			60,500

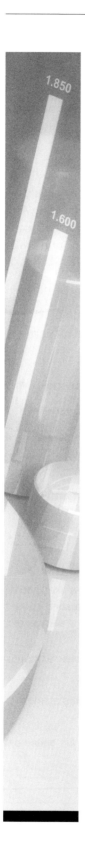

RAMJIT SINGH AND VETA BIX IN PARTNERSHIP, **TRADING AS 'RAVE MUSIC'** **STATEMENT OF FINANCIAL POSITION as at 31 December 20-5**			
	£	£	£
Non-current assets	Cost	Accumulated depreciation	Carrying amount
Premises	200,000	12,000	188,000
Fixtures and fittings	20,000	10,000	10,000
	220,000	22,000	198,000
Current assets			
Inventory (closing)		30,000	
Trade receivables		3,000	
Prepayments		800	
		33,800	
Less Current liabilities			
Trade payables	7,000		
Accruals	1,700		
Value Added Tax	4,000		
Bank	2,000		
		14,700	
Net current assets			19,100
			217,100
Less Non-current liabilities			
Bank loan			80,000
NET ASSETS			137,100
FINANCED BY			
	Ramjit Singh	**Veta Bix**	
Capital accounts	50,000	45,000	95,000
Current accounts			
Opening balance	4,000	1,000	
Add: salary	–	10,000	
interest on capital	5,000	4,500	
profit share	30,250	30,250	
	39,250	45,750	
Less: drawings	24,000	18,000	
goods for own use*	500	400	
	14,750	27,350	42,100
			137,100

*   goods for own use can be incorporated into the amount for drawings – shown here separately so that the accounting treatment can be seen clearly.

PREPARING PARTNERSHIP FINANCIAL STATEMENTS

When partnership financial statements are being prepared, the accounts assistant must take note of:

- the terms of the partnership agreement
- the policies, regulations, procedures and timescales of the partnership

If there are any discrepancies, unusual features or queries, they should be identified and, where possible, resolved by the accounts assistant. Any outstanding issues will need to be referred to the appropriate person – such as the accounts supervisor, the manager of the partnership, or one or more of the partners.

Chapter Summary	■ A partnership is formed when two or more (usually up to a maximum of twenty) people set up in business.
	■ The Partnership Act 1890 states certain accounting rules, principally that profits and losses must be shared equally.
	■ Many partnerships over-ride the accounting rules of the Act by making a partnership agreement which covers the following main points:
	– division of profits and losses between partners
	– partners' salaries
	– whether interest is to be allowed on capital and at what rate
	– whether interest is to be charged on partners' drawings
	■ The usual way to account for partners' capital is to maintain a fixed capital account for each partner. This is complemented by a fluctuating current account which is used as a working account for profit share, drawings, etc.
	■ The financial statements of partnerships are similar to those of sole traders, but incorporate:
	– an appropriation section, as a continuation of the income statement to show the profit (or loss) share
	– capital and current accounts for each partner shown in the statement of financial position

Key Terms		
	partnership	the relation which subsists between persons carrying on a business in common with a view of profit
	Partnership Act 1890	legislation which includes the accounting rules of partnerships
	partnership agreement	agreement between the partners which, amongst other things, often varies the accounting rules of the Partnership Act 1890
	appropriation section	part of the income statement which shows how the profit is shared amongst the partners
	capital account	account which records the amount of capital contributed by a partner; usually for a fixed amount, which only alters where a permanent increase or decrease takes place
	current account	a fluctuating account to which is credited: profit share, salary, interest on capital, and to which is debited: loss share, interest on drawings, and drawings

Activities

15.1 In the absence of a partnership agreement, which one of the following contravenes the provisions of the Partnership Act 1890?

(a)   no partner is entitled to a salary

(b)   profits and losses are to be shared in proportion to capital

(c)   partners are not entitled to receive interest on their capital

(d)   interest is not to be charged on partners' drawings

Answer (a) or (b) or (c) or (d)

15.2 The current account of a partner, Tara Shah, has a balance at the beginning of the financial year of £550 debit. During the year, the following transactions pass through her current account:

- interest on capital, £900
- salary, £10,000
- drawings, £14,000
- profit share, £4,230

What is the balance of Tara Shah's current account at the end of the financial year?

(a) £580 Cr

(b) £1,220 Dr

(c) £1,680 Dr

(d) £120 Cr

Answer (a) or (b) or (c) or (d)

15.3 Lysa and Mark are in partnership and own a shop, 'Trends', which sells fashionable teenage clothes. The following figures are extracted from their accounts for the year ended 31 December 20-8:

	£	
Capital accounts at 1 January 2008:		
Lysa	50,000	Cr
Mark	40,000	Cr
Current accounts at 1 January 20-8:		
Lysa	420	Cr
Mark	1,780	Cr
Drawings:		
Lysa	13,000	
Mark	12,250	
Interest charged on drawings:		
Lysa	300	
Mark	250	
Interest allowed on capital:		
Lysa	2,500	
Mark	2,000	
Profit share:		
Lysa	9,300	
Mark	9,300	

Note: neither partner is entitled to receive a salary

You are to show the partners' capital and current accounts for the year ended 31 December 20-8.

15.4 John James and Steven Hill are in partnership and own a wine shop called 'Grapes'. The following
trial balance has been taken from their accounts for the year ended 31 December 20-5:

	Dr £	Cr £
Capital accounts:		
James		38,000
Hill		32,000
Current accounts:		
James	3,000	
Hill		1,000
Drawings:		
James	10,000	
Hill	22,000	
Sales revenue		174,000
Cost of sales	85,000	
Rent and rates	7,500	
Advertising	12,000	
Heat and light	3,500	
Wages and salaries	18,000	
Sundry expenses	4,000	
Shop fittings at cost	20,000	
*Closing inventory – statement of financial position	35,000	
Bank	29,000	
Sales ledger control	6,000	
Purchases ledger control		8,000
Value Added Tax		2,000
	255,000	255,000

* Only the closing inventory is included in the trial balance because cost of sales has already been calculated.

Notes at 31 December 20-5:
- depreciation is to be charged on the shop fittings at 10 per cent per year
- Steven Hill is to receive a partnership salary of £15,000
- allow interest on partners' capital accounts at 10 per cent per year
- remaining profits and losses are to be shared equally

Task 1

Prepare the partnership financial statements for the year ended 31 December 20-5, using the
extended trial balance method.

Task 2

Show the partners' capital and current accounts for the year ended 31 December 20-5.

Task 3

Prepare the partnership financial statements for the year ended 31 December 20-5 in the conventional format.

Task 4

On receiving the accounts, John James asks a question about the partners' current accounts. He wants to know why the balances brought down at the start of the year for the two partners are on opposite sides.

Draft a note to John James explaining:

- what the balance on a partner's current account represents

- what a debit balance on a partner's current account means

- what a credit balance on a partner's current account means

15.5   You have the following information about a partnership business:

- The financial year ends on 31 March

- The partners are Ian, Jim and Kay

- Partners' annual salaries:

Ian	£20,500
Jim	£14,500
Kay	£10,250

- Partners' capital account balances as at 31 March 20-5:

Ian	£30,000
Jim	£40,000
Kay	£20,000

  Interest on capital is allowed at 5% per annum on the capital account balance at the end of the financial year.

- The partners share the remaining profit of £22,000 as follows:

Ian	40%
Jim	40%
Kay	20%

- Partners' drawings for the year:

Ian	£30,000
Jim	£25,000
Kay	£14,000

Prepare the current accounts for the partners for the year ended 31 March 20-5. Show clearly the balances carried down. You MUST enter zeros where appropriate in order to obtain full mark. Do NOT use brackets, minus signs or dashes.

Current accounts

	Ian £	Jim £	Kay £		Ian £	Jim £	Kay £
Balance b/d	0	0	200	Balance b/d	0	900	0

15.6 This Activity is about preparing a partnership statement of financial position.

You are preparing the statement of financial position for the DE Partnership for the year ended 31 March 20-2. The partners are Don and Eve.

All the necessary year end adjustments have been made, except for the transfer of profit to the current accounts of the partners.

Before sharing profits the balances of the partners' current accounts are:

- Don £750 credit

- Eve £400 debit

Each partner is entitled to £4,000 profit share.

(a) **Calculate the balance of each partner's current account after sharing profits. Fill in the answers below.**

Current account balance: Don	£
Current account balance: Eve	£

Note: these balances will need to be transferred into the statement of financial position of the partnership which follows.

You have the following trial balance. All the necessary year end adjustments have been made.

(b) Prepare a statement of financial position for the partnership as at 31 March 20-2. You need to use the partners' current account balances that you have just calculated. Do NOT use brackets, minus signs or dashes.

DE Partnership
Trial balance as at 31 March 20-2

	Dr £	Cr £
Accruals		550
Administration expenses	28,180	
Allowance for doubtful debts		1,100
Allowance for doubtful debts: adjustment	110	
Bank	11,520	
Capital account – Don		25,000
Capital account – Eve		20,000
Cash	150	
Closing inventory	15,790	15,790
Current account – Don		750
Current account – Eve	400	
Depreciation charge	3,250	
Disposal of non-current asset	650	
Machinery at cost	35,500	
Machinery: accumulated depreciation		12,150
Opening inventory	11,650	
Purchases	70,250	
Purchases ledger control		18,720
Sales revenue		125,240
Sales ledger control	25,690	
Selling expenses	18,940	
Value Added Tax		2,780
Total	222,080	222,080

DE Partnership

Statement of financial position as at 31 March 20-2

Non-current (fixed) assets	Cost £	Accumulated depreciation £	Carrying amount (net book value) £
Current assets			
Current liabilities			
Net current assets			
Net assets			
Financed by:	Don	Eve	Total

16 Changes in partnerships

this chapter covers...

In this chapter we continue our study of partnerships by looking at the principles involved and the accounting entries, for:

- admission of a new partner

- retirement of a partner

- death of a partner

- changes in profit-sharing ratios

- partnership changes when there are split years

Before we look at each of these, we need to consider the goodwill of the business, which features in all of the changes listed above.

GOODWILL

The statement of financial position of a partnership, like that of many businesses, rarely indicates the true value of the business as a going concern: usually the recorded figures underestimate the worth of a business. There are two main reasons for this:

- **Prudence** – if there is any doubt about the value of assets, they are stated at the lowest possible figure.

- **Goodwill** – a going concern business (ie one that continues to trade successfully) will often have a value of goodwill, because of various factors, eg the trade that has been built up, the reputation of the business, the location of the business, the skill of the workforce, and the success at developing new products.

definition of goodwill

Goodwill can be defined formally in accounting terms as:

the difference between the value of a business as a whole, and the net value of its separate assets and liabilities.

For example, an existing business is bought for £500,000, with the separate assets and liabilities being worth £450,000 net; goodwill is, therefore, £50,000.

Thus goodwill has a value as an intangible non-current asset to the owner or owners of a going concern business, whether or not it is recorded on the statement of financial position. As you will see in the sections which follow, a valuation has to be placed on goodwill when changes take place in a partnership.

valuation of goodwill

The valuation of goodwill is always subject to negotiation between the people concerned if, for instance, a partnership business is to be sold. It is, most commonly, based on the profits of the business – eg the average profit over the last, say, three years and multiplied by an agreed figure, perhaps six times.

We will now see how goodwill is created when changes are made to partnerships, such as the admission of a new partner or retirement of an existing partner. For these changes, a value for goodwill is agreed and this amount is temporarily debited to goodwill account, and credited to the partners' capital accounts in their profit-sharing ratio. After the change in the partnership, it is usual practice for the goodwill to be written off – the partners' capital accounts are debited and goodwill account is credited. Thus a 'nil' balance remains on goodwill account and, therefore, it is not recorded on the partnership statement of financial position. This follows the prudence concept, and is the method commonly followed when changes are made to partnerships.

ADMISSION OF A NEW PARTNER

A new partner – who can only be admitted with the consent of all existing partners – is normally charged a premium for goodwill. This is because the new partner will start to share in the profits of the business immediately and will benefit from the goodwill established by the existing partners. If the business was to be sold shortly after the admission of a new partner, a price will again be agreed for goodwill and this will be shared amongst all the partners (including the new partner).

To make allowance for this benefit it is necessary to make double-entry adjustments in the partners' capital accounts. The most common way of doing this is to use a goodwill account which is opened by the old partners with the agreed valuation of goodwill and, immediately after the admission of the new partner, is closed by transfer to the partners' capital accounts, including that of the new partner.

The procedures on admission of a new partner are:

- **agree a valuation for goodwill**

- **old partners: goodwill created**
  - debit goodwill account with the amount of goodwill
  - credit partners' capital accounts (in their old profit-sharing ratio) with the amount of goodwill

- **old partners + new partner: goodwill written off**
  - debit partners' capital accounts (in their new profit-sharing ratio) with the amount of goodwill
  - credit goodwill account with the amount of goodwill

The effect of this is to charge the new partner with a premium for goodwill.

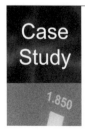

Case Study

AL AND BEN:
ADMISSION OF A NEW PARTNER

situation

Al and Ben are in partnership sharing profits and losses equally. Their statement of financial position as at 31 December 20-1 is as follows:

AL AND BEN	
STATEMENT OF FINANCIAL POSITION as at 31 December 20-1	
	£
Net assets	80,000
Capital accounts:	
Al	45,000
Ben	35,000
	80,000

On 1 January 20-2 the partners agree to admit Col into the partnership, with a new profit-sharing ratio of Al (2), Ben (2) and Col (1). Goodwill has been agreed at a valuation of £25,000. Col will bring £20,000 of cash into the business as his capital, part of which represents a premium for goodwill.

solution

The accounting procedures on the admission of Col into the partnership are as follows:

- goodwill has been valued at £25,000

- old partners: goodwill created

  - debit goodwill account

capital – Al	£12,500
capital – Ben	£12,500

  - credit capital accounts (in their old profit-sharing ratio)

goodwill – Al	£12,500
goodwill – Ben	£12,500

- old partners + new partner: goodwill written off

  - debit capital accounts (in their new profit-sharing ratio)

goodwill – Al	£10,000
goodwill – Ben	£10,000
goodwill – Col	£5,000

  - credit goodwill account £25,000

capital – Al	£10,000
capital – Ben	£10,000
capital – Col	£5,000

The capital accounts of the partners, after the above transactions have been recorded, appear as:

Dr				Partners' capital accounts				Cr
	Al	Ben	Col		Al	Ben	Col
	£	£	£		£	£	£
Goodwill	10,000	10,000	5,000	Balances b/d	45,000	35,000	-
Balances c/d	47,500	37,500	15,000	Goodwill	12,500	12,500	-
				Bank	-	-	20,000
	57,500	47,500	20,000		57,500	47,500	20,000
				Balances b/d	47,500	37,500	15,000

The statement of financial position, following the admission of Col, appears as:

AL, BEN AND COL
STATEMENT OF FINANCIAL POSITION as at 1 January 20-2

	£
Net assets (£80,000 + £20,000)	100,000
Capital accounts:	
Al (£45,000 + £12,500 – £10,000)	47,500
Ben (£35,000 + £12,500 – £10,000)	37,500
Col (£20,000 – £5,000)	15,000
	100,000

In this way, the new partner has paid the existing partners a premium of £5,000 for a one-fifth share of the profits of a business with a goodwill value of £25,000.

Although a goodwill account has been used, it has been fully utilised with adjusting entries made in the capital accounts of the partners, as follows:

Dr			Goodwill account			Cr
		£			£
Capital – Al	goodwill created	12,500	Capital – Al	goodwill written off	10,000
Capital – Ben		12,500	Capital – Ben		10,000
			Capital – Col		5,000
		25,000			25,000

RETIREMENT OF A PARTNER

When a partner retires it is necessary to calculate how much is due to the partner in respect of capital and profits. The partnership agreement normally details the procedures to be followed when a partner retires. The most common procedure requires goodwill to be valued and this operates in a similar way to the admission of a new partner, as follows:

- **agree a valuation for goodwill**
- **old partners: goodwill created**
  - debit goodwill account with the amount of goodwill
  - credit partners' capital accounts (in their old profit-sharing ratio) with the amount of goodwill
- **remaining partners: goodwill written off**
  - debit partners' capital accounts (in their new profit-sharing ratio) with the amount of goodwill
  - credit goodwill account with the amount of goodwill

The effect of this is to credit the retiring partner with the amount of the goodwill built up whilst he or she was a partner. This amount, plus the retiring partner's capital and current account balances can then be paid out of the partnership bank account. (If there is insufficient money for this, it is quite usual for a retiring partner to leave some of the capital in the business as a loan, which is repaid over a period of time.)

Case Study

JAN, KAY AND LIL: RETIREMENT OF A PARTNER

situation

Jan, Kay and Lil are in partnership sharing profit and losses in the ratio of 2:2:1 respectively. Partner Jan decides to retire on 31 December 20-4 when the partnership statement of financial position is as follows:

JAN, KAY AND LIL	
STATEMENT OF FINANCIAL POSITION as at 31 December 20-4	
	£
Net assets	<u>100,000</u>
Capital accounts:	
Jan	35,000
Kay	45,000
Lil	<u>20,000</u>
	<u>100,000</u>

Goodwill is agreed at a valuation of £30,000. Kay and Lil are to continue in partnership and will share profits and losses in the ratio of 2:1 respectively. Jan agrees to leave £20,000 of the amount due to her as a loan to the new partnership.

solution

The accounting procedures on the retirement of Jan from the partnership are as follows:

- goodwill has been valued at £30,000

- old partners: goodwill created

  - debit goodwill account

capital – Jan	£12,000
capital – Kay	£12,000
capital – Lil	£6,000

  - credit capital accounts (in their old profit-sharing ratio of 2:2:1)

goodwill – Jan	£12,000
goodwill – Kay	£12,000
goodwill – Lil	£6,000

- remaining partners: goodwill written off

  - debit capital accounts (in their new profit-sharing ratio of 2:1)

goodwill – Kay	£20,000
goodwill – Lil	£10,000

  - credit goodwill account

capital – Kay	£20,000
capital – Lil	£10,000

The capital accounts of the partners, after the above transactions have been recorded, appear as:

Dr				**Partners' capital accounts**			Cr
	Jan	Kay	Lil		Jan	Kay	Lil
	£	£	£		£	£	£
Goodwill	–	20,000	10,000	Balances b/d	35,000	45,000	20,000
Loan	20,000			Goodwill	12,000	12,000	6,000
Bank	27,000						
Balances c/d	–	37,000	16,000				
	47,000	57,000	26,000		47,000	57,000	26,000
				Balances b/d	–	37,000	16,000

Note: After recording goodwill, the balance of Jan's capital account is £47,000 (ie £35,000 + £12,000, being her share of the goodwill). Of this, £20,000 will be retained in the business as a loan, and £27,000 will be paid to her from the partnership bank account.

The statement of financial position, after the retirement of Jan, appears as follows:

KAY AND LIL	
STATEMENT OF FINANCIAL POSITION as at 1 January 20-5	
	£
Net assets (£100,000 – £27,000 paid to Jan)	73,000
Less Loan account of Jan	20,000
	53,000
Capital accounts:	
Kay (£45,000 + £12,000 – £20,000)	37,000
Lil (£20,000 + £6,000 – £10,000)	16,000
	53,000

The effect of this is that the remaining partners have bought out Jan's £12,000 share of the goodwill of the business, ie it has cost Kay £8,000, and Lil £4,000. If the business was to be sold later, Kay and Lil would share the goodwill obtained from the sale in their new profit-sharing ratio.

DEATH OF A PARTNER

The accounting procedures on the death of a partner are very similar to those for a partner's retirement. The only difference is that the amount due to the deceased partner is placed in an account called 'Executors (or Administrators) of X deceased' pending payment.

CHANGES IN PROFIT-SHARING RATIOS

It may be necessary, from time-to-time, to change the profit-sharing ratios of partners. A partner's share of profits might be increased because of an increase in capital in relation to the other partners, or because of a more active role in running the business. Equally, a share of profits may be decreased if a partner withdraws capital or spends less time in the business.

Clearly, the agreement of all partners is needed to make changes, and the guidance of the partnership agreement should be followed.

Generally, a change in profit-sharing ratios involves establishing a figure for goodwill, even if the partnership is to continue with the same partners; this is to establish how much goodwill was built up while they shared profits in their old ratios. Each partner will, therefore, receive a value for the goodwill based on the old profit-sharing ratio.

Case Study

DES AND EVE:
CHANGES IN PROFIT-SHARING RATIOS

situation

Des and Eve are in partnership sharing profits and losses equally. The statement of financial position at 31 December 20-6 is as follows:

DES AND EVE	
STATEMENT OF FINANCIAL POSITION as at 31 December 20-6	
	£
Net assets	60,000
Capital accounts:	
Des	35,000
Eve	25,000
	60,000

The partners agree that, as from 1 January 20-7, Des will take a two-thirds share of the profits and losses, with Eve taking one-third. It is agreed that goodwill shall be valued at £30,000.

solution

The accounting procedures on the change in the profit-sharing ratio are as follows:

• goodwill has been valued at £30,000

• old profit-sharing ratio: goodwill created

  – debit goodwill account

      capital – Des   £15,000

      capital – Eve   £15,000

  – credit capital accounts (in their old profit-sharing ratio of 1:1)

      goodwill – Des   £15,000

      goodwill – Eve   £15,000

- new profit-sharing ratio: goodwill written off

  - debit capital accounts (in their new profit-sharing ratio of 2:1)

goodwill – Des	£20,000
goodwill – Eve	£10,000

  - credit goodwill account

capital – Des	£20,000
capital – Eve	£10,000

The capital accounts of the partners, after the above transactions have been recorded, appear as:

Dr			**Partners' capital accounts**			Cr
	Des	Eve		Des	Eve
	£	£		£	£
Goodwill	20,000	10,000	Balances b/d	35,000	25,000
Balances c/d	30,000	30,000	Goodwill	15,000	15,000
	50,000	40,000		50,000	40,000
			Balances b/d	30,000	30,000

The statement of financial position at 1 January 20-7 appears as:

DES AND EVE
STATEMENT OF FINANCIAL POSITION as at 1 January 20-7

	£
Net assets	60,000
Capital accounts:	
Des (£35,000 + £15,000 – £20,000)	30,000
Eve (£25,000 + £15,000 – £10,000)	30,000
	60,000

The effect is that Des has 'paid' Eve £5,000 to increase his share of the profits from half to two-thirds. This may seem unfair but neither partner is worse off in the event of the business being sold, assuming that the business is sold for £90,000 (£60,000 assets + £30,000 goodwill). Before the change in the profit-sharing ratio they would have received:

Des £35,000 capital + £15,000 half-share of goodwill	=	£50,000
Eve £25,000 capital + £15,000 half-share of goodwill	=	£40,000

After the change, they will receive:

Des £30,000 capital + £20,000 two-thirds share of goodwill	=	£50,000
Eve £30,000 capital + £10,000 one-third share of goodwill	=	£40,000

As far as the sale amounts are concerned, the position remains unchanged: it is only the profit-sharing ratios that will be different as from 1 January 20-7. Also, any increase in goodwill above the £30,000 figure will be shared in the new ratio.

PARTNERSHIP CHANGES: SPLIT YEARS

Any of the changes in partnerships that we have looked at so far in this chapter may occur during the course of an accounting year, rather than at the end of it.

For example, part-way through the year:

- the partners may decide to admit a new partner
- a partner might retire, or die
- the partners may decide to change their profit-sharing ratios

To avoid having to prepare financial statements at the date of the change, it is usual to continue with the accounts until the normal year end. Then, when profit for the year has been calculated, it is necessary to apportion the profit between the two parts of the financial year, ie to split the year into the period before the change, and the period after the change. This may be done by assuming that the profit for the year has been earned at an even rate throughout the year, but it is important to check in Assessments as profit may not accrue evenly.

The apportionment is done by dividing the appropriation account between the two time periods.

Case Study

RAJ AND SAM: SPLIT YEARS

situation

Raj and Sam are in partnership; their partnership agreement states:

- interest is allowed on partners' capital accounts at the rate of ten per cent per annum
- Sam receives a partnership salary of £18,000 per annum
- the balance of partnership profits and losses are shared between Raj and Sam in the ratio 2:1 respectively

At the beginning of the financial year, on 1 January 20-4, the balances of the partners' capital accounts were:

Raj	£70,000
Sam	£50,000

During the year ended 31 December 20-4, the profit of the partnership was £50,500 before appropriations. The profit arose evenly throughout the year.

On 1 October 20-4, Raj and Sam admitted Tom as a partner. Tom introduced £40,000 of cash into the business as his capital.

The partnership agreement was amended on 1 October 20-4 as follows:

- interest is allowed on partners' capital accounts at the rate of ten per cent per annum
- Sam and Tom are each to receive a partnership salary of £12,000 per annum
- the balance of partnership profits and losses are to be shared between Raj, Sam and Tom in the ratio of 2:2:1 respectively

Note: no accounting entries for goodwill are to be recorded.

solution

RAJ, SAM AND TOM
PARTNERSHIP APPROPRIATION ACCOUNT for the year ended 31 December 20-4

	9 months to 30 September	3 months to 31 December	Total for year
	£	£	£
Profit	37,875	12,625	50,500
Less appropriation of profit:			
Salaries:			
Sam £18,000 pa x 9 months	13,500	–	
£12,000 pa x 3 months		3,000	16,500
Tom £12,000 pa x 3 months		3,000	3,000
Interest on partners' capitals:			
Raj £70,000 @ 10% pa x 9 months	5,250	–	
£70,000 @ 10% pa x 3 months	–	1,750	7,000
Sam £50,000 @ 10% pa x 9 months	3,750	–	
£50,000 @ 10% pa x 3 months	–	1,250	5,000
Tom £40,000 @ 10% pa x 3 months	–	1,000	1,000
	*15,375	**2,625	18,000
Share of remaining profit:			
Raj	(2/3) 10,250	(2/5) 1,050	11,300
Sam	(1/3) 5,125	(2/5) 1,050	6,175
Tom	–	(1/5) 525	525
	15,375	2,625	18,000

*   Raj and Sam shared profits 2:1 respectively
**   Raj, Sam and Tom shared profits 2:2:1

RECORDING PARTNERSHIP CHANGES

The accounting effects of partnership changes usually have a significant impact upon partners' capital accounts and the ratio in which they share profits and losses. Before implementing changes, the accounts assistant must check that the correct actions are being taken. This may mean referring issues to the appropriate person – such as the accounts supervisor, the manager of the partnership, or one or more of the partners.

The accounts assistant must take note of:

- the terms of the partnership agreement
- the policies, regulations, procedures and timescales of the partnership

If there are any discrepancies or queries they should be identified and, where possible, resolved – any outstanding issues will need to be referred to the appropriate person.

Chapter Summary

- ■ Goodwill is an intangible fixed asset.

- ■ With partnerships, goodwill is normally valued for transactions involving changes in the structure of the business to cover:
  - admission of a new partner
  - retirement of a partner
  - death of a partner
  - changes in profit-sharing ratios

  A goodwill account is normally created just before the change, and then written off immediately after the change, ie it does not appear on the partnership statement of financial position.

- ■ When partnership changes take place part-way through the financial year, it is necessary to apportion the profit between the two parts of the financial year, usually by assuming that the profit has been earned at a uniform rate throughout the year.

Key Terms

goodwill	the difference between the value of a business as a whole, and the net value of its separate assets and liabilities
goodwill account	an account to which goodwill, an intangible non-current asset, is debited
premium for goodwill	amount charged to a new partner who joins an existing partnership

Activities

16.1 Where changes in partnerships take place, a goodwill account is opened, usually temporarily. After the change has taken place, goodwill account is usually written off. This follows the accounting concept of:

(a)   prudence

(b)   accruals

(c)   going concern

(d)   consistency

Answer (a) or (b) or (c) or (d)

16.2 Andrew and Barry are in partnership sharing profits equally. Colin is admitted to the partnership and the profit sharing ratios now become Andrew (2), Barry (2) and Colin (1). Goodwill at the time of Colin joining is valued at £50,000. What will be the goodwill adjustments to Andrew's capital account?

(a)   debit £25,000,   credit £25,000

(b)   debit £20,000,   credit £25,000

(c)   debit £20,000,   credit £20,000

(d)   debit £25,000,   credit £20,000

Answer (a) or (b) or (c) or (d)

16.3 Jim and Maisie are in partnership sharing profits and losses in the ratio 3:2 respectively. At 31 December 20-4 the balances of their capital accounts are £60,000 and £40,000 respectively. Current accounts are not used by the partnership.

On 1 January 20-5, Matt is admitted into the partnership, with a new profit-sharing ratio of Jim (3), Maisie (2) and Matt (1). Goodwill has been agreed at a valuation of £48,000. Matt will bring £28,000 of cash into the business as his capital and premium for goodwill. Goodwill is to be eliminated from the accounts.

For the year ended 31 December 20-5, the partnership profits amount to £60,000, and the partners' drawings were:

	£
Jim	12,000
Maisie	12,000
Matt	8,000

You are to show the partners' capital accounts for the period from 31 December 20-4 to 1 January 20-6.

16.4 Reena, Sam and Tamara are in partnership sharing profits in the ratio 4:2:2 respectively. Sam is to retire on 31 August 20-8 and is to be paid the amount due to him from the bank.

The statement of financial position drawn up immediately before Sam's retirement was as follows:

	£
Non-current assets	50,000
Current assets	10,000
Bank	25,000
	85,000
Trade payables	(10,000)
	75,000
Capital accounts:	
Reena	33,000
Sam	12,000
Tamara	30,000
	75,000

Goodwill is to be valued at £16,000. No goodwill is to remain in the accounts after Sam's retirement. In the new partnership Reena and Tamara are to share profits equally.

Note that current accounts are not used by the partnership.

Task 1

Prepare the partners' capital accounts, showing the amount Sam is to be paid upon retirement.

Task 2

Show the statement of financial position immediately after Sam's retirement from the partnership.

16.5 Dave and Elsa are in partnership sharing profits and losses equally. Their statement of financial position at 30 September 20-8 is as follows:

DAVE AND ELSA

STATEMENT OF FINANCIAL POSITION as at 30 September 20-8

	£
Net assets	130,000
Capital Accounts:	
Dave	80,000
Elsa	50,000
	130,000

The partners agree that, as from 1 October 20-8, Dave will take a two-thirds share of the profits and losses, with Elsa taking one-third. It is agreed that goodwill should be valued at £45,000. No goodwill is to remain in the accounts following the change.

Note that current accounts are not used by the partnership.

Task 1

Show the journal entries to record the creation of goodwill and its subsequent elimination for the change in the profit-sharing ratio.

Task 2

Show the partners' capital accounts with the entries to record the change in the profit-sharing ratio.

Task 3

Show the statement of financial position of Dave and Elsa after the change in the profit-sharing ratio.

16.6 Jean and David are in partnership. Profit for the year ended 31 December 20-1 is £32,700 before appropriation of profit. Their capital account balances at 31 December 20-1 are Jean £10,000, David £12,000. Their partnership agreement allows for the following:

- partnership salaries
    - Jean £12,000
    - David £10,000
- interest is allowed on capital at 5 per cent per year on the balance at the year end
- profit share, effective until 30 June 20-1
    - Jean two-thirds
    - David one-third
- profit share, effective from 1 July 20-1
    - Jean one-half
    - David one-half

Notes:

- no accounting entries for goodwill are to be recorded
- profits accrued evenly during the year
- drawings for the year were: Jean £18,600, David £14,200

Task 1

Prepare the partnership appropriation account for Jean and David for the year ended 31 December 20-1

Task 2

Update the current accounts for the partnership for the year ended 31 December 20-1. Show clearly the balances carried down.

Dr				Partners' current accounts			Cr
20-1		Jean	David	20-1		Jean	David
		£	£			£	£
1 Jan	Balance b/d	–	1,250	1 Jan	Balance b/d	2,400	–

16.7 You have the following information about a partnership:

The partners are Kay and Lee.

- Mel was admitted to the partnership on 1 April 20-1 when she introduced £30,000 to the bank account.

- Profit share, effective until 31 March 20-1:
  - Kay   50%
  - Lee   50%

- Profit share, effective from 1 April 20-1:
  - Kay   40%
  - Lee   40%
  - Mel   20%

- Goodwill was valued at £24,000 on 31 March 20-1.

- Goodwill is to be introduced into the partners' capital accounts on 31 March and then eliminated on 1 April

(a) **Prepare the capital account for Mel, the new partner, showing clearly the balance carried down as at 1 April 20-1.**

Capital account – Mel

			Balance b/d	0

(b)   **Complete the following sentence by circling the appropriate phrase in each case:**

Goodwill can be defined as the difference between **(the value of the business/the balance at bank)**, and the **(accumulated depreciation/net value)** of the separate **(receivables and payables/assets and liabilities)**.

16.8   You have the following information about a partnership business:

- The financial year ends on 31 March.

- The partners at the beginning of the year were Amy, Ben and Col.

- Amy retired on 30 September 20-2.

- Partners' annual salaries:

    - Amy   £24,000

    - Ben   £21,000

    - Col   nil

- Partners' interest on capital:

    - Amy   £1,000 per full year

    - Ben   £1,500 per full year

    - Col   £500 per full year

- Profit share, effective until 30 September 20-2:

    - Amy   50%

    - Ben   25%

    - Col   25%

- Profit share, effective from 1 October 20-2:

    - Ben   60%

    - Col   40%

Profit for the year ended 31 March 20-3 was £72,000. You can assume that profits accrued evenly during the year.

Prepare the appropriation account (on the next page) for the partnership for the year ended 31 March 20-3.

Partnership Appropriation account for the year ended 31 March 20-3

	1 Apr 20-2 – 30 Sep 20-2 £	1 Oct 20-2 – 31 Mar 20-3 £	Total £
Profit			
Salaries:			
Amy			
Ben			
Col			
Interest on capital:			
Amy			
Ben			
Col			
Profit available for distribution			

Profit share			
Amy			
Ben			
Col			
Total profit distributed			

Answers to activities

CHAPTER 1: THE ACCOUNTING SYSTEM

1.1   (a)   ledger   (b)   receivable (debtor)   (c)   payable (creditor)

     (d)   sales day book   (e)   cash book   (f)   general ledger *or* nominal ledger

     (g)   assets minus liabilities equals capital, *or* assets equals capital plus liabilities

1.2   (a)   assets – items owned by a business; liabilities – items owed by a business

     (b)   receivables – individuals or businesses who owe money in respect of goods or services supplied by the business; payables – individuals or businesses to whom money is owed by the business

     (c)   purchases – goods bought, either on credit or for cash, which are intended to be resold later; sales – the sale of goods, whether on credit or for cash, in which the business trades

     (d)   credit purchases – goods bought, with payment to be made at a later date; cash purchases – goods bought and paid for immediately

1.3   (a)   asset of bank increases by £8,000
         capital increases by £8,000
         asset £8,000 – liability £0 = capital £8,000

     (b)   asset of computer increases by £4,000
         asset of bank decreases by £4,000
         asset £8,000 – liability £0 = capital £8,000

     (c)   asset of bank increases by £3,000
         liability of loan increases by £3,000
         asset £11,000 – liability £3,000 = capital £8,000

     (d)   asset of van increases by £6,000
         asset of bank decreases by £6,000
         asset £11,000 – liability £3,000 = capital £8,000

1.4   (a)   capital   £20,000
     (b)   capital   £10,000
     (c)   liabilities   £7,550
     (d)   assets   £14,100
     (e)   liabilities   £18,430
     (f)   assets   £21,160

1.5   (a)   owner started in business with capital of £10,000 in the bank
     (b)   bought office equipment for £2,000, paying by cheque
     (c)   received a loan of £6,000 by cheque
     (d)   bought a van for £10,000, paying by cheque
     (e)   owner introduces £2,000 additional capital by cheque
     (f)   loan repayment of £3,000 made by cheque

CHAPTER 2: DOUBLE-ENTRY BOOK-KEEPING

2.1   (d)   **2.2**   (b)   **2.3**   (d)

2.4   **JAMES ANDERSON (summary of transactions)**

			Dr			Cr
Account	**20-4**		**£**	**20-4**		**£**
Capital				2 Feb	Bank	7,500
Computer	6 Feb	Bank	2,000			
Rent paid	9 Feb	Bank	750			
Wages	12 Feb	Bank	425			
	25 Feb	Bank	380			
Bank loan				13 Feb	Bank	2,500
Commission rec'd				20 Feb	Bank	145
Drawings	23 Feb	Bank	200			
Van	27 Feb	Bank	6,000			

CHAPTER 3: BALANCING ACCOUNTS AND THE TRIAL BALANCE

3.1   (c)   **3.2**   (b)   **3.3**   (c)

3.4   (a) and (c)   **ANDREW JOHNSTONE**

Dr			**Bank account**			Cr
20-4		£	20-4			£
1 Jan	Capital	10,000	4 Jan	Rent paid		500
11 Jan	Sales	1,000	5 Jan	Shop fittings		1,500
12 Jan	Sales	1,250	20 Jan	Comp Supplies Ltd		5,000
22 Jan	Sales	1,450	31 Jan	Balance c/d		6,700
		13,700				13,700
1 Feb	Balance b/d	6,700	2 Feb	Rent paid		500
4 Feb	Sales	1,550	15 Feb	Shop fittings		850
10 Feb	Sales	1,300	27 Feb	Comp Supplies Ltd		6,350
12 Feb	Rowcester College	750	28 Feb	Balance c/d		5,300
19 Feb	Sales	1,600				
25 Feb	Sales	1,100				
		13,000				13,000
1 Mar	Balance b/d	5,300				

Dr		**Capital account**			Cr
20-4		£	20-4		£
			1 Jan	Bank	10,000

Dr		**Rent paid account**			Cr
20-4		£	20-4		£
4 Jan	Bank	500	28 Feb	Balance c/d	1,000
2 Feb	Bank	500			
		1,000			1,000
1 Mar	Balance b/d	1,000			

Dr		Shop fittings account				Cr
20-4			£	20-4		£
5 Jan	Bank		1,500	28 Feb	Balance c/d	2,350
15 Feb	Bank		850			
			2,350			2,350
1 Mar	Balance b/d		2,350			

Dr		Purchases account				Cr
20-4			£	20-4		£
7 Jan	Comp Supplies Ltd		5,000	31 Jan	Balance c/d	11,500
25 Jan	Comp Supplies Ltd		6,500			
			11,500			11,500
1 Feb	Balance b/d		11,500	28 Feb	Balance c/d	17,000
24 Feb	Comp Supplies Ltd		5,500			
			17,000			17,000
1 Mar	Balance b/d		17,000			

Dr		Comp Supplies Limited				Cr
20-4			£	20-4		£
20 Jan	Bank		5,000	7 Jan	Purchases	5,000
31 Jan	Balance c/d		6,500	25 Jan	Purchases	6,500
			11,500			11,500
5 Feb	Purchases returns		150	1 Feb	Balance b/d	6,500
27 Feb	Bank		6,350	24 Feb	Purchases	5,500
28 Feb	Balance c/d		5,500			
			12,000			12,000
				1 Mar	Balance b/d	5,500

Dr		Sales account				Cr
20-4			£	20-4		£
31 Jan	Balance c/d		4,550	11 Jan	Bank	1,000
				12 Jan	Bank	1,250
				16 Jan	Rowcester College	850
				22 Jan	Bank	1,450
			4,550			4,550
28 Feb	Balance c/d		11,150	1 Feb	Balance b/d	4,550
				4 Feb	Bank	1,550
				10 Feb	Bank	1,300
				19 Feb	Bank	1,600
				25 Feb	Bank	1,100
				26 Feb	Rowcester College	1,050
			11,150			11,150
				1 Mar	Balance b/d	11,150

Dr		**Rowcester College**			Cr
20-4		£	20-4		£
16 Jan	Sales	850	27 Jan	Sales returns	100
			31 Jan	Balance c/d	750
		850			850
1 Feb	Balance b/d	750	12 Feb	Bank	750
26 Feb	Sales	1,050	28 Feb	Balance c/d	1,050
		1,800			1,800
1 Mar	Balance b/d	1,050			

Dr		**Sales returns account**		Cr
20-4		£	20-4	£
27 Jan	Rowcester College	100		

Dr		**Purchases returns account**		Cr
20-4		£	20-4	£
			5 Feb Comp Supplies Ltd	150

(b)

Trial balance as at 31 January 20-4

	Dr	Cr
	£	£
Bank	6,700	
Capital		10,000
Rent paid	500	
Shop fittings	1,500	
Purchases	11,500	
Comp Supplies Limited		6,500
Sales		4,550
Rowcester College	750	
Sales returns	100	
	21,050	21,050

(d)

Trial balance as at 28 February 20-4

	Dr	Cr
	£	£
Bank	5,300	
Capital		10,000
Rent paid	1,000	
Shop fittings	2,350	
Purchases	17,000	
Comp Supplies Limited		5,500
Sales		11,150
Rowcester College	1,050	
Sales returns	100	
Purchases returns		150
	26,800	26,800

3.5

SAMANTHA WILKES
Trial balance as at 31 March 20-4

	Dr £	Cr £
Bank		2,750
Purchases	14,890	
Sales revenue		35,680
Purchases returns		440
Purchases ledger control		2,360
Office equipment	8,000	
Vehicle	14,000	
Opening inventory	2,810	
Sales returns	550	
Sales ledger control	3,840	
Administration expenses	12,060	
Value Added Tax		1,420
Carriage out	740	
Discount received		210
Capital *(missing figure)*		14,030
	56,890	56,890

CHAPTER 4: FINANCIAL STATEMENTS – THE EXTENDED TRIAL BALANCE

4.1   (b)   **4.2**   (d)

4.3   Business A: profit £40,000; capital £100,000
Business B: expenses £70,000; liabilities £100,000
Business C: income £70,000; assets £90,000
Business D: expenses £75,000; liabilities £60,000
Business E: loss £10,000; assets £100,000

4.4

	TRIAL BALANCE		FINANCIAL STATEMENTS			
			INCOME STATEMENT		STATEMENT OF FINANCIAL POSITION	
	Debit	Credit	Debit	Credit	Debit	Credit
(a) Salaries	✓		✓			
(b) Purchases	✓		✓			
(c) Sales ledger control	✓				✓	
(d) Sales returns	✓		✓			
(e) Discount received		✓		✓		
(f) Vehicle	✓				✓	
(g) Capital		✓				✓

4.5 EXTENDED TRIAL BALANCE

NICK JOHNSON

31 DECEMBER 20-3

Account name	Ledger balances Dr £	Ledger balances Cr £	Adjustments Dr £	Adjustments Cr £	Income statement Dr £	Income statement Cr £	Statement of financial position Dr £	Statement of financial position Cr £
Opening inventory	25,000				25,000			
Purchases	210,000				210,000			
Sales revenue		310,000				310,000		
Administration expenses	12,400				12,400			
Wages	41,000				41,000			
Rent paid	7,500				7,500			
Telephone	1,000				1,000			
Interest paid	9,000				9,000			
Travel expenses	1,100				1,100			
Premises at cost	200,000						200,000	
Machinery at cost	40,000						40,000	
Sales ledger control	31,000						31,000	
Bank	900						900	
Cash	100						100	
Capital		150,000						150,000
Drawings	14,000						14,000	
Loan from bank		100,000						100,000
Purchases ledger control		29,000						29,000
Value Added Tax		4,000						4,000
Closing inventory: income statement				21,000		21,000		
Closing inventory: statement of financial position			21,000				21,000	
Profit/loss for the year					24,000			24,000
	593,000	593,000	21,000	21,000	331,000	331,000	307,000	307,000

4.6 EXTENDED TRIAL BALANCE

ALAN HARRIS

30 JUNE 20-4

Account name	Ledger balances Dr £	Ledger balances Cr £	Adjustments Dr £	Adjustments Cr £	Income statement Dr £	Income statement Cr £	Statement of financial position Dr £	Statement of financial position Cr £
Opening inventory	13,250				13,250			
Capital		70,000						70,000
Premises at cost	65,000						65,000	
Vehicle at cost	5,250						5,250	
Purchases	55,000				55,000			
Sales revenue		85,500				85,500		
Administration expenses	850				850			
Wages	9,220				9,220			
Rent paid	1,200				1,200			
Telephone	680				680			
Interest paid	120				120			
Travel expenses	330				330			
Sales ledger control	1,350						1,350	
Purchases ledger control		6,400						6,400
Value Added Tax		1,150						1,150
Bank	2,100						2,100	
Cash	600						600	
Drawings	8,100						8,100	
Closing inventory: income statement		18,100				18,100		
Closing inventory: statement of financial position	18,100						18,100	
Profit/loss for the year					22,950			22,950
	181,150	181,150			103,600	103,600	100,500	100,500

CHAPTER 5: ACCRUALS AND PREPAYMENTS

5.1   (d)   **5.2**   (c)

5.3

Dr		Vehicle expenses account			Cr
20-7		£	20-7		£
31 Dec	Balance b/d	1,680	31 Dec	Drawings	420
			31 Dec	Income statement	1,260
		1,680			1,680

5.4   (a)   Expenses in income statement of £56,760; statement of financial position shows accruals of £1,120.

(b)   Expenses in income statement of £2,852 (ie £3,565 – £713); statement of financial position shows prepayments of £713.

(c)   Expenses in income statement of £1,800; statement of financial position shows prepayments of £150.

5.5   (a)   **Rent paid**

	£		£
Bank	11,250	Balance b/d	750
		Income statement	9,000
		Balance c/d	1,500
	11,250		11,250

(b)   **Administration expenses**

		£			£
20-6 1 Apr	Balance b/d	250	20-7 31 Mar	Income statement	10,825
20-7 31 Mar	Bank	10,400			
20-7 31 Mar	Balance c/d	175			
		10,825			10,825

(c)

Account	£	£ Dr	£ Cr
Accruals			175
Capital	75,000		75,000
Discount received	680		680
Drawings	10,000	10,000	
Interest received	200		200
Machinery at cost	20,000	20,000	
Prepayments		1,500	
Sales revenue	115,000		115,000

5.6 (a) **Rent received**

	£		£
Income statement	5,400	Balance b/d	450
Balance c/d	900	Bank	5,850
	6,300		6,300

(b) **Vehicle expenses**

		£			£
20-3 30 Jun	Bank	6,450	20-2 1 Jul	Balance b/d	220
20-3 30 Jun	Balance c/d	380	20-3 30 Jun	Income statement	6,610
		6,830			6,830

(c)

Account	£	£ Dr	£ Cr
Accruals			380
Capital	30,000		30,000
Cash	250	250	
Discount allowed	600	600	
Prepayments			900*
Purchases	15,500	15,500	
Sales returns	850	850	
Vehicles at cost	12,000	12,000	

* prepayment of income: rent received

5.7 EXTENDED TRIAL BALANCE

DON SMITH

31 DECEMBER 20-2

Account name	Ledger balances Dr £	Ledger balances Cr £	Adjustments Dr £	Adjustments Cr £	Income statement Dr £	Income statement Cr £	Statement of financial position Dr £	Statement of financial position Cr £
Sales ledger control	24,325						24,325	
Purchases ledger control		15,408						15,408
Value Added Tax		4,276						4,276
Capital		30,000						30,000
Bank		1,083						1,083
Rent and rates	10,862			250	10,612			
Electricity	2,054		110		2,164			
Telephone	1,695				1,695			
Salaries	55,891		365		56,256			
Vehicles at cost	22,250						22,250	
Office equipment at cost	7,500						7,500	
Vehicle expenses	10,855				10,855			
Drawings	15,275						15,275	
Discount allowed	478				478			
Discount received		591				591		
Purchases	138,960				138,960			
Sales revenue		257,258				257,258		
Opening inventory	18,471				18,471			
Closing inventory: income statement				14,075		14,075		
Closing inventory: statement of financial position			14,075				14,075	
Accruals				475				475
Prepayments			250				250	
Profit/loss for the year					32,433			32,433
	308,616	308,616	14,800	14,800	271,924	271,924	83,675	83,675

5.8 EXTENDED TRIAL BALANCE

JOHN BARCLAY
30 JUNE 20-3

Account name	Ledger balances Dr £	Ledger balances Cr £	Adjustments Dr £	Adjustments Cr £	Income statement Dr £	Income statement Cr £	Statement of financial position Dr £	Statement of financial position Cr £
Sales revenue		864,321				864,321		
Purchases	600,128			250	599,878			
Sales returns	2,746				2,746			
Purchases returns		3,894				3,894		
Office expenses	33,947			346	33,601			
Salaries	122,611				122,611			
Vehicle expenses	36,894		1,250		38,144			
Discount allowed	3,187				3,187			
Discount received		4,951				4,951		
Sales and purchases ledger control	74,328	52,919					74,328	52,919
Value Added Tax		10,497						10,497
Opening inventory	63,084				63,084			
Vehicles at cost	83,500						83,500	
Office equipment at cost	23,250						23,250	
Land and buildings at cost	100,000						100,000	
Bank loan		75,000						75,000
Bank	1,197						1,197	
Capital		155,000						155,000
Drawings	21,710		250				21,960	
Closing inventory: income statement				66,941		66,941		
Closing inventory: statement of financial position			66,941				66,941	
Accruals				1,250				1,250
Prepayments			346				346	
Profit/loss for the year					76,856			76,856
	1,166,582	1,166,582	68,787	68,787	940,107	940,107	371,522	371,522

CHAPTER 6: DEPRECIATION OF NON-CURRENT ASSETS

6.1 (a)

6.2
- With reducing balance depreciation a fixed percentage is written off the reduced balance (carrying amount) of the asset each year.
- When compared with straight-line depreciation, reducing balance needs a much higher percentage to be written off each year to achieve the same residual value.
- Thus the money amounts for reducing balance are greater in the early years and smaller in the later years when compared with straight-line depreciation.
- As delivery vans depreciate more in the early years and are unlikely to be kept for the whole of their expected lives, reducing balance depreciation is a more accurate reflection of their worth than is straight-line depreciation.
- The depreciation charge will be high in the early years but smaller in the later years; by contrast repair costs are likely to be low early on but will increase in later years. By using reducing balance depreciation, the total charge to the income statement for both depreciation and repair costs is likely to be similar throughout the assets' lives.

6.3 (a)

Dr			Car: accumulated depreciation account			Cr
20-2		£	20-2			£
31 Dec	Balance c/d	3,000	31 Dec	Depreciation charge		3,000
20-3			20-3			
31 Dec	Balance c/d	5,250	1 Jan	Balance b/d		3,000
			31 Dec	Depreciation charge		2,250
		5,250				5,250
20-4			20-4			
31 Dec	Disposals	6,937	1 Jan	Balance b/d		5,250
			31 Dec	Depreciation charge		1,687
		6,937				6,937

(b)

Year	Statement of financial position	
	Dr *Cost*	Cr *Accumulated depreciation*
	£	£
31 Dec 20-2	12,000	3,000
31 Dec 20-3	12,000	5,250

(c)

Dr		Disposals account		Cr
20-4	£	20-4		£
31 Dec Car at cost	12,000	31 Dec Accumulated depreciation		6,937
31 Dec Income statement		31 Dec Bank		5,500
(profit on disposal)	437			
	12,437			12,437

6.4   (a) **Machinery at cost**

Balance b/d	£20,000		
Bank	£8,000	Balance c/d	£28,000
	£28,000		£28,000

(b) **Machinery: accumulated depreciation**

		Balance b/d	£6,000
Balance c/d	£7,250	Depreciation charge	£1,250
	£7,250		£7,250

Machinery: depreciation charge

Balance b/d	£2,000	Income statement	£3,250
Machinery: accumulated depreciation	£1,250		
	£3,250		£3,250

6.5   (a)

year 1	£3,000
year 2	£2,250
total	£5,250

(b)   **Vehicle at cost**

Balance b/d	£12,000	Disposals	£12,000
	£12,000		£12,000

Vehicle: disposals

Vehicle at cost	£12,000	Vehicle: accumulated depreciation	£5,250
Income statement	£250	Bank/cash	£7,000
	£12,250		£12,250

Bank/cash

Vehicle disposals	£7,000	Balance c/d	£8,400
Value Added Tax	£1,400		
	£8,400		£8,400

(c)

profit	✓
loss	

6.6   **Machinery at cost**

Balance b/d	£4,200	Disposals	£4,200
Disposals	£1,200	Balance c/d	£6,000
Bank	£4,800		
	£10,200		£10,200

Machinery: accumulated depreciation

Disposals	£3,150	Balance b/d	£3,150
Balance c/d	£1,500	Depreciation charge	£1,500
	£4,650		£4,650

Machinery: depreciation charge

Machinery: accumulated depreciation	£1,500	Income statement	£1,500
	£1,500		£1,500

Machinery: disposals

Machinery at cost	£4,200	Machinery: accumulated depreciation	£3,150
Income statement	£150	Machinery at cost	£1,200
	£4,350		£4,350

6.7

Account	£	£ Dr	£ Cr
Accrual of expenses	680		680
Capital	25,000		25,000
Depreciation charge	1,200	1,200	
Drawings	8,000	8,000	
Interest received	200		200
Machinery at cost	6,500	6,500	
Machinery: accumulated depreciation	2,400		2,400
Prepayment of expenses	210	210	

6.8 Extended trial balance – see next page

6.9 A letter incorporating the following points:
- Straight-line method at 20% per year = depreciation charge of £200 per year
- Reducing balance method at 50% per year = depreciation charge of £500 for year 1, £250 for year 2, £125 for year 3, £62 for year 4, and £31 for year 5, leaving a small residual value of £32
- Either method acceptable
- The straight-line method will give larger profits for the first two years
- The cash position is not affected, as depreciation is a non-cash expense (this point should be stressed)

6.8 EXTENDED TRIAL BALANCE

JOHN HENSON

31 DECEMBER 20-1

Account name	Ledger balances		Adjustments		Income statement		Statement of financial position	
	Dr £	Cr £	Dr £	Cr £	Dr £	Cr £	Dr £	Cr £
Purchases	71,600				71,600			
Sales revenue		121,750				121,750		
Opening inventory	6,250				6,250			
Vehicle running expenses	1,480				1,480			
Rent and rates	5,650				5,650			
Office expenses	2,220				2,220			
Discount received		285				285		
Wages and salaries	18,950				18,950			
Office equipment at cost	10,000						10,000	
Office equipment: accumulated depreciation				1,000				1,000
Vehicle at cost	12,000						12,000	
Vehicle: accumulated depreciation				3,000				3,000
Sales ledger control	5,225						5,225	
Purchases ledger control		3,190						3,190
Value Added Tax		1,720						1,720
Capital		20,000						20,000
Drawings	13,095						13,095	
Bank	725						725	
Disposal of non-current asset		250				250		
Closing inventory: income statement				8,500		8,500		
Closing inventory: statement of financial position			8,500				8,500	
Depreciation charge			4,000		4,000			
Profit/loss for the year					20,635			20,635
	147,195	147,195	12,500	12,500	130,785	130,785	49,545	49,545

6.10 EXTENDED TRIAL BALANCE

HAZEL HARRIS

31 DECEMBER 20-8

Account name	Ledger balances		Adjustments		Income statement		Statement of financial position	
	Dr £	Cr £	Dr £	Cr £	Dr £	Cr £	Dr £	Cr £
Bank loan		75,000						75,000
Capital		125,000						125,000
Purchases and sales revenue	465,000	614,000			465,000	614,000		
Building repairs	8,480				8,480			
Vehicle at cost	12,000						12,000	
Vehicle: accumulated depreciation		2,400		1,920				4,320
Vehicle expenses	2,680				2,680			
Premises at cost	100,000						100,000	
Premises: accumulated depreciation		4,000		2,000				6,000
Bank		2,000						2,000
Furniture at cost	25,000						25,000	
Furniture: accumulated depreciation		2,500		2,500				5,000
Wages and salaries	86,060		3,180		89,240			
Discounts	10,610	8,140			10,610	8,140		
Drawings	24,000						24,000	
Rates and insurance	6,070			450	5,620			
Sales and purchases ledger control	52,130	32,600					52,130	32,600
Value Added Tax		5,250						5,250
Administration expenses	15,460				15,460			
Opening inventory	63,000				63,000			
Disposal of non-current asset	400				400			
Closing inventory: income statement				88,000		88,000		
Closing inventory: statement of financial position			88,000				88,000	
Accruals				3,180				3,180
Prepayments			450				450	
Depreciation charge			6,420		6,420			
Profit/loss for the year					43,230			43,230
	870,890	870,890	98,050	98,050	710,140	710,140	301,580	301,580

CHAPTER 7: IRRECOVERABLE DEBTS AND ALLOWANCE FOR DOUBTFUL DEBTS

7.1 (a) *Tutorial note:* where control accounts - see Chapter 10 - are in use, the credit entry will be to sales ledger control account.

7.2 (c)

7.3 • *Income statement*
debit irrecoverable debts, £210
debit allowance for doubtful debts: adjustment, £500

• *Statement of financial position*
debit sales ledger control £20,000, credit allowance for doubtful debts £500

7.4 Dr **Allowance for doubtful debts account** Cr

20-5		£	20-5		£
31 Dec	Balance c/d	400	1 Jan	Balance b/d	300
			31 Dec	Allowance for doubtful debts: adjustment *(increase in allowance)*	100
		400			400
20-6			20-6		
31 Dec	Allowance for doubtful debts: adjustment *(decrease in allowance)*	50	1 Jan	Balance b/d	400
31 Dec	Balance c/d	350			
		400			400
20-7			20-7		
			1 Jan	Balance b/d	350

20-5 *Extracts from financial statements produced for year ended 31 December:*
Income statement:
– debit allowance for doubtful debts: adjustment £100
Statement of financial position:
– debit sales ledger control £8,000
– credit allowance for doubtful debts £400

20-6 *Extracts from financial statements produced for year ended 31 December:*
Income statement:
– credit allowance for doubtful debts: adjustment £50
Statement of financial position:
– debit sales ledger control £7,000
– credit allowance for doubtful debts £350

7.5 (a) **Irrecoverable debts**

	£		£
Sales ledger control (Thompson & Co)	110	Income statement	255
Sales ledger control (T Aziz)	65		
Sales ledger control (Wyvern Traders)	80		
	255		255

(b) **Allowance for doubtful debts**

		£			£
20-8 31 Dec	Balance c/d	700	20-8 1 Jan	Balance b/d	600
			20-8 31 Dec	Allowance for doubtful debts: adjustment	100
		700			700

(c)

	Ledger balances		Adjustments	
Account	Dr £	Cr £	Dr £	Cr £
Allowance for doubtful debts		600		100
Allowance for doubtful debts: adjustment			100	
Irrecoverable debts			255	
Loan interest	790			
Sales ledger control	28,255			255
Vehicles at cost	12,000			
Vehicles: accumulated depreciation		6,400		
Wages	35,470			

7.6 EXTENDED TRIAL BALANCE

PAUL SANDERS

31 DECEMBER 20-4

Account name	Ledger balances Dr £	Ledger balances Cr £	Adjustments Dr £	Adjustments Cr £	Income statement Dr £	Income statement Cr £	Statement of financial position Dr £	Statement of financial position Cr £
Purchases and sales revenue	51,225	81,762			51,225	81,762		
Sales and purchases returns	186	254			186	254		
Opening inventory	6,031				6,031			
Discounts allowed and received	324	238			324	238		
Vehicle expenses	1,086				1,086			
Wages and salaries	20,379				20,379			
Electricity	876		102		978			
Telephone	1,241				1,241			
Rent and rates	4,565			251	4,314			
Sundry expenses	732				732			
Irrecoverable debts	219				219			
Sales and purchases ledger control	1,040	7,671					1,040	7,671
Value Added Tax		1,301						1,301
Bank	3,501						3,501	
Cash	21						21	
Vehicles at cost	15,000						15,000	
Vehicles: accumulated depreciation		3,000		3,000				6,000
Office equipment at cost	10,000						10,000	
Office equipment: accumulated depreciation		5,000		1,000				6,000
Capital		25,000						25,000
Drawings	8,000						8,000	
Disposal of non-current asset		200				200		
Closing inventory: income statement				8,210		8,210		
Closing inventory: statement of financial position			8,210				8,210	
Accruals				102				102
Prepayments			251				251	
Depreciation charge			4,000		4,000			
Allowance for doubtful debts				52				52
Allowance for doubtful debts: adjustment			52		52			
Profit/loss for the year					103		103	
	124,426	124,426	12,615	12,615	90,767	90,767	46,126	46,126

7.7 EXTENDED TRIAL BALANCE

JAMES JENKINS
30 JUNE 20-5

Account name	Ledger balances Dr £	Ledger balances Cr £	Adjustments Dr £	Adjustments Cr £	Income statement Dr £	Income statement Cr £	Statement of financial position Dr £	Statement of financial position Cr £
Capital		36,175						36,175
Drawings	19,050						19,050	
Purchases and sales revenue	105,240	168,432			105,240	168,432		
Opening inventory	9,427				9,427			
Sales and purchases ledger control	3,840	5,294					3,840	5,294
Value Added Tax		1,492						1,492
Sales and purchases returns	975	1,237			975	1,237		
Discounts allowed and received	127	643			127	643		
Wages and salaries	30,841				30,841			
Vehicle expenses	1,021		55		1,076			
Rent and rates	8,796			275	8,521			
Heating and lighting	1,840				1,840			
Telephone	355				355			
General expenses	1,752				1,752			
Irrecoverable debts	85				85			
Vehicle at cost	8,000						8,000	
Vehicle: accumulated depreciation		3,500		1,125				4,625
Shop fittings at cost	6,000						6,000	
Shop fittings: accumulated depreciation		2,000		600				2,600
Cash	155						155	
Bank	21,419						21,419	
Closing inventory: income statement				11,517		11,517		
Closing inventory: statement of financial position			11,517				11,517	
Accruals				55				55
Prepayments			275				275	
Depreciation charge			1,725		1,725			
Allowance for doubtful debts		150	54					96
Allowance for doubtful debts: adjustment				54		54		
Profit/loss for the year					19,919			19,919
	218,923	218,923	13,626	13,626	181,883	181,883	70,256	70,256

CHAPTER 8: THE RULES OF ACCOUNTING

8.1   (d)

8.2   (a)   Prudence: by making an allowance for doubtful debts the business is recording the possibility that the customer may not pay.

(b)   Materiality: although the discs will be kept for a number of years they are not treated as a non-current asset and depreciated because their cost is not material to the business.

(c)   Consistency: the owner of the business should use the most appropriate depreciation method for the type of asset, and apply it consistently from year-to-year. In this way the financial statements of different years are comparable; the depreciation method can be changed provided there are good reasons for so doing, with a note to the financial statements explaining what has happened.

(d)   Accruals (or matching): here the expense of electricity is being matched to the time period in which the cost was incurred.

8.3   (a)   Consistency concept: he should continue to use reducing balance method (it won't make any difference to the bank manager anyway).

(b)   Prudence concept: inventory valuation should be at lower of cost and net realisable value, ie £10,000 in this case.

(c)   Business entity concept: car is an asset of John's firm, not a personal asset (in any case personal assets, for sole traders and partnerships, might well be used to repay debts of firm).

(d)   Prudence concept: the trade receivable should be written off as an irrecoverable debt in the income statement (so reducing profit), and the statement of financial position figure for receivables should be £27,500 (which is closer to the amount he can expect to receive).

(e)   Accruals concept: expenses and revenues must be matched, therefore it must go through the old year's financial statements.

(f)   Going concern concept: presumes that the business will continue to trade in the foreseeable future: alternative is to use liquidation amounts where the assets may have very different values.

8.4   (a)   The purpose of depreciation is to spread the cost of a non-current asset over its useful life.

(b)   D

8.5   (c)

8.6   (a)   Sales for February: 24 tables at £50 each = £1,200

(b)   Closing inventory at 28 February: 6 tables at £31 each = £186

8.7

		£	
•	seeds	1,450	(selling price)
•	fertilisers and insecticides	2,270	(cost price)
•	tools	4,390	(cost price)
		8,110	

8.8 (a) this year's profit is overstated by £1,000

(b) next year's profit will be understated by £1,000

8.9 (a) Inventory is to be valued at the lower of cost and net realisable value.

(b) B

(c) D

(d) decrease

8.10

> EMAIL
>
> **Cost of computer accounting software**
>
> As the cost of the software is relatively low, I recommend that it is treated as revenue expenditure and shown amongst the expenses in the income statement. This is in line with the accounting concept of materiality: at a cost of £99 it is not worth recording it separately. Had the cost been much higher, the software would have been treated as a non-current asset and depreciated over its useful life.

8.11 • The first part of the statement is true – capital expenditure is money spent on non-current assets

• Whilst non-current assets are recorded in the statement of financial position, there is a link with the income statement in that the depreciation charge will be recorded as an expense

• As all non-current assets having a known useful life must be depreciated (IAS 16), there is a clear link between such non-current assets shown in the statement of financial position and the depreciation charge recorded in the income statement

• On disposal of non-current assets the amount of any over or under depreciation is taken to the income statement

8.12

		capital expenditure	revenue expenditure
(a)	purchase of machinery	✓	
(b)	installation of machinery	✓	
(c)	depreciation of machinery		✓
(d)	purchase of property	✓	
(e)	legal fees relating to the purchase of property	✓	
(f)	repairs to property		✓
(g)	insurance of property		✓
(h)	labour costs of own employees used to build extension to property	✓	
(i)	repainting and redecoration of property		✓

CHAPTER 9: ACCOUNTING FOR CAPITAL TRANSACTIONS

9.1 (a)   **9.2** (a)   **9.3** (b)

9.4

EXTRACT FROM NON-CURRENT ASSET REGISTER

Description/serial no	Acquisition date	Cost £	Depreciation £	Carrying amount £	Funding method	Disposal proceeds £	Disposal date
Office equipment							
Computer, Supra ML	12/3/-1	3,000.00			Cash		
Year ended 31/12/-1			1,500.00	1,500.00			
Year ended 31/12/-2			750.00	750.00			
Year ended 31/12/-3			375.00	375.00			
Year ended 31/12/-4						500.00	10/2/-4

9.5 (a)

Date	Details	Reference	Dr	Cr
			£	£
20-1				
10 Jan	Machine	GL	32,000	
	Bank	CB		32,000
	Purchase of machine to develop and print films; capital expenditure authorisation number			

Dr		Machine at cost account		Cr
20-1		£	20-4	£
10 Jan	Bank	32,000	17 Aug Disposals	32,000
20-4				
17 Aug	Disposals (part exchange allowance)	5,000		

Depreciation charge calculations

Depreciation at 40 per cent reducing balance per year is as follows:

year ended 31 December 20-1	£12,800
year ended 31 December 20-2	£7,680
year ended 31 December 20-3	£4,608

Note: the journal entry for the first year only is shown

Date	Details	Reference	Dr	Cr
			£	£
20-1				
31 Dec	Income statement	GL	12,800	
	Depreciation charge	GL		12,800
	Depreciation charge for year on machine			
31 Dec	Depreciation charge	GL	12,800	
	Machine: accumulated depreciation	GL		12,800
	Transfer of depreciation charge for year to accumulated depreciation			

Dr			Depreciation charge account		Cr
20-1		£	20-1		£
31 Dec	Machine: accumulated depreciation	12,800	31 Dec Income statement		12,800
20-2			20-2		
31 Dec	Machine: accumulated depreciation	7,680	31 Dec Income statement		7,680
20-3			20-3		
31 Dec	Machine: accumulated depreciation	4,608	31 Dec Income statement		4,608

Dr			Machine: accumulated depreciation account			Cr
20-1		£	20-1			£
31 Dec	Balance c/d	12,800	31 Dec	Depreciation charge		12,800
20-2			20-2			
31 Dec	Balance c/d	20,480	1 Jan	Balance b/d		12,800
			31 Dec	Depreciation charge		7,680
		20,480				20,480
20-3			20-3			
31 Dec	Balance c/d	25,088	1 Jan	Balance b/d		20,480
			31 Dec	Depreciation charge		4,608
		25,088				25,088
20-4			20-4			
17 Aug	Disposals	25,088	1 Jan	Balance b/d		25,088

Date	Details	Reference	Dr	Cr
20-4			£	£
17 Aug	Disposals	GL	32,000	
	Machine at cost	GL		32,000
	Machine: accumulated depreciation	GL	25,088	
	Disposals	GL		25,088
	Machine at cost	GL	5,000	
	Disposals	GL		5,000
	Income statement	GL	1,912	
	Disposals	GL		1,912
			64,000	64,000
	Part exchange of machine to develop and print films; loss on disposal of £1,912 transferred to income statement			

Dr			**Machine disposals account**		Cr
20-4		£	20-4		£
17 Aug	Machine at cost	32,000	17 Aug	Machine: accumulated depreciation	25,088
			17 Aug	Machine at cost (part exchange)	5,000
			17 Aug	Income statement (loss on disposal)	1,912
		32,000			32,000

(b)

EXTRACT FROM NON-CURRENT ASSET REGISTER

Description/serial no	Acquisition date	Cost £	Depreciation £	Carrying amount £	Funding method	Disposal proceeds £	Disposal date
Machinery							
Automated d&p machine	10/1/-1	32,000.00			Cash		
Year ended 31/12/-1			12,800.00	19,200.00			
Year ended 31/12/-2			7,680.00	11,520.00			
Year ended 31/12/-3			4,608.00	6,912.00			
Year ended 31/12/-4						5,000.00	17/8/-4

9.6   Depreciation calculations:

	20-1 £	20-2 £	20-3 £	TOTAL £
Registration number				
WV01 XNP	4,500	4,500	–	9,000
WV01 YNP	4,500	4,500	4,500	13,500
WV03 ZNP	–	–	5,250	5,250
TOTAL	9,000	9,000	9,750	27,750

Dr			**Vehicles at cost account**			Cr
20-1			£	20-1		£
24 Jan	Bank		15,000	31 Dec	Balance c/d	30,000
24 Jan	Bank		15,000			
			30,000			30,000
20-2				20-2		
1 Jan	Balance b/d		30,000	31 Dec	Balance c/d	30,000
20-3				20-3		
1 Jan	Balance b/d		30,000	13 Oct	Disposals	15,000
17 Feb	Bank		17,500	31 Dec	Balance c/d	32,500
			47,500			47,500
20-4				20-4		
1 Jan	Balance b/d		32,500			

Dr	**Depreciation charge account**			Cr
20-1		£	20-1	£
31 Dec Vehicles: accumulated depreciation		9,000	31 Dec Income statement	9,000
20-2			20-2	
31 Dec Vehicles: accumulated depreciation		9,000	31 Dec Income statement	9,000
20-3			20-3	
31 Dec Vehicles: accumulated depreciation		9,750	31 Dec Income statement	9,750

Dr		**Vehicles: accumulated depreciation account**			Cr
20-1		£	20-1		£
31 Dec	Balance c/d	9,000	31 Dec	Depreciation charge	9,000
20-2			20-2		
31 Dec	Balance c/d	18,000	1 Jan	Balance b/d	9,000
			31 Dec	Depreciation charge	9,000
		18,000			18,000
20-3			20-3		
13 Oct	Disposals	9,000	1 Jan	Balance b/d	18,000
31 Dec	Balance c/d	18,750	31 Dec	Depreciation charge	9,750
		27,750			27,750
20-4			20-4		
			1 Jan	Balance b/d	18,750

Dr		Vehicle disposals account				Cr
20-3			£	20-3		£
13 Oct	Vehicles at cost		15,000	13 Oct	Vehicles: accumulated depreciation	9,000
13 Oct	Income statement (profit on disposal)		500	13 Oct	Bank	6,500
			15,500			15,500

9.7

NON-CURRENT ASSET REGISTER							
Description/serial no	Acquisition date	Cost £	Depreciation £	Carrying amount £	Funding method	Disposal proceeds £	Disposal date
Office equipment							
Telephone system	30/09/-4	1,500.00			Cash		
Year end 31/03/-5			450.00	1,050.00			
Year end 31/03/-6			450.00	600.00			
Year end 31/03/-7			450.00	150.00			
Executive desk	28/03/-7	660.00			Cash		
Year end 31/03/-7			198.00	462.00			
Vehicles							
WV04 JEC	15/04/-4	18,000.00			Cash		
Year end 31/03/-5			4,500.00	13,500.00			
Year end 31/03/-6			3,375.00	10,125.00			
Year end 31/03/-7			–	–		8,500.00	10/03/-7
WV55 DBC	30/10/-5	12,000.00			Part-exchange		
Year end 31/03/-6			3,000.00	9,000.00			
Year end 31/03/-7			2,250.00	6,750.00			

Tutorial note: the delivery cost of the executive desk is capitalised.

9.8 (d)

CHAPTER 10: CONTROL ACCOUNTS

10.1 (c)   **10.2** (b)

10.3 (d)   **10.4** (b)

10.5

Dr			Sales ledger control account				Cr
20-8		£	20-8				£
1 Jun	Balance b/d	17,491	30 Jun	Sales returns			1,045
30 Jun	Credit sales	42,591	30 Jun	Payments from trade receivables			39,024
			30 Jun	Discount allowed			593
			30 Jun	Irrecoverable debts			296
			30 Jun	Balance c/d			19,124
		60,082					60,082
1 Jul	Balance b/d	19,124					

10.6

Dr			Purchases ledger control account		Cr
20-9		£	20-9		£
30 Apr	Purchases returns	653	1 Apr	Balance b/d	14,275
30 Apr	Payments to trade payables	31,074	30 Apr	Credit purchases	36,592
30 Apr	Discount received	1,048			
30 Apr	Set-off: sales ledger	597			
30 Apr	Balance c/d	17,495			
		50,867			50,867
			1 May	Balance b/d	17,495

10.7 (a)

SALES LEDGER

Dr			Arrow Valley Retailers		Cr
20-4		£	20-4		£
1 Feb	Balance b/d	826.40	20 Feb	Bank	805.74
3 Feb	Sales	338.59	20 Feb	Discount allowed	20.66
			29 Feb	Balance c/d	338.59
		1,164.99			1,164.99
1 Mar	Balance b/d	338.59			

Dr	**B Brick (Builders) Limited**			Cr
20-4		£	20-4	£
1 Feb	Balance b/d	59.28	29 Feb Irrecoverable debts	59.28

Dr	**Mereford Manufacturing Company**			Cr
20-4		£	20-4	£
1 Feb	Balance b/d	293.49	24 Feb Sales returns	56.29
3 Feb	Sales	127.48	29 Feb Set-off: purchases ledger	364.68
		420.97		420.97

Dr	**Redgrove Restorations**			Cr
20-4		£	20-4	£
1 Feb	Balance b/d	724.86	7 Feb Sales returns	165.38
17 Feb	Sales	394.78	29 Feb Balance c/d	954.26
		1,119.64		1,119.64
1 Mar	Balance b/d	954.26		

Dr	**Wyvern Warehouse Limited**			Cr
20-4		£	20-4	£
1 Feb	Balance b/d	108.40	15 Feb Bank	105.69
17 Feb	Sales	427.91	15 Feb Discount allowed	2.71
			29 Feb Balance c/d	427.91
		536.31		536.31
1 Mar	Balance b/d	427.91		

(b)

Dr	**Sales ledger control account**			Cr
20-4		£	20-4	£
1 Feb	Balance b/d	2,012.43	29 Feb Sales returns	221.67
29 Feb	Credit sales	1,288.76	29 Feb Payments received	911.43
			29 Feb Discount allowed	23.37
			29 Feb Set-off: purchases ldgr.	364.68
			29 Feb Irrecoverable debts	59.28
			29 Feb Balance c/d	1,720.76
		3,301.19		3,301.19
1 Mar	Balance b/d	1,720.76		

(c)

Reconciliation of sales ledger control account		
	1 February 20-4	29 February 20-4
	£	£
Arrow Valley Retailers	826.40	338.59
B Brick (Builders) Limited	59.28	–
Mereford Manufacturing Company	293.49	nil
Redgrove Restorations	724.86	954.26
Wyvern Warehouse Limited	108.40	427.91
Sales ledger control account	2,012.43	1,720.76

10.8 (a)

10.9

Adjustment number	Amount £	Debit ✓	Credit ✓
1	200		✓
2	150		✓
3	125		✓

10.10

Adjustment number	Amount £	Debit ✓	Credit ✓
1	180		✓
3	400	✓	
4	440	✓	

10.11

Adjustment number	Amount £	Debit ✓	Credit ✓
2	550		✓
3	180	✓	
4	210		✓

CHAPTER 11: THE JOURNAL AND CORRECTION OF ERRORS

11.1 (b)   **11.2** (a)

11.3 (a) *error of omission*

Date	Details	Reference	Dr	Cr
			£	£
	Sales ledger control	GL	150	
	Sales	GL		150
	Sales invoice no .... omitted from the accounts: in the sales ledger – debit J Rigby £150			

(b) *error of principle*

Date	Details	Reference	Dr	Cr
			£	£
	Vehicles at cost	GL	10,000	
	Vehicle expenses	GL		10,000
	Correction of error – vehicle no .... invoice no			

(c) *reversal of entries*

Date	Details	Reference	Dr	Cr
			£	£
	Postages	GL	55	
	Bank	CB		55
	Postages	GL	55	
	Bank	CB		55
			110	110
	Correction of reversal of entries on			

(d) *error of original entry*

Date	Details	Reference	Dr	Cr
			£	£
	Sales ledger control	GL	98	
	Bank	CB		98
	Bank	CB	89	
	Sales ledger control	GL		89
			187	187
	Correction of error – bank payment for £89 received on ......(date)......: in the sales ledger *– debit L Johnson £98* *– credit L Johnson £89*			

(e) *compensating error*

Date	Details	Folio	Dr	Cr
			£	£
	Purchases	GL	100	
	Purchases returns	GL		100
	Correction of under-cast on purchases account and purchases returns account on ....(date).......			

(f) *mispost/error of commission*

Date	Details	Folio	Dr	Cr
			£	£
	Purchases ledger control	GL	125	
	Purchases ledger control	GL		125
	Correction of mispost – bank payment for £125 on ..... in the purchases ledger			
	– debit H Price Limited			
	– credit H Prince			

11.4

	Date	Details	Reference	Dr	Cr
				£	£
(a)		Office expenses	GL	85	
		Suspense	GL		85
		Omission of entry in office expenses account.			
(b)		Suspense	GL	78	
		Photocopying	GL		78
		Photocopying	GL	87	
		Suspense	GL		87
				165	165
		Payment for photocopying £87 entered in photocopying account as £78			
(c)		Suspense	GL	2,500	
		Sales returns	GL		2,500
		Sales returns	GL	2,400	
		Suspense	GL		2,400
				4,900	4,900
		Incorrect balance of sales returns account transferred to the trial balance			
(d)		Commission received	GL	25	
		Suspense	GL		25
		Commission received entered twice in commission received account.			

Dr		Suspense account			Cr
20-7		£	20-7		£
30 Sep	Trial balance difference	19	(a)	Office expenses	85
(b)	Photocopying	78	(b)	Photocopying	87
(c)	Sales returns	2,500	(c)	Sales returns	2,400
			(d)	Commission received	25
		2,597			2,597

11.5 (a)

Date	Details	Reference	Dr	Cr
20-8			£	£
31 Dec	Closing inventory – statement of financial position	GL	22,600	
	Closing inventory – income statement	GL		22,600
	Inventory valuation at 31 December 20-8 transferred to the financial statements			

(b)

Date	Details	Reference	Dr	Cr
20-8			£	£
31 Dec	Income statement	GL	890	
	Telephone expenses	GL		890
	Transfer to income statement of expenditure for the year			

(c)

Date	Details	Reference	Dr	Cr
20-8			£	£
31 Dec	Income statement	GL	23,930	
	Salaries	GL		22,950
	Accruals	GL		980
			23,930	23,930
	Transfer to income statement of expenditure for the year			

(d)

Date	Details	Reference	Dr	Cr
20-8			£	£
31 Dec	Income statement	GL	1,160	
	Prepayments	GL	80	
	Photocopying expenses	GL		1,240
			1,240	1,240
	Transfer to income statement			
	of expenditure for the year			

(e)

Date	Details	Reference	Dr	Cr
20-8			£	£
31 Dec	Rent received	GL	4,800	
	Prepayment of income	GL		400
	Income statement	GL		4,400
			4,800	4,800
	Transfer to income statement			
	of income for year			

(f)

Date	Details	Reference	Dr	Cr
20-8			£	£
31 Dec	Income statement	GL	500	
	Depreciation charge	GL		500
	Transfer to income statement of			
	depreciation charge for year on			
	fixtures and fittings			
31 Dec	Depreciation charge	GL	500	
	Fixtures and fittings: accumulated			
	depreciation	GL		500
	Transfer of depreciation charge for year			
	to accumulated depreciation account			

(g)

Date	Details	Reference	Dr	Cr
20-8			£	£
31 Dec	Disposals	GL	5,000	
	Machinery at cost	GL		5,000
	Machinery: accumulated depreciation	GL	3,750	
	Disposals	GL		3,750
	Bank	CB	2,400	
	Disposals	GL		2,000
	VAT	GL		400
	Income statement	GL		750
	Disposals	GL	750	
			11,900	11,900
	Sale of machine no ....; profit on sale £750 credited to income statement			

(h)

Date	Details	Reference	Dr	Cr
20-8			£	£
31 Dec	Irrecoverable debts	GL	125	
	Sales ledger control	GL		125
	Accounts written off as irrecoverable:			
	in the sales ledger			
	– credit Nick Marshall £55			
	– credit Crabbe & Company £30			
	– credit A Hunt £40			
	Total £125			
31 Dec	Income statement	GL	125	
	Irrecoverable debts	GL		125
	Transfer to income statement of irrecoverable debts for year			

(i)

Date	Details	Reference	Dr	Cr
20-8			£	£
31 Dec	Income statement	GL		100
	Allowance for doubtful debts: adjustment	GL	100	
	Transfer to income statement of decrease in allowance for doubtful debts			
31 Dec	Allowance for doubtful debts: adjustment	GL		100
	Allowance for doubtful debts	GL	100	
	Transfer of reduction for year to allowance for doubtful debts account			

11.6 (a) **Journal**

	Dr £	Cr £
Irrecoverable debts	220	
Sales ledger control		220

(b) **Journal**

	Dr £	Cr £
Vehicles	12,500	
Suspense		12,500

(c) **Journal**

	Dr £	Cr £
Closing inventory – statement of financial position	*24,750	
Closing inventory – income statement		*24,750

* lower of cost and net realisable value: £25,400 – £650

(d) **Journal**

	Dr £	Cr £
Suspense	1,400	
VAT		1,400
Suspense	1,400	
VAT		1,400

11.7   (a)   **Extract from extended trial balance**

	Ledger balances		Adjustments	
	Dr	Cr	Dr	Cr
	£	£	£	£
Allowance for doubtful debts		720		
Bank	9,500			2,500
Closing inventory – statement of financial position			*41,200	
Closing inventory – income statement				*41,200
Depreciation charge	2,000			
Irrecoverable debts			78	
Office expenses	5,300			
Rent paid	14,200			
Sales		245,000		
Sales ledger control	47,400		350	78
Suspense		2,150	2,500	350
VAT		7,300		
Vehicles – accumulated depreciation		6,000		

* lower of cost and net realisable value: £42,000 – £800

(b)

Account	Dr ✓	Cr ✓
Income statement	✓	
Office expenses		✓
Narrative: Transfer to income statement of expenditure for the year		

11.8   Extended trial balance

Ledger account	Ledger balances		Adjustments		Income statement		Statement of financial position	
	£ Dr	£ Cr	£ Dr	£ Cr	£ Dr	£ Cr	£ Dr	£ Cr
Allowance for doubtful debts		1,700		200				1,900
Allowance for doubtful debts adjustment			200		200			
Bank		16,200		300				16,500
Capital		20,500						20,500
Closing inventory			18,500	18,500		18,500	18,500	
Depreciation charge			3,500		3,500			
Office expenses	18,600		400		19,000			
Opening inventory	12,500				12,500			
Payroll expenses	40,800		200		41,000			
Purchases	260,000		1,000		261,000			
Purchases ledger control		32,500						32,500
Sales revenue		375,000				375,000		
Sales ledger control	60,100						60,100	
Selling expenses	21,000				21,000			
Suspense	1,300		300	1,600				
VAT		2,900						2,900
Vehicles at cost	45,000						45,000	
Vehicles accumulated depreciation		10,500		3,500				14,000
Profit/loss for the year					35,300			35,300
	459,300	459,300	24,100	24,100	393,500	393,500	123,600	123,600

Tutorial notes:

- two amounts are shown on the same line in the adjustments column for closing inventory: the debit entry is shown in the debit column of the statement of financial position; the credit entry is shown in the credit column of the income statement (see the journal entries in this Chapter)

- in suspense account the debit balance of £1,300 is cleared by the credit adjustments for £400, £200 and £1,000 (total £1,600), and the debit adjustment of £300

- depreciation charge and allowance for doubtful debts are adjusted in the way that has been shown in Chapters 6 and 7

CHAPTER 12: SOLE TRADER FINANCIAL STATEMENTS

12.1 (a) | £23,480 |

(b)

	Debit ✓	Credit ✓	No change ✓
Non-current assets	✓		
Trade receivables			✓
Trade payables		✓	
Bank			✓
Capital			✓

(c)

	✓
A bank loan repayable in two years' time	
A bank overdraft	✓
Drawings by the owner of the business	
Inventory sold and awaiting collection by the customer	

12.2

NICK JOHNSON

INCOME STATEMENT
for the year ended 31 December 20-3

	£	£
Sales revenue		310,000
Opening inventory	25,000	
Purchases	210,000	
	235,000	
Less Closing inventory	21,000	
Cost of sales		214,000
Gross profit		96,000
Less expenses:		
Administration expenses	12,400	
Wages	41,000	
Rent paid	7,500	
Telephone	1,000	
Interest paid	9,000	
Travel expenses	1,100	
		72,000
Profit for the year		24,000

STATEMENT OF FINANCIAL POSITION as at 31 December 20-3

	£	£	£
Non-current assets			
Premises			200,000
Machinery			40,000
			240,000
Current assets			
Inventory (closing)		21,000	
Receivables		31,000	
Bank		900	
Cash		100	
		53,000	
Less Current liabilities			
Payables	29,000		
Value Added Tax	4,000		
		33,000	
Net current assets			20,000
			260,000
Less Non-current liabilities			
Loan from bank			100,000
NET ASSETS			160,000
FINANCED BY			
Capital			
Opening capital			150,000
Add Profit for the year			24,000
			174,000
Less Drawings			14,000
Closing capital			160,000

12.3

ALAN HARRIS
INCOME STATEMENT
for the year ended 30 JUNE 20-4

	£	£
Sales revenue		85,500
Opening inventory	13,250	
Purchases	55,000	
	68,250	
Less Closing inventory	18,100	
Cost of sales		50,150
Gross profit		35,350
Less expenses:		
Administration expenses	850	
Wages	9,220	
Rent paid	1,200	
Telephone	680	
Interest paid	120	
Travel expenses	330	
		12,400
Profit for the year		22,950

STATEMENT OF FINANCIAL POSITION
as at 30 June 20-4

	£	£	£
Non-current assets			
Premises			65,000
Vehicle			5,250
			70,250
Current assets			
Inventory (closing)		18,100	
Receivables		1,350	
Bank		2,100	
Cash		600	
		22,150	
Less Current liabilities			
Payables	6,400		
Value Added Tax	1,150		
		7,550	
Net current assets			14,600
NET ASSETS			84,850
FINANCED BY			
Capital			
Opening capital			70,000
Add Profit for the year			22,950
			92,950
Less Drawings			8,100
Closing capital			84,850

12.4

CHRISTINE LORRAINE
INCOME STATEMENT
for the year ended 30 June 20-1

	£	£	£
Sales revenue			175,000
Less Sales returns			4,100
Net sales revenue			170,900
Opening inventory		15,140	
Purchases	102,000		
Add Carriage in	1,210		
	103,210		
Less Purchases returns	8,300		
Net purchases		94,910	
		110,050	
Less Closing inventory		18,350	
Cost of sales			91,700
Gross profit			79,200
Add income: Discount received			790
			79,990
Less expenses:			
Discount allowed		1,460	
Carriage out		5,680	
Other expenses		58,230	
			65,370
Profit for the year			14,620

CHAPTER 13: ADJUSTMENTS TO SOLE TRADER FINANCIAL STATEMENTS

13.1 (c)

13.2 (a)

13.3 (c)

13.4 (a)

Zelah Trading Income statement for the year ended 31 March 20-4	£	£
Sales revenue		155,210
Opening inventory	4,850	
Purchases	85,260	
Closing inventory	(6,500)	
Cost of sales		83,610
Gross profit		71,600
Less expenses:		
Depreciation charge	3,400	
Discounts allowed	750	
General expenses	21,240	
Rent	8,900	
Selling expenses	27,890	
Total expenses		62,180
Profit for the year		9,420

(b)

	✓
As a non-current asset	
As a current asset	✓
As a current liability	
As a deduction from capital	

(c)

	✓
HM Revenue and Customs owes the business	
HM Revenue and Customs is a receivable of the business	
There is an error – VAT is always a debit balance	
The business owes HM Revenue and Customs	✓

13.5

HELENA OSTROWSKA
INCOME STATEMENT
for the year ended 31 March 20-5

	£	£
Sales revenue		243,820
Opening inventory	30,030	
Purchases	140,950	
	170,980	
Less Closing inventory	34,080	
Cost of sales		136,900
Gross profit		106,920
Less expenses:		
Shop wages	40,270	
Heat and light	3,470	
Rent and rates	12,045	
Depreciation charge: shop fittings	5,000	
Loss on disposal of non-current asset	850	
Irrecoverable debts	200	
		61,835
Profit for the year		45,085

STATEMENT OF FINANCIAL POSITION
as at 31 March 20-5

	£	£	£
Non-current assets	Cost	Accumulated depreciation	Carrying amount
Shop fittings	30,000	15,000	15,000
Current assets			
Inventory		34,080	
Trade receivables		46,280	
Prepayment of expenses		220	
Bank		10,180	
		90,760	
Less Current liabilities			
Trade payables	24,930		
Accrual of expenses	940		
Value Added Tax	3,860		
		29,730	
Net current assets			61,030
NET ASSETS			76,030
FINANCED BY			
Capital			
Opening capital			62,000
Add Profit for the year			45,085
			107,085
Less Drawings			31,055
Closing capital			76,030

13.6

MARK PELISI
INCOME STATEMENT
for the year ended 31 March 20-7

	£	£
Sales revenue		100,330
Less Sales returns		120
		100,210
Less Cost of sales		35,710
Gross profit		64,500
Add other income:		
Discounts received		240
Profit on disposal of non-current asset		160
Allowance for doubtful debts: adjustment		180
		65,080
Less expenses:		
Discounts allowed	170	
Depreciation charges: vehicles	6,000	
equipment	3,500	
Wages	24,110	
Advertising	770	
Administration expenses	14,830	
Irrecoverable debts	350	
		49,730
Profit for the year		15,350

STATEMENT OF FINANCIAL POSITION
as at 31 March 20-7

	£	£	£
Non-current assets	Cost	Accumulated depreciation	Carrying amount
Vehicles	24,000	12,500	11,500
Equipment	18,500	8,000	10,500
	42,500	20,500	22,000
Current assets			
Inventory		5,640	
Trade receivables	3,480		
Less allowance for doubtful debts	620		
		2,860	
Bank		3,800	
		12,300	
Less Current liabilities			
Trade payables	2,760		
Accrual of expenses	400		
Value Added Tax	1,840		
		5,000	
Net current assets			7,300
			29,300
Less Non-current liabilities			
Bank loan			9,000
NET ASSETS			20,300
FINANCED BY			
Capital			
Opening capital			35,040
Add Profit for the year			15,350
			50,390
Less Drawings			30,090
Closing capital			20,300

CHAPTER 14: INCOMPLETE RECORDS

14.1 (c) **14.2** (b) **14.3** (d)

14.4

			£
(a)	•	receipts from sales	153,500
	•	add trade receivables at year end	2,500
	•	**sales for year**	156,000
(b)	•	payments to suppliers	95,000
	•	add trade payables at year end	65,000
	•	**purchases for year**	160,000
(c)	•	payments for rent and rates	8,750
	•	less rent prepaid at 31 Dec 20-4	250
	•	**rent and rates for year**	8,500
	•	payments for wages	15,000
	•	add wages accrued at 31 Dec 20-4	550
	•	**wages for year**	15,550

(d)

JANE PRICE
INCOME STATEMENT
for the year ended 31 December 20-4

	£	£
Sales revenue		156,000
Purchases	160,000	
Less Closing inventory	73,900	
Cost of sales		86,100
Gross profit		69,900
Less expenses:		
Advertising	4,830	
Rent and rates	8,500	
Wages	15,550	
Administration expenses	5,000	
Depreciation charge: shop fittings	10,000	
		43,880
Profit for the year		26,020

(e)

JANE PRICE
STATEMENT OF FINANCIAL POSITION
as at 31 December 20-4

	£	£	£
Non-current assets	Cost	Accumulated depreciation	Carrying amount
Shop fittings	50,000	10,000	40,000
Current assets			
Inventory		73,900	
Trade receivables		2,500	
Prepayment of rent		250	
Bank*		19,900	
		96,550	
Less Current liabilities			
Trade payables	65,000		
Accrual of wages	550		
		65,550	
Net current assets			31,000
NET ASSETS			71,000
FINANCED BY			
Capital			
Opening capital (introduced at start of year)			60,000
Add Profit for the year			26,020
			86,020
Less Drawings			15,020
Closing capital			71,000

* Cash book summary:

	£
• total receipts for year	213,500
• less total payments for year	193,600
• **balance at year end**	19,900

14.5

JAMES HARVEY
CALCULATION OF INVENTORY LOSS FOR THE YEAR

	£	£
Opening inventory		21,500
Purchases		132,000
Cost of inventory available for sale		153,500
Sales	180,000	
Less Normal gross profit margin (30%)	54,000	
Cost of sales		126,000
Estimated closing inventory		27,500
Less Actual closing inventory		26,000
Value of inventory loss		1,500

14.6 (a)

	•	receipts from sales	121,000
	•	less trade receivables at beginning of year	36,000
	•	add irrecoverable debts written off during year	550
	•	add trade receivables at end of year	35,000
	•	**sales for year**	120,550

(b)

	•	payments to suppliers	62,500
	•	less trade payables at beginning of year	32,500
	•	add trade payables at end of year	30,000
	•	**purchases for year**	60,000

(c)

	•	payments for administration expenses	30,000
	•	less accrual at beginning of year	500
	•	add accrual at end of year	700
	•	**administration expenses for year**	30,200

(d)

COLIN SMITH
INCOME STATEMENT
for the year ended 30 June 20-5

	£	£
Sales revenue		120,550
Opening inventory	25,000	
Purchases	60,000	
	85,000	
Less Closing inventory	27,500	
Cost of sales		57,500
Gross profit		63,050
Less expenses:		
Administration expenses	30,200	
Depreciation charge: fixtures and fittings	5,000	
Irrecoverable debts	550	
		35,750
Profit for the year		27,300

(e)

COLIN SMITH
STATEMENT OF FINANCIAL POSITION as at 30 June 20-5

	£	£	£
Non-current assets	Cost	Accumulated depreciation	Carrying amount
Fixtures and fittings	50,000	15,000	35,000
Current assets			
Inventory		27,500	
Trade receivables		35,000	
Bank		1,210	
		63,710	
Less Current liabilities			
Trade payables	30,000		
Accrual of administration expenses	700		
		30,700	
Net current assets			33,010
NET ASSETS			68,010
FINANCED BY			
Capital			
Opening capital*			69,500
Add Profit for the year			27,300
			96,800
Less Drawings			28,790
Closing capital			68,010

* Opening capital:	£
• assets at 1 July 20-4	102,500
• less liabilities at 1 July 20-4	33,000
• **capital at 1 July 20-4**	69,500

14.7 (a)   **Sales ledger control account**

Balance b/d	20,400	Bank	192,650
Sales day book	201,600	Discounts allowed	2,250
		Balance c/d	27,100
	222,000		222,000

(b)   **VAT control account**

Purchases day book	19,200	Balance b/d	3,050
Selling expenses	2,480	Sales day book	33,600
Bank	10,425		
Balance c/d	4,545		
	36,650		36,650

CHAPTER 15: PARTNERSHIP FINANCIAL STATEMENTS

15.1   (b)   **15.2**   (a)

15.3

Dr			Partners' capital accounts		Cr
	Lysa	Mark		Lysa	Mark
20-8	£	£	20-8	£	£
31 Dec Balances c/d	50,000	40,000	1 Jan Balances b/d	50,000	40,000
20-9			20-9		
			1 Jan Balances b/d	50,000	40,000

Dr			Partners' current accounts		Cr
	Lysa	Mark		Lysa	Mark
20-8	£	£	20-8	£	£
31 Dec Drawings	13,000	12,250	1 Jan Balances b/d	420	1,780
31 Dec Interest on drawings	300	250	31 Dec Interest on capital	2,500	2,000
31 Dec Balance c/d	–	580	31 Dec Profit share	9,300	9,300
			31 Dec Balance c/d	1,080	–
	13,300	13,080		13,300	13,080
20-9			20-9		
1 Jan Balance b/d	1,080	–	1 Jan Balance b/d	–	580

15.4 Task 1   EXTENDED TRIAL BALANCE

J JAMES & S HILL T/A "GRAPES"

31 DECEMBER 20-5

Account name	Ledger balances Dr £	Cr £	Adjustments Dr £	Cr £	Income statement Dr £	Cr £	Statement of financial position Dr £	Cr £
Capital account: James		38,000						38,000
Capital account: Hill		32,000						32,000
Current account: James	3,000						3,000	
Current account: Hill		1,000						1,000
Drawings: James	10,000						10,000	
Drawings: Hill	22,000						22,000	
Gross profit		89,000				89,000		
Rent and rates	7,500				7,500			
Advertising	12,000				12,000			
Heat and light	3,500				3,500			
Wages and salaries	18,000				18,000			
Sundry expenses	4,000				4,000			
Shop fittings at cost	20,000						20,000	
Shop fittings: accumulated depreciation				2,000				2,000
Bank	29,000						29,000	
Sales ledger control	6,000						6,000	
Purchases ledger control		8,000						8,000
Value Added Tax		2,000						2,000
Closing inventory: statement of financial position	35,000						35,000	
Depreciation charge			2,000		2,000			
Partnership salary: Hill					15,000			15,000
Interest on capital: James					3,800			3,800
Interest on capital: Hill					3,200			3,200
Profit/loss: James					10,000			10,000
Profit/loss: Hill					10,000			10,000
	170,000	**170,000**	**2,000**	**2,000**	**89,000**	**89,000**	**125,000**	**125,000**

Task 2

Dr			Partners' capital accounts			Cr
	James £	Hill £		James £	Hill £	
20-5			20-5			
31 Dec Balances c/d	38,000	32,000	1 Jan Balances b/d	38,000	32,000	
20-6			20-6			
			1 Jan Balances b/d	38,000	32,000	

Dr			Partners' current accounts			Cr
	James £	Hill £		James £	Hill £	
20-5			20-5			
1 Jan Balance b/d	3,000	–	1 Jan Balance b/d	–	1,000	
31 Dec Drawings	10,000	22,000	31 Dec Salary	–	15,000	
31 Dec Balances c/d	800	7,200	31 Dec Interest on capital	3,800	3,200	
			31 Dec Profit share	10,000	10,000	
	13,800	29,200		13,800	29,200	
20-6			20-6			
			1 Jan Balances b/d	800	7,200	

Task 3

JOHN JAMES AND STEVEN HILL IN PARTNERSHIP, TRADING AS "GRAPES"
INCOME STATEMENT
for the year ended 31 December 20-5

	£	£
Sales revenue		174,000
Less cost of sales		85,000
Gross profit		89,000
Less expenses:		
Rent and rates	7,500	
Advertising	12,000	
Heat and light	3,500	
Wages and salaries	18,000	
Sundry expenses	4,000	
Depreciation charge: shop fittings	2,000	
		47,000
Profit for the year		42,000
Less appropriation of profit:		
Salary: Hill		15,000
Interest allowed on partners' capitals		
James £38,000 x 10%	3,800	
Hill £32,000 x 10%	3,200	
		7,000
Profit available for distribution		20,000
Profit share:		
James		10,000
Hill		10,000
Total profit distributed		20,000

continued on next page

STATEMENT OF FINANCIAL POSITION as at 31 December 20-5

	£ Cost	£ Accumulated depreciation	£ Carrying amount
Non-current assets			
Shop fittings	20,000	2,000	18,000
Current assets			
Inventory (closing)		35,000	
Trade receivables		6,000	
Bank		29,000	
		70,000	
Less Current liabilities			
Trade payables	8,000		
Value Added Tax	2,000		
		10,000	
Net current assets			60,000
NET ASSETS			78,000

FINANCED BY

	James	Hill	Total
Capital accounts	38,000	32,000	70,000
Current accounts	800	7,200	8,000
	38,800	39,200	78,000

Tutorial note: only the balances of the partners' capital and current accounts have been shown in the statement of financial position.

Task 4

- The balance on the partners' current accounts represents the balance owed or owing between the business and the individual partners after transactions such as salaries, interest on capitals, profit share, and drawings have been taken into account.

- A debit balance on a partner's current account means that the partner has drawn out more than his/her entitlement of salary, interest on capital and profit share.

- A credit balance on a partner's current account means that the partner has drawn out less than his/her entitlement of salary, interest on capital and profit share.

15.5   Current accounts

	Ian £	Jim £	Kay £		Ian £	Jim £	Kay £
Balance b/d	0	0	200	Balance b/d	0	900	0
Drawings	30,000	25,000	14,000	Salaries	20,500	14,500	10,250
Balance c/d	800	1,200	1,450	Interest on capital	1,500	2,000	1,000
				Profit share	8,800	8,800	4,400
	30,800	26,200	15,650		30,800	26,200	15,650

15.6 (a)

Current account balance: Don	£4,750
Current account balance: Eve	£3,600

(b)

DE Partnership

Statement of financial position as at 31 March 20-2

Non-current (fixed) assets	Cost £	Accumulated depreciation £	Carrying amount (net book value) £
Machinery	35,500	12,150	23,350
Current assets			
Inventory		15,790	
Trade receivables		*24,590	
Bank		11,520	
Cash		150	
		52,050	
Current liabilities			
Trade payables	18,720		
Value Added Tax	2,780		
Accruals	550		
		22,050	
Net current assets			30,000
Net assets			53,350

Financed by:	Don	Eve	Total
Capital accounts	25,000	20,000	45,000
Current accounts	4,750	3,600	8,350
	29,750	23,600	53,350

* sales ledger control £25,690 *minus* allowance for doubtful debts £1,100
= trade receivables £24,590

CHAPTER 16: CHANGES IN PARTNERSHIPS

16.1 (a)   **16.2** (b)

16.3 Dr   **Partners' capital accounts**   Cr

		Jim	Maisie	Matt			Jim	Maisie	Matt
20-4		£	£	£	20-4		£	£	£
					31 Dec	Balances b/d	60,000	40,000	–
20-5					20-5				
1 Jan	Goodwill	24,000	16,000	8,000	1 Jan	Goodwill	28,800	19,200	–
31 Dec	Drawings	12,000	12,000	8,000	1 Jan	Bank			28,000
31 Dec	Balances c/d	82,800	51,200	22,000	31 Dec	Profit share	30,000	20,000	10,000
		118,800	79,200	38,000			118,800	79,200	38,000
20-6					20-6				
					1 Jan	Balances b/d	82,800	51,200	22,000

16.4 **Task 1**

Dr   **Partners' capital accounts**   Cr

	Reena	Sam	Tamara		Reena	Sam	Tamara
	£	£	£		£	£	£
Goodwill	8,000	–	8,000	Balances b/d	33,000	12,000	30,000
Bank		16,000		Goodwill	8,000	4,000	4,000
Balances c/d	33,000	–	26,000				
	41,000	16,000	34,000		41,000	16,000	34,000
				Balances b/d	33,000	–	26,000

Task 2   **REENA AND TAMARA IN PARTNERSHIP**
STATEMENT OF FINANCIAL POSITION as at 1 September 20-8

	£
Non-current assets	50,000
Current assets	10,000
Cash at bank (£25,000 – £16,000)	9,000
	69,000
Trade payables	(10,000)
	59,000
Capital accounts	
Reena	33,000
Tamara	26,000
	59,000

16.5   Task 1

Date	Details	Reference	Dr	Cr
20-8			£	£
1 Oct	Goodwill	GL	45,000	
	Capital – Dave	GL		22,500
	Capital – Elsa	GL		22,500
			45,000	45,000
	Goodwill created for the change in the profit-sharing ratio; credited to capital accounts in the partners' old profit-sharing ratio of 1:1			
1 Oct	Capital – Dave	GL	30,000	
	Capital – Elsa	GL	15,000	
	Goodwill	GL		45,000
			45,000	45,000
	Goodwill written off for the change in the profit-sharing ratio; debited to capital accounts in the partners' new profit-sharing ratio of 2:1			

Task 2

Dr   **Partners' capital accounts**   Cr

		Dave	Elsa			Dave	Elsa
20-8		£	£	20-8		£	£
1 Oct	Goodwill	30,000	15,000	1 Oct	Balances b/d	80,000	50,000
1 Oct	Balances c/d	72,500	57,500	1 Oct	Goodwill	22,500	22,500
		102,500	72,500			102,500	72,500
				1 Oct	Balances b/d	72,500	57,500

Task 3

DAVE AND ELSA IN PARTNERSHIP	
STATEMENT OF FINANCIAL POSITION as at 1 October 20-8	
	£
Net assets	130,000
Capital accounts:	
Dave	72,500
Elsa	57,500
	130,000

16.6   Task 1

JEAN AND DAVID
PARTNERSHIP APPROPRIATION ACCOUNT for the year ended 31 December 20-1

	Total	Jean	David
	£	£	£
Profit for the year	32,700		
Salaries	(22,000)	12,000	10,000
Interest on capital @ 5%	(1,100)	500	600
Profit available for distribution	9,600		
Profit share:			
6 months to 30 June (six-twelfths)	4,800	3,200	1,600
6 months to 31 December (six-twelfths)	4,800	2,400	2,400
Total profit distributed	9,600	5,600	4,000

Task 2

Dr   **Partners' current accounts**   Cr

		Jean	David			Jean	David
20-1		£	£	20-1		£	£
1 Jan	Balance b/d	–	1,250	1 Jan	Balance b/d	2,400	–
31 Dec	Drawings	18,600	14,200	31 Dec	Salaries	12,000	10,000
31 Dec	Balance c/d	1,900	–	31 Dec	Interest on capital	500	600
				31 Dec	Profit share	5,600	4,000
				31 Dec	Balance c/d	–	850
		20,500	15,450			20,500	15,450
20-2				20-2			
1 Jan	Balance b/d	–	850	1 Jan	Balance b/d	1,900	–

16.7 **(a)** **Capital account – Mel**

Goodwill	4,800	Balance b/d	0
Balance c/d	25,200	Bank	30,000
	30,000		30,000

(b) Goodwill can be defined as the difference between **the value of the business**, and the **net value** of the separate **assets and liabilities**.

16.8 **Partnership Appropriation account for the year ended 31 March 20-3**

	1 Apr 20-2 – 30 Sep 20-2 £	1 Oct 20-2 – 31 Mar 20-3 £	Total £
Profit	36,000	36,000	72,000
Salaries:			
Amy	12,000	0	12,000
Ben	10,500	10,500	21,000
Col	0	0	0
Interest on capital:			
Amy	500	0	500
Ben	750	750	1,500
Col	250	250	500
Profit available for distribution	12,000	24,500	36,500

Profit share			
Amy	6,000	0	6,000
Ben	3,000	14,700	17,700
Col	3,000	9,800	12,800
Total profit distributed	12,000	24,500	36,500

Appendix:

Photocopiable resources

These pages may be photocopied for student use, but remain the copyright of the author. It is recommended that they are enlarged to A4 size.

These pages are also available for download from the Resources Section of www.osbornebooks.co.uk

The forms and formats include:

| Dr | | | account | | Cr |
Date	Details	Amount	Date	Details	Amount
		£			£

| Dr | | | account | | Cr |
Date	Details	Amount	Date	Details	Amount
		£			£

| Dr | | | account | | Cr |
Date	Details	Amount	Date	Details	Amount
		£			£

| Dr | | | account | | Cr |
Date	Details	Amount	Date	Details	Amount
		£			£

Journal

Date	Details	Reference	Dr	Cr
			£	£

Journal

Date	Details	Reference	Dr	Cr
			£	£

Journal

Date	Details	Reference	Dr	Cr
			£	£

Journal

Date	Details	Reference	Dr	Cr
			£	£

EXTENDED TRIAL BALANCE

name ....   date ....

Account name	Ledger balances		Adjustments		Income statement		Statement of financial position	
	Dr £	Cr £	Dr £	Cr £	Dr £	Cr £	Dr £	Cr £
Closing inventory: income statement								
Closing inventory: statement of financial position								
Accruals								
Prepayments								
Depreciation charge								
Irrecoverable debts								
Allowance for doubtful debts								
Allowance for doubtful debts: adjustment								
Profit/loss for the year								

NON-CURRENT ASSET REGISTER

Description/serial no	Acquisition date	Cost £	Depreciation £	Carrying amount* £	Funding method	Disposal proceeds £	Disposal date

* carrying amount (net book value), ie cost less accumulated depreciation

INCOME STATEMENT
(PROFIT AND LOSS ACCOUNT)

of ....

for the year ended ....

	£	£
Sales revenue		
Cost of sales		
Gross profit		
Less expenses:		
Total expenses		
Profit for the year		

STATEMENT OF FINANCIAL POSITION
(BALANCE SHEET)

of ....

as at ....

	Cost £	Accumulated depreciation £	Carrying amount (net book value) £
Non-current (fixed) assets			
Current assets			
Current liabilities			
Net current assets			
Less Non-current (long-term) liabilities			
Net assets			
Financed by:			Total

Index

RECOVERY OF A DEBT

Recovery of a debt is when a former trade receivable, whose account has been written off as irrecoverable, makes a payment.

From time-to-time, a former trade receivable whose account has been written off as irrecoverable may make a payment – either voluntarily, or as a result of debt collection procedures. For such a recovery the book-keeping transactions are:

- debit cash/bank account (with the amount of the recovery)
- credit debts recovered account

Note that recovery of a debt paid after being previously written off should be a rare event because a debt should not be treated as irrecoverable unless certain.

At the end of the financial year the amount of any debts recovered during the year is transferred, as income, to the credit column of the income statement.

The payment received – either in cash or by cheque – is debited to cash/bank account and credited to debts recovered account.

Having recovered payment from a former trade receivable, if the customer now wishes to buy goods or services, it is prudent to insist on cash payment for some time to come!

Case Study

CASE STUDY: RECOVERY OF A DEBT

T Hughes is a customer – the balance of £25 on his account was written off as an irrecoverable debt on 15 December 20-7.

Today, on 15 April 20-8, T Hughes wishes to pay off the amount of the debt – with a cheque for £25.

The book-keeping entries to record the debt recovered on 15 April 20-8 are as follows:

Dr		Bank Account			Cr
20-8		£	20-8		£
15 Apr Debts recovered		25			

Dr		Debts Recovered Account			Cr
20-8		£	20-8		£
			15 Apr Bank (T Hughes)		25

Debts recovered account is a 'holding account' to which any other recoveries can be credited. At the end of the financial year, the total of the account is transferred to the credit column of the income statement:

Dr		**Debts recovered account**		Cr
20-8	£	20-8		£
31 Dec Income statement	25	15 Apr Bank (T Hughes)		25

In financial statements, the effect of debts recovered is to increase the previously reported profit for the year – by £25 in this case.

Note that debts recovered must not be recorded in sales ledger control account – see Chapter 10.

Tutorial note:

Some businesses may have an accounting policy of crediting debt recoveries to irrecoverable debts account – instead of using debts recovered account. Such a policy would make sense where debt recoveries were few and far between. As a consequence, this could result in a credit balance on irrecoverable debts account during an accounting period where, for example, the only transaction was a recovery. If you do see a trial balance with a credit balance for irrecoverable debts, simply show the amount in the income statement credit column: this will have the effect of increasing profit for the year.

406

for your notes

for your notes

for your notes

for your notes

for your notes